THE
OLD TESTAMENT

Its Background, Growth, and Content

THE
OLD TESTAMENT

Its Background, Growth, and Content

PETER C. CRAIGIE

Abingdon Press
Nashville

THE OLD TESTAMENT: Its Background, Growth, and Content

Copyright © 1986 by Abingdon Press

Library of Congress Cataloging-in-Publication Data

CRAIGIE, PETER C.
  The Old Testament.
  Bibliography; p.
  Includes index.
  1. Bible. O.T.—Introductions. I. Title.
  BS1140.2.C65   1986   221.6'1   86-14115

ISBN 0-687-28751-0 (alk. paper)

Scripture quotations in this publication are from the Revised Standard Version of the Bible, copyrighted 1946, 1952, © 1971, 1973 by the Division of Christian Education of the National Council of the Churches of Christ in the U.S.A., and are used by permission.

Figure numbers 6, 7, 8, 9, 10, 14, and 38 are reproduced by courtesy of The University Museum, University of Pennsylvania.

Figure numbers 12, 13, and 35 are reproduced by courtesy of The Metropolitan Museum of Art. Figure 13 is a gift of the Edward S. Harkness Collection, 1926.

Figure numbers 15 and 26 are reproduced by courtesy of The Brooklyn Museum. Gift of Theodora Wilbour from the estate of her father, Charles Edwin Wilbour.

Figure numbers 16, 17, and 18 are reproduced by courtesy of Hirmer Verlag.

Figure number 21 is reproduced by courtesy of the British Museum, Schweich Lectures, 1937.

Figure numbers 23 and 40 are reproduced by permission of The American Schools of Oriental Research.

Figure number 27 is reproduced by permission of The University of Chicago Press.

Figure number 36 is reproduced by permission of Mrs. Elizabeth Frank. Gift of her husband H. T. Frank.

Figure number 41 is used by permission of Paul Leslie Garber, Agnes Scott College.

MANUFACTURED BY THE PARTHENON PRESS AT
NASHVILLE, TENNESSEE, UNITED STATES OF AMERICA

CONTENTS

LIST OF
PHOTOS, CHARTS
AND MAPS

PREFACE

THIS book was written as a basic introductory study for undergraduates. Given this audience, I have had the difficult task of covering an enormous subject in as concise a fashion as possible, being fully aware that in doing so I run the risk of omitting much that is important. I have tried to convey not only something of the substance and character of the Old Testament, but also an understanding of the world from which it emerged. In addition, I have attempted to give some indication of how the Old Testament is treated in modern biblical scholarship. I am very aware of all that is missing in this introductory textbook, but it is my hope that it might open for many the first door in the study of the Old Testament.

I have taught introductory courses in Old Testament studies for many years in various Canadian universities. This book reflects, in part, what I have learned from my students and the information they wanted to know. The students came from many different backgrounds and included Jews, Christians, Muslims, and persons of no particular faith or religious affiliation. Teaching in such a context, I traditionally began by "confessing" my potential for bias (namely the Christian faith), for none of us can escape bias and achieve total objectivity. My approach to the Old Testament text, in terms of contemporary biblical scholarship, has offered common ground upon which we all, regardless of religious affiliation or otherwise, can approach the text with the shared goal of understanding it and learning to appreciate its content. I am very aware that the expression *Old Testament* in the title of this study is a Christian term for what is primarily a Jewish book; my only justification for continuing to use the expression in a book which attempts openness toward both Jewish and Christian understanding is that *Old Testament* has become, for practical purposes, the commonly accepted title for the Hebrew Bible in the modern secular world. When I use the proper expression, *Tanak*, I have to explain what it means to 98 percent of my students, regardless of their religious affiliation. When I talk about the *Old Testament*, at least they have all heard of it!

In the study of the Old Testament, there are a number of difficult issues which are constantly the focus of debate. Sometimes the debate is of a conventional academic kind, pertaining to the interpretation of evidence. Sometimes it is of a more theological nature, when the scholarly interpretation of evidence may seem to conflict with either Jewish or Christian faith. In matters such as these, I have tried to retain a balanced perspective, indicating both sides of the issues and attempting to be fair to both parties. Where I have erred, I should warn the reader that it is probably in being too cautious and conservative, unwilling to go along with every new trend in scholarly research. I hope the volume contains a fairly balanced view of biblical scholarship and introduces the vitality of the contemporary scholarly enterprise.

Finally, I should like to convey a word to those students who may be so unfortunate as to have to toil through the late night hours with this and similar books. I began my own undergraduate studies of the Old Testament quite by accident; a course was offered at the University of Edinburgh which happened to fit my timetable. From that casual beginning I have never ceased reading and enjoying the Old Testament. It is important to me as Scripture, but more than that it has been a continual source of insight, inspiration, challenge to thought, and, indeed, pleasure. Frankly, I would never have believed as an undergraduate student that I would have lived to write words like these! It is my hope that you too may eventually be surprised by the Old Testament.

Peter C. Craigie

THE
OLD TESTAMENT
Its Background, Growth, and Content

INTRODUCTION

PART I

THE
PHENOMENON
OF THE
OLD TESTAMENT

F OR many decades the Bible has been the best-selling book in the Western world. And yet, despite its continuing popularity in the marketplace, it is a book more respected than read; the contents of the Bible, so familiar to so many, can no longer be considered a part of the property of common knowledge. The Old Testament, which in the Christian Bible is more than three times as long as its New Testament counterpart, has become the least known part of this little read book. According to a 1979 Gallup poll conducted in the United States, only 49 percent of Protestants and 44 percent of Roman Catholics could name as many as four of the Ten Commandments. While a Jewish response no doubt would have been higher, a secular response would have been much lower. Yet, the Old Testament is a fundamental book, not only for the faith of both Judaism and Christianity, but also in the wider context of Western civilization.

There are many reasons for the decline in knowledge of the Bible, some of which will be described later in this chapter. But from the beginning it is wise to recognize that, while almost all people have heard of the Old Testament, few any longer know of its contents or significance. If we are to know the book in a little more detail, we must start at the very beginning with some basic questions: What is the Old Testament? How did it come into existence? What was its original language? How did it survive? And perhaps the most important question: Why should we know about the Old Testament and try to come to terms with its contents? These introductory questions are addressed in this opening chapter. Only after some preliminary answers have been provided will we turn to the more specific matters of the background, growth, and content of the Old Testament.

1. The Nature of the Old Testament

When one opens the pages of the Old Testament, one is opening a library, not a single book. The Old Testament is a collection of ancient Hebrew writings that have been brought together to form an anthology (the process by which they were brought together is described in section 3). In most English translations, the collection extends to more than one thousand pages of text.

There are many ways of expressing the total number of originally separate books and writings that comprise the collection as a whole. In a traditional, or modern, Protestant translation of the Bible, the Old Testament contains thirty-nine books. This division of contents, in turn, is based essentially on the Jewish Bible, which contains twenty-four books; the difference in numbers is largely accounted for by the different methods of counting (see figure 1). The single book *Samuel* in the Jewish Bible is divided into two books, I and II Samuel, in Christian Bibles. To use another example, the twelve minor prophets in the Christian Bible (from Hosea to Malachi) are called simply "The Twelve" in the Jewish Bible, a single book. For all practical purposes, the Jewish and Protestant versions of the Old Testament are the same. Some additions, or "deutero-canonical" works, are recognized by the Roman Catholic and Orthodox churches. These books, though not recognized as canonical writings in the ancient Jewish traditions, compose the contents of the *Apocrypha*. Thus the Roman Catholic Old Testament contains seven books more than those recognized in the Jewish and Protestant forms of the Old Testament. Despite the minor variations, the Old Testament, whether viewed from a Jewish or Christian perspective, is essentially the same book. When it comes to the interpretation and significance of the ancient texts, however, a greater variety of views begins to emerge.

Figure 1. THE CANON OF THE OLD TESTAMENT

The Books of the Law (Torah)	The Books of the Prophets (Nebhi'im)	The Books of the Writings (Kethubim)	The Books of the Apocrypha (R.C. Canon)
Genesis Exodus Leviticus Numbers Deuteronomy	*Former Prophets* Joshua Judges I Samuel II Samuel I Kings II Kings *Latter Prophets* Isaiah Jeremiah Ezekiel The Book of the Twelve	Psalms Job Proverbs Ruth Song of Songs Ecclesiastes Lamentations Esther Daniel Ezra-Nehemiah I Chronicles II Chronicles	Tobit Judith Wisdom of Solomon Ecclesiasticus Baruch I Maccabees II Maccabees Additions to Esther Additions to Daniel
			Apocrypha (Orthodox) The above, less the Book of Baruch

The recognition of the nature of the Old Testament as a collection is important if it is to be read intelligently. The works that make up the whole were written by different hands, sometimes in widely separated historical periods. Sometimes an author is known, sometimes unknown. Sometimes a book is written in prose, sometimes in poetry. Some books are long, equivalent in length to a modern book (for example, Genesis, Jeremiah), others are very short, no longer than a letter to a friend (for example, Obadiah). The language varies, too, though it has been made uniform in most English translations; some books and poems are in very archaic Hebrew, whereas others are in a more modern and smoother style. Some books are splendid when viewed as literature (for example, Job), whereas others have a more mundane character (for example, Chronicles).

Thus the Old Testament is in some ways a kind of patchwork quilt of language and letters from old Israel. One can only begin to imagine its diverse character if one tries to recreate a parallel in the English language. Imagine an anthology that contained the following works: *Beowulf,* stories from Chaucer, selected plays of Shakespeare, poetry from Robert Burns to Robert Frost, *Hymns Ancient and Modern,* the Declaration of Independence, and Sir Winston Churchill's *History of the English Speaking Peoples.* (I should extend the list to thirty-nine, but enough examples have been provided to make the point). This imaginary anthology is incredibly diverse. The average English-speaking person would have no difficulty understanding Churchill, but Chaucer's writings would be difficult because English has changed with the passing of time. The average American would have little difficulty in reading the language of Robert Frost, but might find the Scottish terms of Robert Burns difficult to understand. While most modern readers would understand Shakespeare's English, all would recognize it as the language of another century. The Old Testament is not so different from this imaginary English language anthology. Its vocabulary reflects variations of time and of regional dialects. It contains some documents of literary importance and others of political or national importance. It contains not only mundane prose, but also magnificent poetry.

As we read the pages that now comprise the Old Testament, we enter not only the legacy left to us by ancient Israel, but also a profoundly spiritual work which has left its mark on other peoples and on later generations.

2. Titles of the Book

In the opening pages of this volume, the book (or collection of books) under discussion has been consistently called the Old Testament. Yet Old Testament is a relatively new name for the book; it is also essentially a Christian name for what is, first and foremost, a Jewish book. The only justification for using Old Testament both in the title of this textbook and throughout its chapters, is that this is the name by which the work has become commonly known throughout the Western world, largely as a consequence of the spread and influence of Christian culture.

The book is primarily Jewish, and a variety of terms may be employed to designate the book within the context of Judaism. It may be called, simply, the *Bible* (based on the Greek *ta biblia,* "the books"), which is an appropriate enough title, provided that it is remembered that Jews and Christians use the word *bible* in a slightly different manner (the Christian use of the word also incorporates the New Testament). It is commonly called the *Hebrew Bible* to clarify precisely which Bible is intended (the New Testament was written in Greek). It may be called, in the Jewish context, the *Torah,* but this term is used with various senses so extensively in Judaism that it is potentially ambiguous. Torah may refer to the five books of Moses (or the Pentateuch), to the entire Hebrew Bible, to Jewish sacred writings as a whole (including post-biblical works), and to the life of *studying* the Scriptures, a vocation traditionally held in high esteem in Judaism. Perhaps the most suitable name for the book in Judaism is *Tanak* (the meaning is described in section 3, following). This term describes precisely and unambiguously the same canonical work that is referred to outside Judaism as the Old Testament.

The common Christian title of the book is Old Testament; as the English word *testament* has changed somewhat in common use during the last century, *Old Covenant* might be a more appropriate rendition of the title. It is called *old* to differentiate it from the *new,* for there are two covenants in the Christian Bible. The expression *new covenant* (drawn from the language of Jeremiah 31:31) designates the Christian self-understanding of the new faith established in Jesus

Christ; the new relationship between Christ and church was understood as a new covenant in Jeremiah's words; so the Scripture of the new community was descriptively named. The expression Old Testament, as a title, thus designates the antecedent character of the Hebrew Scripture in the Christian conception, though the Christian Bible contains both testaments, each being fully a part of Scripture. The adjectives "old" and "new" should not be taken to imply that the books of the Hebrew Bible are in some sense second-class citizens in the community of books comprised in the entire Christian Bible.

Having clarified the various titles of the book, I shall continue to employ the title Old Testament. The only reason for so doing, as indicated above, is the common acceptance of this title in the Western world as a whole, both secular and religious. In employing this title, it is wise to recall at all times that it is Christian in origin and that the Scripture, so labeled, is primarily Jewish and continues with different labels as a common legacy of both Judaism and Christianity.

3. The Canon and Formation of the Book

The sheer size of the Old Testament might suggest at first that it is simply a collection of *all* the ancient books of the Hebrews in the biblical period. Such, however, is not the case; many other books were written in the biblical period, some of which have survived, others of which are known only by name (for example, The Book of the Wars of the Lord mentioned in Numbers 21:14 is no longer extant). The books which now compose the contents of the Old Testament reflect only a portion of the literary output of the ancient Hebrews, and the process by which the collection came into being was not a random one.

The collection of books which comprise the Old Testament is called the *canon;* the canon specifies those books which belonged to Scripture, were recognized as authoritative for both faith and practice, and were believed to be inspired by God in some special manner. Concurrently, the notion of canon excludes from Scripture, and therefore from special divine authority, all those other books which it does not encompass. Thus within both Judaism and Christianity the canon of the Old Testament specifies the limits of the collection; it specifically limits the contents, invests them with authority, prohibits them from being changed, and implies that their inspired contents are sacrosanct. The formation of a canon is the end of a long process. The books which now constitute the Bible were not consciously written as parts of the Bible. Indeed, the "biblical books" were originally independent, not part of any Bible, until with the passing of time they were incorporated into what we now call the canon of the Old Testament.

A study of the Old Testament canon must begin from a Jewish perspective. One of the titles of the book, as has been noted above, is Tanak. This is, in a sense, an artificial word constructed from the first letters of the names of the three principal divisions in the Jewish canon of Scripture—namely T, N, and K.

(i) *Torah*—The first and most authoritative division of the Jewish canon contains the five books of Moses from Genesis to Deuteronomy, which are also called the Pentateuch.

(ii) *Nebi'im* (Prophets)—This division of the canon includes both those books conventionally thought of as "prophetic" (Isaiah, Jeremiah, Ezekiel, and the "Book of the Twelve"—namely from Hosea to Malachi), and books of a more historical character (I and II Samuel, I and II Kings, Joshua, and Judges).

(iii) *Kethubim* (Writings)—This is the most miscellaneous division of the canon, including Psalms, Job, Proverbs, Ruth, Song of Songs, Ecclesiastes, Lamentations, Esther, Daniel, Ezra, Nehemiah, and I and II Chronicles.

This threefold division of the Hebrew canon goes back to ancient times, and the precise process by which it came into being can no longer be determined with certainty. The process which eventually lead to the development of the canon probably began during the Hebrew monarchy (approximately the tenth to sixth centuries B.C.) in the ancient Israelite school system. There is some evidence, both biblical and archaeological, to suggest that in the schools of ancient Israel, as in other parts of the Near East, important texts were copied out and preserved for subsequent generations. These texts were later to become a part of the canon.

By the second century B.C. it seems to be clear from the surviving evidence that the first division of the canon, the Torah, was accepted within Judaism as being authoritative and inspired. The second division, the *Nebi'im*, was known, but apparently had not yet achieved the status of the Torah. Although most of the books that now compose the third division were recognized, the Kethubhim still lacked any clear status as a division of canon. By the beginning of the first century A.D., both the *Torah* and the Nebi'im seem to have been widely accepted as authoritative Scripture, though there remained a degree of fluidity as to the contents of the Kethubim. Between 70 and 100 A.D., the Hebrew canon reached its final and fixed form. In that period, following the destruction of Jerusalem's temple in 70 A.D., the Pharisees came into a role of leadership in Judaism and set about the important task of defining the boundaries of Scripture for the faith of a new era. The status of contentious books was established (for example, there was considerable debate as to whether books such as Ecclesiastes, Song of Songs, and Esther should be included or excluded from the Kethubim); the canon was fixed.

The canonical process within Christianity differed somewhat from that taking place in Judaism, for the Christian church was already established and growing rapidly prior to the final fixing of the Hebrew canon between 70 and 100 A.D. The early Christians shared with the Jews the "Law and the Prophets" (Torah and Nebi'im), but went their own way with respect to the "Writings," which remained fluid with respect to canon in the first century.

It was for this reason that the so-called Apocrypha became a part of the canon of the early church (see section 1, above), though there continued to be debate during the first four centuries of Christianity as to the precise canon of the Old Testament. Apart from a minority who advocated the church's acceptance of the Hebrew canon, the majority of the Christian church, throughout its first fifteen centuries, had an Old Testament which included both the books of the Jewish Bible and the books of the Apocrypha. Only in the fifteenth century A.D. with the rebirth of interest in Hebrew learning in Gentile Europe, and in the Protestant Reformation in the sixteenth century, did one portion of Christianity return to what had been a minority position in the early church, namely that the most appropriate canon for Christianity was the Jewish canon. The presence of this double tradition with respect to canon in the history of Christianity can be seen in the custom of printing the books of the Apocrypha in many modern versions of the English Bible (a contemporary example is the *New English Bible*).

4. The Languages of the Old Testament

The original texts of the Old Testament were written in two languages, Hebrew and Aramaic. For practical purposes, one can say that Hebrew is the language of the Old Testament, for less than 2 percent of the entire biblical corpus is in the Aramaic language. Both these languages use essentially the same alphabet.

(a) Biblical Hebrew

The principal language spoken in Old Testament times was also the language in which the biblical books were written. It has survived primarily in the biblical text; only a few short inscriptions in biblical Hebrew have been recovered through the work of archaeologists. Because the language has survived only in the written texts, there are several limitations to our knowledge of the language. For example, the Old Testament preserves approximately seven thousand words of distinct meaning, in contrast to something like two hundred thousand in modern French and five hundred thousand in modern English. Presumably the original Hebrew language had a much larger vocabulary, but all that has survived is the vocabulary that happened to be employed in the writing of the biblical books. Therefore, only a portion of the ancient language is known, and even in what has survived there is often doubt as to the precise meaning of certain words.

Hebrew belongs to the Semitic family of languages, which includes Assyrian and Babylonian in the ancient world and such languages as Arabic in the modern world (see figure 2). Its closest linguistic relatives are languages such as Phoenician, Ugaritic, and Moabite. Phoenician was the language used by the inhabitants of the Phoenician states on the Mediterranean coast during the biblical period; the language became widespread throughout the Mediterranean world as a consequence of Phoenician trading and colonization. Ugaritic was the language spoken until about 1200 B.C. in the city state of Ugarit, the remains of which can still be seen on the coast of modern Syria, just north of the city of Latakia. Moabite, the language of Israel's neighbors in the territory that is now the kingdom of Jordan, has survived only in a few short inscriptions. Hebrew, together with Phoenician, Ugaritic, and Moabite, is generally classified as a Northwest Semitic language, a sub-group within the larger family of Semitic languages.

Figure 2. THE FAMILY OF SEMITIC LANGUAGES

Group	Examples of Specific Languages	Area of Use
(1) East Semitic Languages	(Akkadian) Babylonian Assyrian	Southern Mesopotamia Northern Mesopatamia
(2) Northwest Semitic Languages	Hebrew Ugaritic Moabite Phoenician	Israel Coast of Syria East of Dead Sea Southeast Mediterranean Coast
(3) South Semitic Languages	Arabic Ethiopic	Arabia Northeast Africa

It is important for the reader of the English Old Testament to recognize not only that the book was written in a foreign language, but also that the language in question has a fundamentally different character from English or European languages. Things are expressed very differently in Hebrew than they would be in English. If one is to progress with the study of the Old Testament, the language must be learned, for however good a translation may be, it can never recapture the flavor and essence of a text in its original language. Nevertheless, the translations of the Old Testament, and especially the Authorized (or King James) Version, have been so pervasive in the English speaking world that the Hebrew language has influenced to a large extent our own language. The words and imagery of the biblical text have thoroughly penetrated English language and literature. Indeed, a number of English words still in common use have entered our language from Hebrew, for example: hallelujah, sack (container), shekel, Satan, sabbath, and several others.

Hebrew is written from right to left in a semi-alphabetic script. The script is semi-alphabetic in that during the biblical period only consonants were employed, with a very limited system of vowels. Later on, in the sixth or seventh centuries A.D., a complete system of vowels was developed and the new vowel signs were added to the original consonantal script. Thus if one turns now to a standard edition of the Hebrew Bible, the text will contain both consonants and vowels, but the complex vowel system was added to the original text through the work of scribes who preserved the text through later centuries (see figure 3). The addition of vowels was of great assistance in clarifying the precise meaning of the original text. By way of example, the following phrase in English, written with consonants only, is thoroughly ambiguous: th ct n th mt. If vowels are added, we can be sure it is "the cat on the mat," not "the cut in the meat," or "the cot in the moat," or one of several other possibilities. So the addition of vowels helped enormously to clarify the sense of the ancient Hebrew text. Conversely, because the vowels were added several centuries after the original writing, there is often debate as to whether or not the later scribes added the correct vowels. Likewise, we cannot be sure that Hebrew was pronounced in the same way at the time the vowels were added and at the time the text was originally written. As a consequence, there is no absolute certainty as to how Hebrew was spoken and pronounced in Old Testament times.

Figure 3. HEBREW WRITING

(1) Script without vowels (Genesis 1:1):

בראשית ברא האלהים את־השמים

(Transliteration) br'shyth br' h'lhym 'th-hshmym

(2) Script with vowels added:

בְּרֵאשִׁית בָּרָא הָאֱלֹהִים אֶת־הַשָּׁמַיִם

(Transliteration) berē'shîth bārā' hā'elōhîm 'eth-hashāmayim

The ancient character of the Hebrew language, together with the limitations of the semi-alphabetic system with which it was recorded, explains in part the difficulties in translating the Old Testament and the varieties of phrasing found in modern translations. In many modern versions of the Bible, notes are added to indicate such things as "Hebrew obscure." The Hebrew word may be rare and, therefore, of uncertain meaning; or perhaps the vowels do not seem to make good sense out of the consonants, so that the translator has to judge as to the best sense. In other cases, the differences in English translations may be results of quite different approaches to translating strange Hebrew expressions into appropriate English. Consider the following renditions of Jeremiah 4:19.

King James Version	"My bowels, my bowels!"
Revised Standard Version	"My anguish, my anguish!"
New English Bible	"Oh, the writhing of my bowels. . ."

The King James Version is technically correct, for the Hebrew word means *bowels* or *intestines*. But the Revised Standard Version has an equally appropriate, and perhaps better, translation. In the Hebrew conception, the bowels were the seat of the emotions (just as we might talk about "butterflies in the stomach"), and the sense of the text is clearly an expression of anguish. The New English Bible paraphrases slightly, in an attempt not only to translate, but also to convey appropriately the literary character of the original text.

The student of the Old Testament who does not know Hebrew must depend on an English translation in the study of the text. In choosing an appropriate version for study, the first and most important principle is to choose a *translation* (for example, the Revised Standard Version), not a *paraphrase* (for example, *The Living Bible*). There is a place for paraphrases, especially in making the text available to a large audience, but they are unsuited to careful study. Having established the first principle, there follows the dilemma of choice, for a plethora of English versions of the Old Testament has appeared in recent years. Although the Revised Standard Version (1977) is not the most modern translation, it is one of the most reliable in respect to the Old Testament; it is an extremely useful version for the detailed study of the text.

The Hebrew of the Old Testament is not exactly the same as modern (Israeli) Hebrew, although a direct line of descent runs between the two languages. Modern Hebrew has grown directly from the language of the Old Testament and from post-biblical (the Talmud and Midrashic literature) and medieval Hebrew. Its existence is largely a consequence of the pioneering work in the late nineteenth and early twentieth centuries of Elieser Perlman, who later changed his surname to Ben-Yahuda. Through education and the preparation of a multi-volume dictionary, Ben-Yahuda restored the ancient Hebrew language to life. But there are clear differences between the ancient and the modern languages. Whereas the Old Testament provided a little more than seven thousand words, the vocabulary of modern Hebrew, under the direction of the Israeli Academy of Hebrew Language, is moving quickly toward one hundred thousand. If words cannot be found in the ancient sources, new ones are created following the sense of ancient texts where possible. Therefore, the modern word for "helicopter" is *massoq*, but there are helicopters in neither the Old Testament nor the Talmud. The word is derived from a rare word, *nasaq*, used only once in the Bible (Psalm 139:8) with the sense "go directly upwards." Indeed, the rarity of the word in the Bible is such that many consider it to be an error for *saleq*, "ascend." In either case, it provides the origin of the modern term for "helicopter."

Not only does the vocabulary of modern Hebrew differ from that of biblical Hebrew, but so also do the grammar and pronunciation. Some of the phonetic distinctions observed in the ancient language are no longer observed in the modern, and the grammar and literary style of the Old Testament have been adapted in numerous ways for the everyday usage of the modern language. What this means is that someone who approaches the study of the Old Testament with a knowledge of modern Hebrew is clearly at an advantage over one with no knowledge of the language. Concurrently, the person conversant in modern Hebrew must be careful not to read the modern language, with all its post-biblical developments, into the biblical text.

(b) Aramaic

The second language of the Old Testament is used principally in two biblical books: Daniel 2:4b–7:28, and Ezra 4:8–6:18 and 7:12-26. In addition, occasional Aramaic words and clauses have survived in other biblical texts (for example, Genesis 31:47 and Jeremiah 10:11).

Aramaic is also a Semitic language, though it is by no means as closely related to Hebrew as are languages like Phoenician and Ugaritic. Aramaic, from about the seventh to the third centuries B.C., became the principal language of commerce and international affairs throughout the Near East. Prior to that it had been the language of the Arameans, who were present in the biblical world during both the second and first millennia B.C. Not a great deal is known about the Arameans, though the Hebrews identified themselves with them through their ancestors (Deuteronomy 26:5). Inscriptions in the Aramaic language from the biblical world are known through archaeological discovery (from approximately the tenth century B.C. onward), so that something of the nature of the Aramaic language is known from sources external to the Bible. (Several books of the Apocrypha and many post–Old Testament Jewish texts have also survived in the Aramaic language.)

The international use of the Aramaic language flourished during the Persian Empire and for a short time afterward. Its use in the books of Ezra and Daniel reflects this period of internationalism and the Jews' use of the language of the day in addition to their own native tongue. The use of Aramaic in certain Jewish circles was to survive until New Testament times and beyond; it is possible that Aramaic was the normal language employed by Jesus and some early members of the Christian church.

5. Chronological Perspectives of the Old Testament

The details of chronology will be examined later in this book, in respect to both Israel's history and that of the ancient Near East. But some general chronological perspectives may be useful at the beginning of the study for two reasons. First, when we look back in time, we have a natural human tendency to "telescope" time, to shrink it to a size our minds can comprehend. Time, as we experience it in our daily lives, takes on an altogether different character when we reflect on bygone centuries. Second, it is an arrogance of our era to think that we live in a "modern and advanced world," whereas the Israelites lived in an ancient and primitive one. Certainly, the two differ, but we will understand the ancient biblical world better if we perceive it in the larger context of the history of civilization.

The subject matter of the Old Testament, from Abraham to Ezra, extends over a period of more than a millennium. A millennium, especially when followed by the letters B.C., does not seem to be a long period of time when viewed in the distant past. But let us remember that the period covered within the Old Testament is indeed a vast one, considerably greater than the entire histories of modern nations, such as the United States or Canada. The expanse of time encompassed by the biblical narrative and the relative absence of details concerning its successive centuries are such that we cannot know Israel's story in its entirety. Though it contains history, the Old Testament is not a history book; rather, it recounts the story of a nation's life with God, thus penetrating the realm of faith. The time span in this story of faith is such that the story is told with perspective and maturity. Our own nation has not existed long enough for us to be able to use the wisdom and maturity with which the Israelites reflected upon their national story.

The Old Testament narrative, though it covers a long period of time, should not be read as though it reflected the background of the emergence of civilization. Human civilization in the ancient Near East, in a fairly advanced form, was thoroughly established by about 3,000 B.C.; the story of Israel does not begin until the late second millennium B.C. When we read of Abraham, Moses, or David, we are reading of the pioneers of faith, but not of pioneers of civilization in the more general sense. The civilized world of the time had long been established before Israel stepped upon the stage of human history.

There is a further chronological perspective that is important. The story of the Old Testament establishes the groundwork from which the religion of Judaism was to flourish. Out of Judaism, Christianity emerged in the first century A.D., and the birth and growth of Islam were to be influenced by both Judaism and Christianity. The Old Testament is, from a chronological perspective, the foundational soil from which the three great religions of the western world were to grow. Great religions were also emerging in other parts of the world during this period, though their existence is not reflected in the biblical books. In South Asia, throughout the Old Testament period, the teachings and traditions were taking the shape of what we call Hinduism, and while the biblical prophets ministered in old Israel, other prophets and religious leaders were serving in other parts of the world. In Iran there was the ministry of Zarathustra, from which Zoroastrianism (modern Parsiism) was developed. In South Asia, Gautama Buddha began a ministry of teaching which was to extend rapidly to East Asia. In China the teachings of Confucius and Lao Tzu were to develop into the traditions of Confucianism and Taoism. These chronological and geographical perspectives serve as a reminder that the story of the Old Testament should not be read in isolation. Our text reflects one part of the world and one extraordinary adventure of faith. During the same period in other places contemporary and significant religious movements were taking place. All are important and all are worth studying. What makes the Old Testament take on particular importance for us, citizens of the Western world, is its formative role in the development of what is now Western civilization and its central place in the great religions of the West, both past and present.

6. The Survival of the Old Testament

It is extraordinary that a collection of books written between two and three thousand years ago has survived at all into the period of the modern world. How did the Old Testament survive? How can we be sure that the books that have survived are unchanged, the original works as originally written?

In responding to these questions, there is an important starting point for all that follows: No original manuscripts of the Old Testament exist. They have long since perished, which is hardly surprising given the passage of time and the perishable nature of paper (parchment or papyrus) and ink. There is no original copy of any Old Testament book; indeed, not even a single verse has survived in its original autograph. This is not a radical statement, simply a statement of fact.

If there are no original manuscripts, then upon what text is our English translation of the Old Testament based? When we read the English, we are in fact reading a translation of medieval Hebrew manuscripts, some of which go back to the late ninth century A.D. Therefore, we are left with a gap that must be accounted for, the gap in time between the oldest surviving complete Hebrew manuscripts from the medieval period to the no longer extant original manuscripts which were written more than one thousand years earlier. This chronological gap can be only partially bridged.

Perhaps the greatest series of advances in the knowledge of the ancient Hebrew texts began in 1947. In that year, the first of a series of discoveries was made in a cave near Qumran, a site located in the region of the northwestern end of the Dead Sea. The cave contained ancient manuscripts written in Hebrew. In the years following 1947 more caves were discovered in the same vicinity and were found to contain further manuscripts; these are popularly referred to as the *Dead Sea Scrolls*. Other ancient manuscripts have since been found in the great wilderness area lying to the west of the Dead Sea. These collections of ancient scrolls contain various types of writing from a Jewish community that had once lived in that wilderness region, but of most immediate interest is the fact that the scrolls include manuscripts from the Hebrew Bible. Some of these manuscripts are merely fragments (see figure 4), others are virtually illegible, yet some are of crucial importance and considerable size. Major scrolls, for example, contain large portions of Isaiah, the Psalms, and other biblical books. Some of these scrolls from Qumran and the neighboring wilderness sites may be dated to a period as early as the second century B.C., and almost all are from the period before A.D. 70.

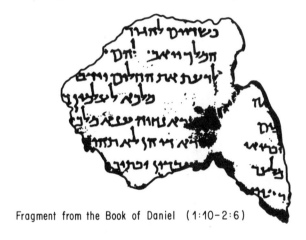

Fragment from the Book of Daniel (1:10–2:6)

Figure 4. Manuscript Fragment from Qumran

Another approach to bridging the gap between the medieval manuscripts on which the English Old Testament is based and the original, but no longer extant, manuscripts of the books is to turn to the evidence of the early translation of the Old Testament into other languages. The first language into which the Old Testament was translated, and therefore the most pertinent to our purpose, is Greek. In the middle of the third century B.C., the Old Testament was translated into Greek in Alexandria, Egypt, for the benefit of the

Jewish community there, who had come to use Greek as the normal language of everyday life. Subsequently, many other Greek translations were made from the Hebrew, both Jewish and Christian, just as today we have a multitude of English translations. Greek manuscripts of the Old Testament, more or less complete, go back to approximately the fourth century A.D., and help to bridge the chronological gap still further. But it must be emphasized again that the gap cannot be bridged entirely. At the moment, the earliest (and very incomplete) witnesses to the Old Testament text come from the second century B.C. There is a gap several centuries, the time varying from one Old Testament book to another, between the earliest extant manuscripts and the no longer existing original manuscripts. Furthermore, the most ancient manuscripts, such as those from Qumran, cannot form the basis of new biblical translations, for they are far from complete. The most modern English translations are still based primarily on the medieval manuscripts, though the translator is now able to take the earlier evidence into account.

Only part of the problem has been solved (and inadequately at that) in this attempt to bridge the gap between medieval and original manuscripts. Granted that it is possible to trace the manuscript evidence back many centuries, how can we be sure that the words of those manuscripts on which our Old Testament is based are precisely the same words that were written by the original author? The answer, from a strictly scientific and historical perspective, is that we cannot be absolutely certain. On the other hand, we can go a long way toward having confidence in the fidelity and authenticity of the medieval manuscript tradition.

To gain this confidence, we need to envision the process involved from the time of a document's first writing to the later evidence of that document that has survived. Let us say, by way of illustration, that in the eighth century B.C. a Hebrew author writes a book which, centuries later, will become a part of the Old Testament. He writes the original book, perhaps, on a scroll, using ink that is a mixture of resin and soot; this is the original manuscript. It will survive for a while; it may even survive longer than its author, but a manuscript is not eternal. If it is stored and used in one of the damper parts of the Promised Land, its "shelf life" will be limited. If it were hidden in a cave near the Dead Sea, which is a dry area with virtually no humidity, its life expectancy would be considerably longer. The book exists originally in a single manuscript; it is not printed or mass produced as are modern books.

The book may be recognized as important; perhaps it is a work that can be used in the context of worship or instruction; so, while the author is still alive, copies of the original manuscript may be made by hand. If the book continues to be used and read over a long period of time, as was certainly the case with the books that were to become part of the Old Testament, further copies will be made. Some copies will be made because more are needed for use, others will be made because the originals are wearing out with the passage of time. So, a manuscript tradition is born, one that will eventually span many centuries continuing on into our modern world.

Now in this whole process of manuscript copying and preservation, the possibility of error occurs. If, for example, the first person to copy the original manuscript makes a small error, all subsequent copyists who make use of the first copy will faithfully perpetuate that error, and every subsequent act of copying leaves open the possibility of further error. Indeed, when you begin to think about the possibilities of such a process being extended over many centuries, it is difficult not to wonder whether the later (surviving) manuscripts will have any direct resemblance to the earlier and original manuscript.

While the possibility of error must be recognized, there are certain other mitigating factors. Any student knows that you can copy a text carefully or casually; the careful copying can be error free, but the casual one is unlikely to be. What is clear from the study of the Hebrew scribal tradition, from ancient times to modern, is the extraordinary care with which the ancient manuscripts were copied and recopied. Every precaution was taken, with countless checks, to preserve the integrity of the manuscript tradition.

One of the most valuable treasures in my library is an enormous four-volume work from the nineteenth century compiled by J. B. de Rossi; it is in Latin, but its title in English would be *Variant Readings of the Old Testament*. De Rossi was one of a few scholars who set himself the task of examining the Hebrew text, in the light of the numerous manuscripts that had survived, to establish the authenticity and clarity of the text according to the manuscript tradition. In the course of his work, he consulted more than seven hundred Hebrew manuscripts and about three hundred other editions of the Bible, including the early versions. He compiled long lists of variant readings, but the overwhelming conclusion of his work is that there was extraordinary uniformity among the manuscripts; he concluded that they must all go back to a single and uniform manuscript tradition.

De Rossi undertook his work, however, before the discovery of the Dead Sea Scrolls, and those manuscripts have slightly changed the scholarly view of the long history of manuscript transmission from the original texts to the surviving documents. The new picture that has emerged goes something like this: From approximately the second century A.D., by which time the Jewish canon of the Hebrew Bible was fixed, there was a single and authoritative text that was transmitted over the centuries. In this text tradition, the variations that appear are of the minor kind (virtually insignificant in meaning) that were compiled by de Rossi. Until the second century A.D., there remained a degree of fluidity with respect to some books. Before the Dead Sea Scrolls were discovered in 1947, for example, it was known that there appeared to have been two early versions of the book of Jeremiah. The version of Jeremiah that survived in the Hebrew manuscripts was quite a bit longer than the Greek Jeremiah, and the chapters and contents were arranged differently. In other words, the people who first translated the book of Jeremiah into Greek used a different manuscript from that which has survived as the main Hebrew text. When the scrolls from Qumran were examined in the years following 1947, it became clear that evidence had survived in those Hebrew manuscripts of *both* versions of Jeremiah, the long and the short text.

To summarize this complicated story, it should be clear that we have not been able to resolve adequately all the questions raised at the beginning. We do not have any original manuscripts, but we can trace some of the manuscript evidence to the second century B.C. There are minor scribal variations among the various Hebrew manuscripts that have survived, the vast majority being relatively insignificant, but we know also of the incredible care and accuracy with which the Jewish scribes preserved and copied their texts from one generation to the next. There are various editions or versions of some ancient books from a very early period (for example, Jeremiah), but by the time the Jewish canon was established (and before the final establishment of the Christian canon), the text of the Old Testament had become fixed and firm. In other words, we do not know with absolute scientific certainty that we have the exact words written by each individual author, but considering the antiquity of the work we have more evidence establishing the general authenticity of the text than we have any right to expect.

There is a final point, though one that cannot be developed in the context of a textbook like this. It is the conviction of both the Jewish and the Christian faiths (though expressed in different ways), that the Hebrew Bible, or Old Testament, is more than just an ancient book. It is the Word of God, the divine revelation, a sacred text. In this sense, the Old Testament books differ fundamentally from works such as those of the Jewish historian Josephus, or the Christian theologian Augustine. Thus from the perspective of Christian or Jewish faith there is an aspect of the authenticity and preservation of the ancient manuscripts that cannot be easily submitted to the historian's investigation or the scientist's microscope. The faith that believes this ancient Scripture to be the Word of God may also exercise faith that in some mysterious fashion God has preserved the integrity of that word in its transmission. This approach is one of faith, consistent with the larger religious belief to which it belongs; it may be informed by a knowledge of the history of the transmission of the Hebrew texts, and indeed should be so informed, but it is not a natural consequence of that study.

7. The Tanak/Old Testament in Contemporary Religion

In the study of the Tanak (Torah, Nebi'im, Kethubim abbreviated), or Old Testament, it is important to remember that although the subject matter is an ancient text, it is also a book of continuing significance for contemporary religions. It is possible to study the Old Testament much as one would the works of Plato—both come to us from the ancient world and both have wisdom to impart. One must go further with the Old Testament; it is not merely an ancient work, but one which has continuing vitality in the modern world. The book plays a central role in two contemporary religions, Judaism and Christianity, and must be differentiated sharply from ancient texts, such as those of Plato.

In the *Qur'an,* the sacred text of Islam, Christians and Jews are referred to as *Al al-Kitab;* the expression means "People of the Book." It is an appropriate expression for designating the members of both faiths, for in each Scripture has an important role to play. At the heart of each religion is a belief in God, but the knowledge of that God is believed to be revealed, in part, through the pages of Scripture. Jews and Christians are thus "People of the Book"—they do not worship the book; its pages point to the substance of both belief and practice.

It is a central perspective of the faith of Judaism that the Tanak constitutes divine revelation. It is not the whole revelation, and the later Mishnah and Talmud complement it. The Tanak is central, and within it the Torah (in the sense of Pentateuch) has pre-eminence. The Torah scrolls, traditionally kept in the ark on the eastern wall of the synagogue, are both the symbol and the substance of Judaism. When the words of the Torah are read to an assembled congregation, they are not merely the words of an ancient text, but the substance of a present and relevant truth. For all the varieties of the modern forms of Judaism (principally Orthodox, Conservative, and Reformed), the Torah provides a common ground, a binding link.

The Old Testament, as a part of the Christian Bible, is no less significant to Christianity. There are varieties of views within the different parts of Christianity (Roman Catholicism, Protestantism, and the Orthodox churches) as to the precise role and authority of the Bible, but the Scripture is shared by all. It affects what is believed and what is practiced; it is read both privately in devotion and publicly in worship. It is never merely an ancient text; it is God's revelation, divine knowledge graciously imparted to mankind in human and physical form.

The precise place and role of the Tanak/Old Testament in Judaism and Christianity are too large a topic to be described adequately in this introductory chapter. All that is stressed here is the importance of recognizing that this ancient book is still, in a special way, modern and living. If we think of it only as a work of antiquity, we will miss much of its power and significance. For all its age, it is still constantly read and proclaimed. It has survived through the centuries not because of the care of antiquarian bibliophiles, but because from one generation to the next it has continued to have a role in living religions. Jews and Christians alike, though they hear and interpret its words with different ears, have listened to the voice of God in this ancient Scripture. Regardless of our own personal perspectives of either belief or unbelief, we shall not perceive the true force of the Old Testament unless we read its words with an awareness that the same words still live in the synagogue and in the church.

The awareness of the continuing life of the Old Testament in contemporary religions should also alert us to the fact that there are different ways of reading this book. The orthodox rabbi, the Christian believer, and the secular scholar will all read the same words, but they will not understand the text in precisely the same manner. They will bring differing faiths, or sets of presuppositions, to bear in their reading. They will bring different questions to the text, and, given the different starting points, they will frequently arrive at different conclusions. All this is pertinent to the perspective from which this textbook on the Old Testament is written. The approach taken here is that of contemporary biblical scholarship, with an inclination toward being conservative rather than radical in contentious matters. Biblical scholarship nowadays is essentially a secular enterprise; therefore, in addition to the standard historical perspectives brought to bear in the examination of an ancient text, an attempt has been made to be sensitive to religious perspectives on the Old Testament, both Jewish and Christian.

8. The Old Testament and the Humanities

The significance of this ancient book in both synagogue and church has naturally secured for it a place of importance in the curriculum of religious colleges and seminaries. Not only future rabbis, priests, and pastors need to know its substance, but also ordinary Christians and Jews may develop an understanding of their faiths through a knowledge of the contents of the Old Testament. That such is the case is hardly surprising; a "Bible" should certainly be known by the adherents to the religion of which it is a part. What is less commonly recognized is that the Old Testament holds a position of considerable prominence outside its immediate religious context; it is an important work, to be studied and read in the context of the humanities or the arts. Although the humanities cannot be restricted to colleges and universities, it is nevertheless instructive to perceive the historical role of Hebrew and Old Testament studies in our educational institutions.

England's King Henry VIII, who is better remembered for his practice of inhumanity than for his contributions to the humanities, established a chair of Hebrew studies at the University of Cambridge in 1540. The study of biblical Hebrew was thus established in that already ancient university, as it was in most other universities of that period. Most of the early European and British universities had a place in their curriculum for the study of the Old Testament, in part as a consequence of their roots in the life of the church.

In the New World, the more ancient practices were continued. Harvard College, four years after its establishment, introduced Hebrew into its curriculum in 1640. Yale University offered classes in Hebrew from its beginning in 1701, and the President of Yale, Ezra Stiles, delivered his inaugural address in Hebrew in 1778; Hebrew, the language of the Old Testament, had become a hallmark of scholarship. It was not only in the universities and colleges that Scripture found its place. In 1647, the Massachusetts Bay Colony passed *Ye olde deluder satan Act,* establishing a school system based upon a knowledge of Scripture (thereby thwarting Satan!). In Canada, as in the United States, Scripture found its place in the educational curriculum from an early date. The study of the Bible and biblical languages was encouraged not only in the religious educational institutions established in the eighteenth century, but also in the secular institutions and colleges that began to emerge in the nineteenth century. Indeed, in the nineteenth century, the study of biblical languages flourished more in Toronto's secular University College than it did in the more numerous church-related colleges.

While it is true that Hebrew and Old Testament studies were introduced into colleges and universities initially on the basis of the religious affiliation of those institutions, the subjects continued to flourish in the arts faculties (and later humanities faculties) of both secular and religious institutions. With the increasing growth of secular and public institutions of higher education in the twentieth century, Hebrew and Old Testament studies have retained a place in the curriculum of most institutions, despite the general pressures and trends in education which tend to downplay the humanities at the expense of educational programs with a more professional focus. There are good reasons for the retention of the Old Testament in the curriculum of the secular institution.

Western civilization, to which we belong, has its roots in the distant past. It has been shaped and influenced by a multitude of disparate forces, but amid the plethora of roots of our civilization two are of particular significance. These two roots are frequently symbolized by the terms *Athens* and *Jerusalem. Athens* represents the civilization of the classical world, with its origins in Greece and its later development in the expansion of the Roman world. It was a civilization in which the arts flourished, but above all one in which philosophy, with its distinctive use of human reason, came into pre-eminence. The importance of Athens in shaping the world is recognized in modern educational systems through the study of classics and of ancient philosophy.

Jerusalem symbolizes the biblical world, with its joint legacy from Judaism and Christianity. Its heritage is preserved primarily in the Bible itself, which is characterized by the perspective of faith, rather than the more rational perspective of Athens. In both ancient Judaism and Christianity various approaches were taken to bring together these traditions of reason and faith, and the tension in the relationship between the two continues to be a distinctive thread throughout the history of Western thought down into our own century.

Because of this joint legacy from Athens and Jerusalem, the classics and the Bible have continued to play influential roles, both positive and negative, in each century of our history. The Old Testament has had a highly significant place in the development of Western civilization, in part, because of the variety of its substance, which touches on literature, politics, history, and many other matters in addition to faith. Consider the following random examples. With respect to modern political thought and philosophy, the writings of Hobbes and of Spinoza are of considerable importance. Hobbes's *Leviathan* and Spinoza's *Theological-Political Tractate* are both thoroughly penetrated by the Old Testament; indeed, both seek to establish a kind of political theory in contradistinction to that implicit in the Old Testament. To take another example, almost any corpus of European literature will be found, upon examination, to contain the influences of the Old Testament. A multivolume *Dictionary of the Bible in English Literature,* currently being prepared for publication in Canada, illustrates the extraordinarily pervasive influence of the Old Testament on English language and letters.

The influence of the Old Testament can be seen not only in intellectual history, but also in the series of persons and events that have shaped our civilization. The New England Puritans, who molded so much of later American thought, understood themselves in Old Testament terms. John Winthrop and his fellow Puritans on the flagship *Arbella,* believed themselves to be participating in an exodus from the European "Egypt" toward the new promised land of America. In an entirely different sense, the image of the exodus became a significant symbol in the theology of black Americans in their continuing struggle for liberation. It has been estimated that in the United States there are forty-seven places called Bethel, sixty-one called Eden, and ninety-five called Salem; obviously the Old Testament used to be a well-read book!

What is true of the United States is also true of Canada, though perhaps in a less distinctive fashion. Whether one looks at the millennial writings of a revolutionary figure like Louis Riel, or the intellectual roots of the Social Gospel movement in the eastern Prairies, the influence of the Bible can be seen. In my own university, which is modern and secular, there is an inscription on the university coat of arms: *Mo shuile togam suas,* a Gaelic translation of Psalm 121:1: "I will lift up my eyes." There may be a certain irony in the fact that a self-consciously secular university has a verse from the Old Testament in its coat of arms; yet, really it is no more than a small symbol of the pervasiveness of the Old Testament, not only in the major intellectual aspects of civilization, but also in the minor characteristics of culture.

The examples that have been given above, both of the place of the Old Testament in the humanities and of its influence in North American history, have been randomly chosen. They are merely signs of a more widespread phenomenon. The Old Testament has had a great deal to do with the shaping of our civilization; so, if we are to understand ourselves, if we are to learn from whence we have come, it would be wise to know the Old Testament and its substance. Whether we belong to the major religious traditions of our society—Judaism and Christianity—whether we are persons of belief or unbelief, we should attempt to read and to understand the Old Testament. In part, it will help us to understand what we are, what we have become. But, in a distinctive fashion, it might also afford us a glimpse of what we might be and of what our society might yet become.

THE
BACKGROUND
OF THE OLD
TESTAMENT PERIOD

THE
CIVILIZATIONS
OF THE ANCIENT
NEAR EAST

C   H   A   P   T   E   R   T   W   O

W E have seen in the opening chapter something of the nature of the Old Testament as a whole. It is a collection of books of extraordinary diversity, and the size of the collection alone is enough to deter the average reader from tackling its thousand or more pages. We may have come across people from time to time who have determined to read the whole Bible. They begin, reasonably enough, with the first chapter of Genesis. The less stalwart flounder somewhere in the middle of Leviticus or Numbers. A few may make it to the books of Chronicles, but only the most determined will reach the final goal—Malachi, chapter 4. To those who have reached the end of the English Old Testament, it may reasonably be asked how much they have understood. If the answer is "Relatively little," it is only fair to add that the fault may not lie entirely with the reader; there are real difficulties encountered in the reading of any ancient text.

1. The Context for Reading the Old Testament

The average North American can read a book written by a twentieth-century author with little difficulty. It is possible to read

John Steinbeck's fiction, set, for example, in California, or the stories of John D. MacDonald, set in Florida, or the popular histories of Pierre Berton—concerning the building of the railroad across Canada—with reasonable ease and speedy comprehension. All these authors, chosen at random, write well, but what we can easily forget is that our capacity to understand a modern book depends not only on the skill of its author, but also on the foreknowledge which we bring to our reading. We are members of the civilization concerning which these authors write. We may have visited, or read about, the settings which form the backgrounds of their stories. We are part and parcel of the same culture from which such books were written; so we are prepared to read these modern books in a way that is quite different from our preparation for reading the Old Testament.

The Old Testament books are not intrinsically more difficult than modern books. Most of us are ill-prepared, by virtue of living in the modern world, for reading books that have emerged from the ancient world. Some of us may be deceived in our approach to the Old Testament; it has influenced so profoundly our own civilization that many portions of it will seem familiar even to the first-time reader. The familiarity, though, may be misleading, for we may be reading the ancient texts through the lenses of later centuries. We should recognize at the outset that we are not so well equipped to read this ancient work as, for example, a Jew of the first century would have been. We may read the Old Testament in excellent translations, but its original languages are not familiar to us. We may read of its culture and civilization, but our own are totally different. It is not so easy to break out of the straitjacket of twentieth-century thinking as we might like to think.

There is a danger, too, in the approach which many will take quite unconsciously in their reading of the Old Testament. The danger might be described as the arrogance of modernity, the assumption that only in our own century has civilization come of age, and that the ancient world was savage and primitive. In the nineteenth century many books about the Old Testament had a paternalistic air, the deep-seated conviction that its stories described simple and primitive peoples when compared to "modern man." This arrogance has not left us in the twentieth century. We may be rightly impressed by the advances in science, technology, medicine, and other areas, but we should not too quickly assume that the people of the biblical world were all primitive savages. We need to read with open minds and a willingness to understand and to learn—this is no easy task for a twentieth-century citizen.

An example of this twentieth-century arrogance can be seen in the various writings of Erich Von Daniken, notably in his popular work *Chariots of the Gods*. Posing as a serious writer (but more seriously committed to a kind of science fiction), Von Daniken explains many of the wonders of ancient Near Eastern civilizations, including the Old Testament miracles, as the work of extra-terrestrial visitors to this planet. The premise has a certain genius, for it is as hard to disprove as it is to prove, but the success of this notion lies in the modern and arrogant conviction that people in ancient times, primitive savages that they were, could not by themselves have produced such extraordinary achievements as the pyramids of Egypt. After all, even we would have difficulty with such projects; so they must have been impossible for the Egyptians. The solution to the dilemma created by modern arrogance emerges from the hatches of spaceships.

What we must do, then, in our attempt to approach the Old Testament with understanding is to bring to our reading some knowledge of the biblical world and its various civilizations. Recognizing the gap between the twentieth century and the biblical centuries, we can seek to bridge it, thereby enabling a more intelligent approach to and reading of the text of the Old Testament. Thus the purpose of Part II of this book is to provide, in very general terms, a broad overview of the world in which the biblical story is set, noting something of its civilization, its history, and its interaction with the Old Testament narrative. It is true, of course, that the civilizations of the ancient Near East form a vast field of study in and of themselves; therefore, we can only scratch the surface of that larger field of study, but enough may emerge to illuminate the background of the Old Testament. First, however, before developing the Near Eastern context, a very brief synopsis of the Old Testament story should be given with an emphasis on the points of contact between that story and the surrounding civilizations.

2. A Synopsis of the Old Testament Story

The Old Testament is not, strictly speaking, a historical work, but it contains a kind of historical framework within which much of its substance is set. At this stage in our study, the story will be told without attention to the critical problems of history; these will be addressed in more detail in chapter ten. For the moment, it is sufficient to convey a broad grasp of the story as it emerges from the text read uncritically, which in turn will provide the overall context within which the component parts of the Old Testament are set.

The antecedents to the story of Israel begin with the patriarchal figure Abraham, who, with his descendants, forms the focus of Genesis 12–50. The story is one of a family's adventures in life and in faith, extending over many generations and several centuries. It begins with Abraham in Haran, a city in northern Mesopotamia (now within the southeastern borders of Turkey). The travels of the patriarch and his successors involve passage through Syria and Palestine, ending up at last in Egypt. The chronological setting implied by this narrative concerning the Hebrew patriarchs is mid-second millennium B.C., and the geographical setting of the story spans the great empires of the biblical world from Mesopotamia to Egypt.

The aspirations of the patriarchs for a land of their own and for the status of nationhood began to take on shape and substance in the books following Genesis. The Hebrew people—who had become, by the fourteenth century B.C., slaves in Egypt—are led out of Egyptian slavery by a new leader, Moses. Escaping via Egypt's eastern boundaries, the former slaves begin a long series of journeys which will take them at last to a land they will make their own and will eventually call Israel. This escape, perhaps to be dated at the beginning of the thirteenth century B.C., is followed a little more than two centuries later by the establishment of a kingdom, with its capital in Jerusalem in the region we still think of as Israel. This kingdom, headed by Saul, David, and Solomon, survived intact for about a century and was for a brief time a superpower in the world of nations. But the fragile unity of the kingdom could not survive the changing of circumstances. In about 922 B.C., following the death of King Solomon, the kingdom broke up into two separate states, Israel in the north and Judah in the south. The northern kingdom maintained its independence until 722 B.C., when it was destroyed by the invading armies of the Assyrian Empire from the north. The southern kingdom lasted a little longer, but by 586 B.C., it too had been defeated in war, this time by the Babylonian Empire. In 586 B.C., it is as if the story that started in the dreams of Abraham more than a millennium earlier had come at last to an end, but such is not the case.

The defeat of Judah and the sack of Jerusalem, occurring in the year 586 B.C., are followed by the dispatch into exile of a significant portion of the population of Jerusalem. The exiles take up residence in Babylon, cut off from their homeland, in a part of the world belonging nowadays to Iraq. In the sixth century B.C. the international situation was in a state of flux. When the Persians conquered the Babylonians, many of those Jewish people in exile were permitted to return home. Back in Jerusalem, they set about the task of restoring the ruined city and rebuilding the once splendid temple. There was also extensive religious reformation, especially in the fifth century B.C., and there emerged the essentially new religion of Judaism from what had formerly been the state religion of Israel. The restoration of an independent Israelite state was not to prove possible in the Old Testament period. The Jews were to remain a subject people, ruled at first on their return from exile by the Persians and later by the Greeks. Whereas during the years of the kingdoms the people had lived in their own land, from the time of the exile onward, Jewish communities lived in various parts of the then known world; the Diaspora, or dispersion of Jewish communities throughout the world, had been born.

Such, in bare outline, is the Old Testament story; it is of course subject to much debate in modern historical study, especially with respect to the earlier period. What is intriguing about the story at this stage in our study is the way in which it spans the millennia (from approximately 1800 B.C. to 200 B.C.) and encroaches upon the various civilizations of the ancient Near Eastern world. We will need to know something more about Israel's history in order to understand better the books of the Old Testament that emerged from that historical experience. In order to understand this whole biblical story better, it must first be seen in the larger context of its times and contemporary civilizations. The story of Israel, however, does not begin with the rise of civilization; that had already been well established before our story begins.

3. The Beginnings of Civilization

The beginnings of the civilized world impinge only indirectly on the biblical story, but insofar as Israel emerges, albeit as a latecomer, within one of the principal cradles of human civilizations, a brief account of the beginnings of civilization helps to set the stage. The word *civilization* can be used in various contexts, but in this sense it describes the emergence of complex forms of human society out of earlier, more simple configurations.

In very general terms, the world's earliest civilizations appear to have arisen, probably independently, in three areas—the Middle East, China, and America. In chronological terms, the civilized societies emerging in the Middle East came first, antedating the birth of Chinese civilization and the somewhat later developments in Central and South America. From the Middle East, civilization appears to have spread in at least two directions—westward into the Mediterranean world and eastward, via Iran, to the Indus Valley in South Asia (though the Indus civilization may also have arisen relatively independently).

In the Middle East, several separate civilizations developed, though with some degree of interaction, in three regions—Mesopotamia (essentially the region of modern Iraq), Egypt, and the territory lying between these two regions (commonly called Syria-Palestine). The development of these societies occurred gradually between the fifth and the third millennia B.C. During this period, there was a slow transition from simple communities (villages, tribal settlements) to complex communities, from rural settlements to urban culture. Building capacities developed, from the simple homes of the early period to the large and complex temples which were being erected around 3000 B.C. Agricultural methods advanced, irrigation was practiced in both Mesopotamia and Egypt, various metals began to be employed, and gradually the shape of human settlement in this world moved toward the complex urban forms that are still with us today. The complexities of this developing civilization brought with them new requirements; the development of writing was one of the major servants of this newly emerging society, being used in Mesopotamia shortly before 3000 B.C. and in Egypt soon thereafter.

From the perspective of reading the Bible, the important point to remember is that this complex variety of emerging Middle Eastern civilizations was already well established long before the Old Testament story begins. Abraham, if we accept him for the moment as a real figure of human history, would have lived around 1800 B.C.; by that time, civilization would have flourished both in his native Mesopotamia and in Egypt for more than a millennium. The civilized world was marked by large and prospering cities; many of the great temples of Mesopotamia and the extraordinary pyramids of Egypt had been built long in the past, and must have seemed as permanent as the mountains and the rivers. Writing, which had been employed initially for business and administrative purposes, had been harnessed for the service of literature, and though literacy was relatively limited, there were competent scribes and gifted authors in many parts of the civilized world. In Mesopotamia, mathematics and science were developed in simple forms. In Egypt, medicine of a fairly sophisticated kind is known to have been practiced. In all regions, religions flourished, temples were built, and notions of law and morality were being developed.

It is possible, of course, to paint too rosy a picture of civilization in the era preceding Abraham. It had its dark side, as does our own civilization in the twentieth century. War between nations was as common then as it is now; beyond the boundaries of the civilized state there always lay the threat of invasion from less civilized but very powerful peoples and tribes. Syria-Palestine, lying between the principal centers of Egypt and Mesopotamia, was frequently in a state of turmoil; it was characterized not only by internal strife between the small city-states that sought to control its land, but it was also the natural battleground on which the successive empires of Mesopotamia and Egypt fought their battles. In some ways little has changed from ancient times to modern; each step in the advance of civilization seems to have been accompanied by an advance in the technology of warfare. Though mankind has advanced from the simple social existence of the village and camp to the complex life of city and nation, human beings did not escape from the prevalence of violence and the common experience of warfare.

The biblical story thus begins in a world already long civilized, as human civilizations go, but one frequently marred by warfare. As the story develops over more than a millennium, it constantly interacts with the surrounding civilizations, being influenced by them and concurrently reacting to them. The Hebrew people shape their own destiny and faith in a world which they cannot ignore. Even when they reject aspects of the religions and civilizations of their neighbors they are being shaped by them. Thus if we are to understand the key figures in the Old Testament story, we should know a little more of the world in which they live. Let us now look more closely at the three regions of the biblical world as they were during the Old Testament period.

4. Mesopotamia and Its Empires

The word *Mesopotamia*, meaning literally the land between the rivers, is used more generally to describe the larger region through which two great rivers flow—the Tigris and the Euphrates. The western river, the Euphrates, arises in the Taurus mountains of southern Turkey and follows a southeasterly route toward the Persian Gulf along a course of more than seventeen hundred miles. The shorter Tigris River, approximately eleven hundred miles long, has its sources in the eastern Taurus mountains and the mountains of Armenia and flows south toward the Gulf, east of the Euphrates.

Figure 5. *Map of Mesopotamia*

The land between and around these rivers was one of the earliest seedbeds of human civilization. In geographical terms, the territory forms a natural unity, bordered on the west and south by the great Arabian desert, on the east by the foothills of the Iranian plateau, and to the north by a further range of mountains. In modern political terms, the territory is divided; most of ancient Mesopotamia lies in the

Figure 6. *Headdress of the lady Pu-abi, from the royal tombs of Ur (ca. 2650-2550 B.C.)*

modern state of Iraq, but in the north and west the ancient territory is now part of the modern states of Turkey and Syria. It was a land in which the development of civilization was made possible principally because of the rivers. The Tigris and Euphrates provided water which in the north made for fertile lands and in the south could be used for irrigation, but more than that, the rivers were waterways providing means of transportation between the regions. The importance of the rivers can be seen in the fact that all the great cities of ancient Mesopotamia were beside or close to one of the great rivers—Ur, Nippur, Babylon, Assur, and Nineveh all found their lifeblood in the Tigris or the Euphrates.

Figure 7. *Gold helmet from the tomb of Mes-kalam-dug; found at Ur, Early Dynastic period*

The cities grew first; then as their power was established there emerged the city-state as the primary form of national and economic life in ancient Mesopotamia. The economy was based initially upon agriculture, upon the crops sustained in the rich soil of the two river valleys, and upon herds of cattle. The land could produce more food than the population required; so the excess could be bartered for those commodities which were absent in Mesopotamia—wood and stone for construction purposes and various kinds of metals. Based on this mixed economy, with an agricultural base and a growing international trade with less developed regions, the city-states became more powerful and expanded their holdings of land. Throughout Mesopotamia's history there was continuing tension, and frequently warfare, between the centers of power in southern Mesopotamia and those in the north, each region trying to control the other. During the biblical period, the two principal areas of strength were Babylon (both a city and a state in southern Mesopotamia) and Assyria (in northern Mesopotamia). Both states rose to periods of imperial power, and both, in their desire to be the world power of the time, extended for a while their control of the biblical world. The frequent references to Babylon and Assyria in the Old Testament indicate the extent to which these two Mesopotamian superpowers alternated in their attempts to control the land settled by the Hebrews.

Figure 8. *Gold cup and lamp, from Ur royal tombs, Early Dynastic period*

The general term used to describe the languages of Mesopotamia is *Akkadian*, a Semitic language which was employed in different dialects in the various regions. In the biblical period, Babylonian and Assyrian were the languages used in the southern and northern regions respectively, each in turn being a subdivision of Akkadian. The languages have been preserved in a variety of written texts recovered by means of archaeological exploration. The texts, in turn, indicate something of the diversity of Mesopotamian culture. Some Akkadian texts reflect the normal business of daily life in ancient Mesopotamia. There are business documents, administrative texts, medical texts,

Figure 9. *Statuette of a he-goat standing by a tree; made of gold, silver, lapis lazuli, and white shell on a wooden core; from Ur, Early Dynastic period*

political treaties, and various kinds of contracts. Several examples of legal texts have survived, including the famous Law Code of Hammurabi, which sheds light on the judiciary and legislative system of the time. Other texts include religious works, literary creations, and historical annals. From the examination of these texts, the fabric of daily life and thought in ancient Mesopotamia can be partially reconstructed, but equally important, the texts shed light on the study of the Old Testament. In later chapters, as we study the particular forms of Hebrew literature, we shall return to these Mesopotamian writings to see the manner in which they illuminate the context of the biblical texts.

Literary works, together with the remains of temples and other physical artifacts, also make possible a preliminary reconstruction of

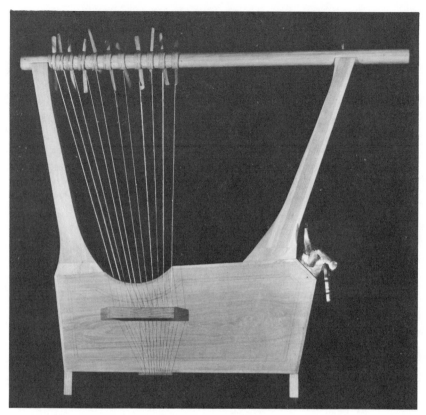

Figure 10. Lyre with gold and lapis bull's head from the death pit at Ur

the religions of the Mesopotamian world. Although each sub-region within the larger area had its own distinctive religious traditions, there was a large commonality of religious thought and practice throughout Mesopotamia. Religion was essentially polytheistic, involving the belief in and worship of numerous gods. The gods, in turn, represented for the most part aspects of the natural world. There was a god of sky and a god of land, a god of rain and a god of grain, gods who represented life and those who threatened death. In addition, certain deities represented particular places, especially cities, and became identified as the patrons or rulers of those cities or states. The gods were classified in a hierarchy of both high and low gods, the former being particularly powerful. The cities and city-states, although ruled in practical terms by a human king, were the domains of particular gods for whom the king acted as regent. Thus Marduk was not only a prominent god in Babylon, but was in effect the absolute ruler of Babylon who was represented before the citizens through his appointed king. The temples of the gods were the central and most splendid buildings in the cities. The worship of the gods and the making of offerings to them were not free options, but requirements of citizenship. Therefore, the kings, holding authority believed to be delegated directly by the chief god, exercised enormous powers in the states they ruled in ancient Mesopotamia. Religion saturated the lives of human beings in the ancient Mesopotamian states; this, too, was to have its influence on the biblical world.

This bird's-eye sketch of civilization in ancient Mesopotamia is hardly sufficient for a careful study of the Old Testament. It will be necessary to return and to examine the details in subsequent chapters as we study particular parts of the Old Testament, but it is important to stress from the beginning the significance of Mesopotamia for Old Testament study. Abraham and his ancestors emerged from Mesopotamian civilization, particularly from the context of its northern manifestations. The great empires of Assyria and Babylon constantly hovered on the horizons of Israel's political and national history; it was the Assyrians who destroyed the northern state of Israel in 722 B.C. and the Babylonians who defeated Judah and Jerusalem in 586 B.C. Babylon became the home of those Hebrews exiled from Judah after 586 B.C., and it left its dark stamp on many of the chapters of the Old Testament. In these and many other ways the civilization of ancient Mesopotamia has marked the pages of the Bible, sometimes for the better and frequently for the worse. One thing is clear—if we are to understand fully the text of the Old Testament, we should know something about Mesopotamia.

5. Ancient Egypt

Whereas the ancient Mesopotamian civilizations developed in the region of two great rivers, the Tigris and the Euphrates, Egypt grew along the banks of a single river, the Nile. Were it not for the Nile, there could have been no Egypt, for its waters flowed north toward the Mediterranean through land that would otherwise be desert. The river's waters and the silt it deposited in the valley made human habitation possible along its banks. The Nile is one of the world's longest rivers, flowing approximately forty-two hundred miles from its furthest headstream in central Africa (the Luvironza) via Lake Victoria to the Mediterranean Sea.

There were two quite distinct regions in the territory that constituted the ancient kingdom of Egypt. Upper Egypt, the southern region, was the portion of the Nile Valley that extended northward from the river's first cataract (modern Aswan) to approximately the region of the modern city of Cairo. This territory was no more than a long strip of land following the course of the river, the inhabitable areas being in places only a few hundred yards wide and occasionally widening to a breadth of about twelve miles. To the east and west of the strip lies the inhospitable desert. North of Cairo, the river branches out into several streams which flow toward the Mediterranean; this triangular northern region, the delta area, was known as Lower Egypt.

From an early date in the third millennium B.C., these two regions of the Nile were united to form a single kingdom. The centuries of the third millennium saw the initial, and in many ways the greatest, period of the development of Egyptian civilization. During the course of the third millennium, some of the earliest and largest pyramids were constructed—Djoser's famous step pyramid, constructed from blocks of cut stone, was erected around 2650 B.C., and several of the great pyramids at Giza were constructed in this period. What made the growth of civilization and the development of a powerful kingdom possible was the river. All regions of Egypt have extremely

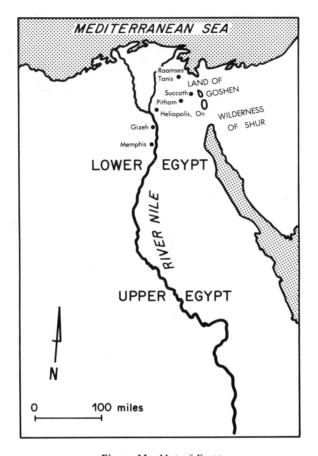

Figure 11. Map of Egypt

low amounts of precipitation, and only the river waters make the production of crops possible. The regular supply of river water made it feasible to harvest crops three times a year in good periods, producing an abundant food supply. The silt, carried from the Ethiopian highlands via the Blue Nile in the annual autumnal flood, constantly enriched the Egyptian Nile Valley, increasing its capacity to bear crops.

The civilization of Egypt, which had reached a highly developed form by the first half of the third millennium B.C., was to continue with very little change for almost three thousand years. Within the kingdom there were, of course, high and low points, with the transition from one royal dynasty to the next and the changes in international conditions. But the main features of Egyptian civilization were to remain without fundamental change until around 332 B.C., when the military advances of Alexander the Great changed much of the face of the ancient world.

Figure 12. Egyptian wall painting showing Apuy's house and garden, from Nineteenth Dynasty, Thebes

The Egyptian state took the form of a monarchy, though it differed in several ways from that of the Mesopotamian city-states. It was ruled by a king, or *pharaoh,* but rather than simply being a regent of the god, the pharaoh was believed to be a god, or divine being in human form. As such he had enormous authority, but he was also responsible for maintaining and governing the state according to certain principles of justice. Whereas in Mesopotamia the focus of power had shifted from time to time with the rise to imperial power of different city-states—notably Assyria and Babylonia—there was more continuity and stability in Egypt. Although its dynasties changed from time to time, as did its capital cities, Egypt was essentially one nation with a unified culture. Its geographical boundaries, of desert and ocean, not only gave to it a natural internal unity, but also made it relatively easy to defend against external aggressors. Although it succumbed on a few occasions to foreign enemies, such defeats were primarily a consequence of internal weakness and dissension. It is fair to say that ancient Egyptian civilization, though now long dead, was the longest continuing form of a single culture that has yet been seen through the centuries of human history.

Figure 13. *Statuette of the god Amon in the precinct of the Great Temple of Amon at Karnak*

Of the remains of ancient Egypt the most remarkable are those which testify to the achievements in architecture and construction. The largest of the pyramids—that of Cheops at Giza—was traditionally one of the Seven Wonders of the World. It covers an area, in total, of approximately thirteen acres, and the dimensions of

Figure 14. An Egyptian painted wooden mummy case, used for burial

6 3

the pyramid were originally 756 feet square at the base and 482 feet high. The construction of such a monument from blocks of limestone—to house a royal tomb—is an extraordinary achievement in terms not only of architecture, but also of organization, management, and engineering competence. In addition to the pyramids, there remain also the temples and monuments of ancient Egypt which, despite their age of several thousands of years, can still be observed by the traveler in modern Egypt.

In ancient Egypt there was a sense of continuity and changelessness in the culture that is rare in the annals of human history. Perhaps the flow of the Nile, with its regular and predictable annual flooding, together with the sense of timelessness provided by the immense pyramids, caused this distinct mindset for the Egyptians of ancient times. There is a calmness and optimism in Egyptian religion, for example, that is in marked contrast to the more turbulent and pessimistic spirit of religion in Mesopotamia. The Egyptians, like

Figure 15. *A hawk, wearing a crown, represents the Egyptian god Horus*

their neighbors in Asia, had a polytheistic religion—different aspects of the natural world were represented by different deities, and certain regional deities were worshiped in particular places. Egyptian religion breathes not only with a certain contentment in earthly life, but also with a very optimistic anticipation of the life to come; beyond the grave, there lay another and better world. Whereas in Egypt's earlier history such a belief may have focused on the royal family, this belief in a happy life after death later spread to become a part of popular religion.

Egypt, like Mesopotamia, was also to impinge in many ways on the biblical world. In the latter half of the second millennium B.C., according to the biblical narrative the descendants of Abraham became residents of Egypt for several centuries. At about the beginning of the thirteenth century B.C. the Hebrews, who by then had become virtual slaves in the construction industry, escaped from their Egyptian servitude under the leadership of Moses. Throughout the history of the Hebrew kingdoms, Egypt was perennially one of the world's great superpowers that had to be taken into account in international and political affairs. Egypt was at times an uncertain ally of the Israelites, at times a threatening enemy, but always a symbol of the slavery of the past. Lying to the south of the nation of God's chosen people, Egypt could never be ignored, and its ominous shadow is cast over many of the chapters of the Old Testament.

Influence, though, is a hard reality to pin down. In matters of faith and religion, the Israelites developed their thinking in direct contrast to the civilization of Egypt. But in other areas, the interactions between the two cultures can be seen in a more positive light. There existed in the Egyptian language (which is not Semitic, but a Hamitic language) a great body of literature, ranging from historical annals to religious and literary texts. As we shall see in subsequent chapters, a knowledge of Egyptian language and literature can be most helpful in the study of Old Testament texts, just as Egyptian history provides a backdrop to the unfolding story of Israel.

6. Syria and Palestine

Lying between Mesopotamia and Egypt is the land along the eastern seaboard of the Mediterranean which is the focal point, in geographical terms, of the Old Testament story. Unlike the neighboring regions to the northeast and southwest, the territory commonly labeled Syria-Palestine does not have any natural geographical or cultural unity. Indeed, what little unity the region has is created by virtue of its being a "land between"—it is between the Mediterranean Sea to the west and the desert to the east, and it is between Egypt in the southwest and Mesopotamia in the northeast. On the positive side, this "betweenness" made Syria-Palestine a region through which many trade routes passed, creating the potential of wealth for its inhabitants. On the negative side, Syria-Palestine became a kind of buffer zone between the various superpowers of the ancient world, and its lands were frequently the fields of battle upon which alien nations fought their wars.

In part, the lack of unity in the region is the consequence of its mixed and divergent geographical character. The western area, bordering the Mediterranean, is hemmed in for much of its length by mountain ranges rising just east of the coastal plain. It is an area affording the possibility of a mixed economy based on shipping, fishing, dye-making (from murex shells), agriculture, fruit farming, and various other enterprises. East of the coastal plain are ranges of mountains, hills, and plateaus, higher in the north than they are in the south. Moving farther east, the terrain changes considerably from north to south. The flatter lands of Syria in the north give way to the Jordan Valley in the south, which sinks eventually more than one thousand feet below sea level to the Dead Sea in a harsh and barren landscape. Moving still further east, the inhabitable land gives way gradually to the northern portion of the great desert region that reaches up from central Arabia.

This large territory is like a patchwork quilt stitched together from almost every conceivable variety of land that is known on earth. Within a short distance one can travel from lush coastal plains to high barren mountains, and then drop into the near-jungle of the Jordan before passing on into desert terrain. Movement from place to place was possible by means of a network of roads developed in ancient times, but the roads did not so much join the parts of a single area as link more or less independent regions. Syria-Palestine is a mosaic of smaller territories separated by geographical boundaries, but linked together into a largely common history by the tides of international fortune.

Figure 16. *The Pyramids of Mycerinus (ca. 2470 B.C.), Chefren (ca. 2500 B.C.), and Cheops (ca. 2530 B.C.), Giza*

Figure 17. *Court and pylon of Ramses II (ca. 1260 b.c.) and Colonnade and court of Amenhotep III (ca. 1390 b.c.), Temple of Amun-Mut-Khons, Luxor*

Figure 18. The Great Sphinx (ca. 2500 B.C.), Giza

Figure 19. *Map of Syria-Palestine*

The "promised land," which for a time was to be the home of the Hebrew kingdoms, lay in the south of this larger region. It was much closer to Egypt than it was to Mesopotamia, being separated from that large southern state only by the desert region around Gaza at the southeastern corner of the Mediterranean. The variety of terrain in Syria-Palestine as a whole is reproduced in the southern territory that was occupied by the Israelites. The coastal plain was bordered by the highlands of Samaria and Judea, which in turn gave way to the great rift of the Jordan Valley. Beyond the Jordan there were pasture lands and forests before the desert boundary, and to the south of Judea the hill country and inhabitable regions also gave way eventually to the desert of the northern region of the Sinai peninsula.

The physical diversity of Syria-Palestine explains in part the difficulties of nomenclature, for the expression *Syria-Palestine* is not entirely satisfactory. There was no single civilization or culture that ever dominated the region in such a way as to give it a single name. The word *Canaan* in the Bible almost fills the bill, but Canaan did not include the northernmost portion of the land being described. Even today the lack of unity from the ancient world continues; in modern times, the nations inhabiting the region include Israel, Jordan, Lebanon, and Syria. Likewise, in the biblical world many different states were present in the region, and a separate list of nations would have to be provided for each of the centuries of ancient history, such was the rapidity of change. Early in the biblical period, there were numerous Canaanite city-states in the south, and somewhat larger and more powerful states, such as the kingdom of Ugarit (until around 1150 B.C.) in the north. In the first millenium, in addition to Israel and Judah there were Phoenician states, such as Tyre and Sidon (in the region that is now Lebanon), Edom and Moab to the east of the Jordan and the Dead Sea, and Syria to the north. The fluctuating tides of history resulted in rapid change and the rise and fall of small states that are now scarcely remembered—we shall examine some of the facets of this history in a little more detail in a later chapter. For the whole region of Syria-Palestine, the history of development and change can only be understood in terms of the involvement of Mesopotamia and Egypt in that area. For only brief periods of the history of Syria-Palestine could the states that were established there claim total independence; much of the time they were either in alliance with, or in subservience to, Egypt or some Mesopotamian empire.

For all the diversity of geography and the proliferation of separate states, there were some commonalities of culture and religion. The general religious tenor of the region was more akin to that of Mesopotamia than to Egypt. Each region had its own gods, both those associated with the natural world and those associated with particular places and nations. But the belief in, and worship of, some gods crossed both geographical and national boundaries. The god Baal, for example, who was identified with rain and storm, and thus associated with the fertility of the ground and its potential for crop-production, is known to have been worshiped in many areas, both north and south. Strictly speaking, each Baal may have been viewed by its followers in the various regions as a distinct deity, but the evidence that has survived indicates that what was believed of Baal on the Syrian coast was not too different from what was believed in the interior of Canaan.

There was, therefore, an element of religious unity penetrating the

7 1

geographical and national diversity of Syria-Palestine. There was also a degree of linguistic unity. The languages spoken in the north of the region have certain fundamental similarities to those spoken in the south. Although there is insufficient evidence to provide the basis for firm judgment, there may also have been a degree of unity throughout the region in areas such as literature and the arts. Certainly the various sub-regions of Syria and Palestine have more in common when compared with one another than they do with either Mesopotamia or Egypt.

Perhaps because of the lack of natural unity in the region, the various indigenous cultures and civilizations were supplemented and enriched from time to time by the invasions, or settlements, of persons from other regions. Hurrians, Hittites, Philistines, Arameans, and others penetrated the region during the second and first millennia B.C. They brought with them cultures of their own, but also adapted the native culture and made it a part of their own. Syria-Palestine was in some ways a cultural and religious melting pot, a region in which various kinds of syncretism were taking place and producing a new and mixed culture distinctive of the region. When we read in the Old Testament, for example, of the "Hittites, the Girgashites, the Amorites, the Canaanites, the Perizzites, the Hivites, and the Jebusites" (Deuteronomy 7:1), we are afforded a glimpse both of native and foreign elements in the land and of the melting-pot character of ancient Syria-Palestine.

This geographical region, then, is the immediate setting for much of the Old Testament story. In one sense, Syria-Palestine is the geographical and political context within which we may read and understand Israel's story. The Hebrew people were constantly engaged in every kind of interaction with their neighbors. But in another sense, on the larger canvas of history the story of Israel is an integral, though small, part of the history of Syria-Palestine. The Hebrew peoples, and later the Hebrew kingdoms, contribute relatively brief episodes to the history of Syria-Palestine. It is the Old Testament, the legacy to subsequent faith and civilization, which puts the Hebrews on center stage in our present study. However, we should not project that significance back into history; during the second and first millennia B.C., the Hebrews played for the most part small roles on the stage of human history.

7. The Beginnings of a New World: the Persians and the Greeks

Up to this point, our survey of the context of the biblical story has traced the outlines of surrounding civilizations in terms of geographical regions. Toward the end of the fourth century B.C., a radical change was to take place which would transform the ancient Near Eastern world and provide a somewhat different setting for the last chapters of the Old Testament story. At the beginning of the fourth century B.C., the old world was coming to an end. A new age was dawning, and its herald was Alexander the Great.

Even before the coming of the new world change had been in the air, and in some ways it was the Persians who not only dominated the last two centuries of the old world, but also paved the way for the new. Lying to the east of the great valleys of the Tigris and Euphrates, Persia (or Iran) seems to be a considerable distance from the biblical world. But the accession of Cyrus II to the Persian throne around 559 B.C. was the first of a series of events that were to catapult the Persians into the spotlight of the biblical story. Cyrus was a part of the Achaemenid Dynasty, which was to extend Persian power beyond the boundaries of the Iranian homeland to control much of the Middle Eastern world for approximately two centuries. In 539 B.C., Cyrus conquered the city of Babylon and attained much of what had been the Babylonian Empire. He was succeeded in 530 B.C. by his son, Cambyses. He and his successors gradually consolidated the Persian hold on the empire built by Cyrus. By about 500 B.C., the Persian Empire included both the traditional centers of power in the old world—Mesopotamia and Egypt—but it extended much further than any of the older empires had. To the west, Asia Minor (modern Turkey) and parts of southeastern Europe (Macedonia) were within the imperial boundaries; in the east, Persian territories extended to the Indus River, including much of the region that is now called Afghanistan and (west) Pakistan.

As in the sixth century B.C. the pendulum of power had swung to the east with the rise of Persia, so in the fourth century B.C. it swung to the west. A young man in Macedonia (a part of the Greek world) had succeeded his father, Philip II, to the throne at the age of twenty. His name was Alexander (more precisely, Alexander III of Macedonia, later to be called "Alexander the Great"). Alexander began a series of military campaigns in 336 B.C., invading Asia Minor to liberate the Greeks there from Persian control. What was initially a military mission quickly became a march toward world control. In 333 B.C., he defeated the Persian Emperor, Darius III, at Issus in northern Syria. From there he marched southward, taking control of Syria-Palestine and Egypt by the end of 332 B.C. Having secured his southern front, he continued his eastward march, taking Mesopotamia, Persia itself, and territories as far east as the Indus Valley and the Punjab (in South Asia) into the control of his rapidly expanding empire. Alexander died in 323 B.C. while still a young man (approximately thirty-three years of age), but by then the shape of the known world had been radically transformed.

Alexander's military achievements were extraordinary—taken alone, they would have won him a permanent place in military history and the *Guinness Book of Records*. But he did more than conquer; he took with him wherever he went the Hellenic culture from the Greek states of his homeland (he had been a pupil of Aristotle). Thus he traveled the world not only as military leader, but also as a "civilizer," in the sense of planting Greek (or Hellenic) culture wherever he went, founding new cities based on the Greek pattern, and transforming the very shape of the territories that came under his control. Alexander's empire did not last long, breaking apart after his death into several smaller (though still very large) regions that were taken over by his generals. But his impact on civilization and culture was to last long after his death, still permeating the entire Middle Eastern world in New Testament times.

The empires of the Persians and the Greeks provide the background for the final scenes in the Old Testament story and for the period in which the Old Testament, as a collection of books, was gradually to develop its present form. It was the rise of the Persians and their conquest of the Babylonians that made possible the first return of Jewish exiles to Jerusalem from Babylon. It was under the overall control of the Persians that Judaism, largely under the influence of Ezra and Nehemiah, was to emerge as the new form of the ancient faith of Israel. There are few, if any, direct references to Alexander and the Greek empire in the Old Testament, though it remains probable that several biblical books assumed their final form

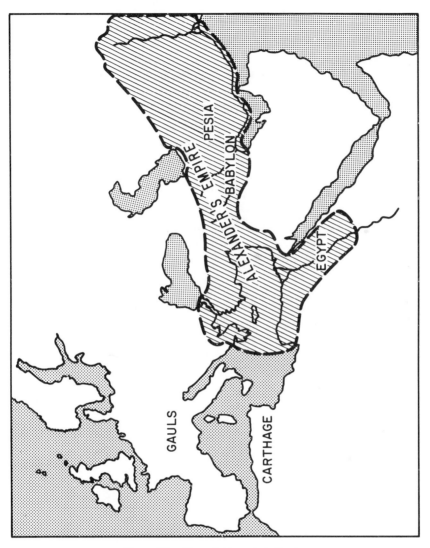

Figure 20. *Map of Alexander's Empire*

in the context of the Greek world. But it was in the Egyptian city of Alexandria, named after the great conqueror, that a significant event took place for the study of the Old Testament. By the third century B.C. there was a large Jewish community in Alexandria, and for their benefit the biblical books were translated from Hebrew to Greek—the translation being referred to as the *Septuagint*. This translation was to be influential both in the later history of the Jewish faith and in the rise of Christianity some three centuries later.

8. Summary: the Context of the Old Testament Story

It may at first seem strange to spend so much time on the biblical world before turning to the study of the Old Testament. Nevertheless, the attempt to understand the context of the biblical story is important.

Consider a more recent analogy. If one were to study and understand the history of the United States, the task could not be undertaken in isolation from the larger currents of history. The beginnings of American history are tied intimately not only to what was happening in England, but also to the religious and political events in various European countries. Modern American history is set equally firmly in an international context. The Soviet Union, the Middle East, Latin America, and other regions all directly influence an understanding of the United States, with respect to both its internal and external policies. To use another example, it would be equally impossible to understand Canada divorced from its relation to the external world and other cultures. Canada's historic attempts to establish its own identity in the context of its British and French legacies, and in recent times to establish a national and economic identity distinct from that of its powerful neighbor, the United States, all require that the study of Canada be conducted in a wide context with a knowledge of the surrounding world.

The study of ancient Israel is no different. To understand both Israel and the books of the Old Testament, we must bring with us some knowledge of the biblical world. This principle would be important in any such study, but its importance is emphasized in this context by virtue of the fact that the Old Testament constantly refers to its environment. Babylon, Assyria, Canaan, Egypt, and many other places are frequently referred to in the biblical texts. It is in the context of these civilizations, with their different cultures and alien faiths, that Israel's journey of faith moves from one century to the next and is eventually deposited for us in the pages of the Old Testament.

There is one further area which we must explore, by way of background, before we turn to the substance of the Old Testament. In this survey of the biblical world, how is it that so much is known of Israel's neighbors? What can we learn of ancient Israel and early Judaism apart from what is written in the biblical books? Are we entirely dependent on the pages of the Old Testament, or are there other sources of information? To respond to questions such as these, we need to turn to archaeology and its contribution to the study of the Bible.

THE
OLD TESTAMENT
AND ARCHAEOLOGY

T HE study of the Old Testament involves a journey into the past. Although the various books that comprise the collection may be read for a variety of modern reasons, for the illumination of contemporary faith or for humane understanding, we must initially travel back in time to the world in which the biblical books were first written; their original historical context will provide assistance in grasping their current relevance. How can we travel back to the biblical world? There are essentially two routes from the twentieth century back to the Old Testament world. One is to be found in the Old Testament, along with other ancient writings that have been preserved from ancient into modern times. Simply by reading the biblical books we can recapture something of the history and civilization of the original settings. But this approach, for all its value, is limited; the biblical writers, while they referred to the history and cultural conditions of the times in which they lived, had another purpose in writing—what they tell us of their world is peripheral to their central purpose in putting pen to paper.

The second route backward in time into the biblical world is provided by archaeology. The modern science of archaeology involves the systematic recovery of evidence that may be found of former civilizations and societies and the careful examination of that recovered evidence in the attempt to reconstruct something of the nature of a former world. In many parts of the world, archaeological work involves, first of all, excavation, for frequently the remains of former societies lie beneath sand or soil. Excavation is only the initial part of the archaeological task; the classification, study, and interpretation of the evidence that is found makes possible the gradual re-creation of ancient societies. We can learn where people used to live and how they lived. We can learn about their history—their hopes and fears. In general we may attain a more rounded and complete picture of life in the ancient world than is available in a written text.

The preceding chapter, which summarizes the Near Eastern environment in which the Old Testament story was set, was informed in part by evidence recovered by archaeologists. In the subsequent chapters of this book, archaeology has an extensive role to play; sometimes archaeological evidence will be referred to explicitly, but more frequently it lies behind the statements that are made about the biblical story and faith. Archaeological evidence, however, has become so important in the study of the Old Testament in the twentieth century that it is useful for any reader to have some broad grasp of the nature of the discipline before engaging in contemporary biblical study.

1. Biblical Archaeology

There is no area of the world in which the modern archaeologist does not have potential interest. There are archaeological excavations undertaken in Israel, and archaeologists are at work in the Banff National Park in the Canadian Rockies. Large-scale archaeological activities are undertaken in Mexico and Syria, while small-scale explorations are conducted from the Orkney Islands in Scotland to equally small islands in the Pacific Ocean. Archaeology is an international activity. Nevertheless, the roots of modern scientific archaeology, going back to the nineteenth century, are to be found largely in the Middle East; the popular thrust that gave rise to exploration in that part of the world was interest in the background of the Bible. The study of the Old Testament and archaeological exploration have gone hand in hand for more than a century.

The expression *biblical archaeology* should be understood and interpreted in a broad sense. It refers to the archaeological exploration of the biblical world. It is limited with respect to time, from approximately 3000 B.C. to the first century A.D., namely the period of both the substance and the formation of the biblical books. It is limited in geographical terms to those areas in which the biblical story is set and the neighboring regions which had an influence on that story. In modern terms, biblical archaeology is undertaken in the following countries (though the list is not exclusive): Turkey, Iraq, Syria, Lebanon, Israel, Jordan, Saudi Arabia, and Egypt.

It should be acknowledged at the outset that there are certain difficulties with the expression *biblical archaeology* and that it should be used only with caution. It does not refer to a different *type* of archaeology—archaeological work should follow the same scientific principles whether conducted in the biblical world or in Mexico. Nor is the expression intended to imply that the only important results of Middle Eastern excavation are those that pertain directly to the Bible. Indeed, many modern archaeologists dislike the expression *biblical archaeology,* preferring to pursue their scientific enterprise without any association, direct or implied, with the study of the Bible. The political tensions in the modern Middle East are such that archaeological excavation has assumed nationalistic importance in many states; conversely, an association of archaeological finds with the Bible may seem to conflict with the nationalistic enterprise.

These comments are made by way of a warning—we should use the expression *biblical archaeology* with caution. It is a legitimate enough approach; when properly understood, it designates an approach by the student of the Old Testament to the findings of Middle Eastern archaeology in order to discover what light may be shed on the biblical text. The importance of the Old Testament, for both the Jewish and the Christian religions, and also for an understanding of Western civilization, inevitably places Middle Eastern archaeology on a somewhat different scale of significance and importance. All archaeological work is, or may be, equally important from a scientific perspective. Yet, my own fascination (rooted in ethnic reasons) with the early history of the Okney Islands, is not shared by a great mass of the population of the Western world. On the other hand, there is very extensive interest in the archaeology of the Middle East, beyond any fascination that is essentially ethnic, precisely because the Bible has so profoundly shaped both our civilization and our religious traditions. The rise of archaeology in the Middle East, though now it may have very different interests and aspirations, was rooted initially in this broadly based interest in the biblical world. So we must use the expression *biblical archaeology* with caution, but we can use it nevertheless, if we are aware of its history and implications and attempt to learn in the broadest terms something more of the world in which the Old Testament was born.

2. The Nature of Archaeological Discovery

In the nineteenth century, archaeology in the Middle East was a fairly primitive enterprise. It has been described fairly positively as "treasure hunting" and more negatively as "looting." It was rooted, then as now, in a fascination with the past and a desire to learn about former ages in human history. But the methods were primitive, and so much that would be considered important nowadays was lost or destroyed in early archaeological work. A considerable part of the interest in early nineteenth-century archaeology, reflected frequently in the source of funding for exploration, was the acquisition of monuments and treasures that could be shipped from the soils in which they were found to the museums of the great cities of Europe. The splendid objects which may now be viewed in the British Museum in London or the Louvre in Paris, for example, were largely the products of nineteenth- and early twentieth-century archaeological expeditions. More recently, and especially since World War II, the ancient treasures recovered from the soil are retained in the country of their origin—the museums of Damascus and Jerusalem, to use only two examples, are beginning to rival those of Europe and North America.

Toward the end of the nineteenth century, the passion for treasure gave way to the sounder principles of scientific exploration and analysis. Greater caution was used in the excavations, the principles of stratigraphy were established, and topographical analysis was developed. Stratigraphy involves the description and classification of various levels in an excavation. When a tell, or mound, is excavated, there may be several layers, each representing periods of occupation on the site. To reach lower layers, the upper layers must be removed, but the detailed description of the various layers, or strata, together with the objects found at that level, enables the determination of both period and type of human habitation represented in that layer. In general terms, the upper strata of an excavated site contain evidence of more recent periods of settlement; the lower strata represent more ancient periods. The objects found in an excavation, particularly pottery, may be used to develop a topography, which in turn enables the interpretation of data from a particular site with respect to both chronology and the type of civilization. In recent decades, more advanced scientific methods of dating ancient objects have been developed.

It is not our purpose to present an account of the nature and method of archaeological work. It is enough to stress that, while innovations in method are still constantly taking place, archaeological work in the strict sense has become a relatively exact science—though the interpretation of archaeological data is perhaps closer to an art than to a science. As a consequence of the results of archaeological excavation and discovery, our knowledge of the biblical world today is considerably greater than it was a century ago. Vast areas of history and civilization in the ancient world, of which until recently we were totally ignorant, are now being filled in. There remains, of course, a great deal of work to be done, but the archaeology of the biblical world has shown massive progress in the last four decades. Whereas it might have been possible half a century ago for a scholar to specialize in the archaeology of the Middle East, most scholars must content themselves today with specializing in a single site, or a particular period or topic. In archaeology, as in so many other areas of contemporary knowledge, we are encountering an "information explosion."

For all the scientific character of modern archaeological work, many of the more important discoveries are not planned in the cool atmosphere of the ivory tower. Several of the most significant discoveries of this century began as a result of an accidental find by a local resident of the area in question (two will be described in section 3, below). Other discoveries of significance are accidental by-products of some other kind of activity. For example, a joint United States–Saudi Arabian geological survey of the central regions of Saudi Arabia in the 1970s revealed evidence of gold mining taking place in the region of Mahd-az-Zahab as early as Old Testament times. Or when the ground was cleared in 1975 to build a seaside hotel, just north of Latakia, on the Mediterranean coast of Syria, the remains of a more ancient summer resort dating to the late Bronze Age (from about the fifteenth to the twelfth centuries B.C.) were discovered. The location of the hotel was moved, and explorations began to uncover more of the ancient settlement. In other areas, salvage excavations have been undertaken to rescue ancient objects from the progress of modern civilization. The erection of dams on rivers such as the Nile and the Euphrates has had the indirect result of increasing archaeological activity upstream from the dams prior to their construction. From various places and for various reasons the remains of ancient civilizations are frequently coming to light and are increasing our knowledge of the biblical world.

3. Significant Discoveries

In one sense, everything that is recovered pertaining to the ancient world is important. The remains of great buildings and fragments of pottery, sewage pipes, and gold plates all provide small pieces of evidence that can be fitted into a larger mosaic to eventually reveal a picture of ancient civilization. The excavations at some sites have been so rich in the diversity of their finds, or so significant in the rarity of what has been discovered, that the public takes a particular interest in them. Even with limited discoveries such as these, there is a large number of significant discoveries in the Middle East that pertain directly to the Old Testament; they could not be adequately described in a single book, let alone a small portion of this chapter. But in the paragraphs that follow, three significant discoveries are described in a little more detail; the purpose is to illustrate the character of archaeological explorations and the evidence they can provide toward the understanding of the Old Testament. It should be stressed, though, that the three discoveries summarized here are but the tip of the iceberg—an enormous number of significant discoveries have been made in recent decades.

(a) The Rediscovery of Ancient Ugarit

For most of the second millennium B.C., a city called Ugarit flourished on the Mediterranean coast of Syria, just north of the region of the modern city of Latakia. Early in the twelfth century B.C.

the city was invaded and destroyed by a powerful group called the Sea Peoples, who were penetrating the eastern Mediterranean world from southern Europe. Following its destruction around 1150 B.C., Ugarit was not rebuilt; the winds blew sand and dirt into the deserted streets and ruined houses until gradually there was only a hill where once there had been a great city. In modern times, the hill is called, in Arabic, *Ras Shamra* (Fennel Head), but apart from the survival of a few local legends the ancient city of Ugarit has long been forgotten, obliterated from human memory.

Figure 21. *El seated on a throne accepting an offering from the king of Ugarit; from Ras Shamra*

The rediscovery of this ancient city after more than three thousand years beneath the soil came about by accident. A farm worker called Mahmoud Mella az-Zir, who lived close to the mound of Ras Shamra, was plowing the land west of the mound in the spring of 1928 when the tip of his plow ran into an obstruction just beneath the surface soil. Clearing away the dirt, he found a flagstone and beneath it some steps leading into an underground tomb in which were a number of ancient objects he was able to sell to a dealer. The news of Mahmoud's discovery quickly spread, and in the spring of 1929 a French archaeological expedition began its work in the vicinity of Ras Shamra under the able leadership of Claude Schaeffer. Although they have been disrupted from time to time by war, the excavations of Ras Shamra are still continuing after more than half a century. Gradually, the excavators at Ras Shamra have cleared away the dirt of centuries and uncovered many of the streets and buildings of ancient Ugarit.

Among the earliest buildings to be laid bare are two large temples in the northern sector of the city, believed to have been dedicated to the gods Baal and Dagon (both deities are mentioned in the Old Testament). Later excavations were to reveal a massive palace complex in the western region of the city, houses of prosperous citizens, homes of priests, and suburbs where workers and artisans lived. Adjoining the city, in the region where the first accidental discovery had been made, was a large necropolis area, and west of that again a small port town serving the city proper, which was a short distance inland. After more than five decades, less than half of the ancient city has been uncovered; nevertheless, as one walks through the streets and stands amid the remains of the ancient buildings, it is possible to re-create in the mind's eye life as it must have been in ancient Ugarit more than three thousand years ago.

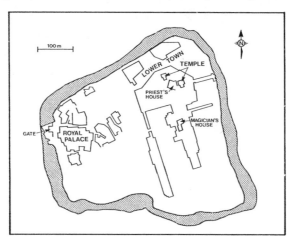

Figure 22. *Map of the City of Ugarit*

The excavations at Ugarit are better known for the written texts that were discovered there than for the physical remains. In 1929, the first season of excavation, clay tablets were discovered which contained writing in a kind of alphabetic cuneiform. The wedge-shaped symbols of cuneiform writing had been imprinted into soft clay, which had then been baked hard; the durability of the baked clay contributed to the survival of these written texts. Once the writing system had been deciphered, the language could be examined—it was called Ugaritic after the city in which it was employed. What is striking about the language is its close linguistic similarity to the Hebrew of the Old Testament. Over the decades, more than one thousand clay tablets in the Ugaritic script have been discovered, and the contents of the tablets are varied; there are letters, administrative texts, religious texts, myths, and legends. While some texts are in prose, others are written in poetry.

Figure 23. *Clay tablet with cuneiform writing (Ugaritic)*

The impact of the discovery of ancient Ugarit on Old Testament studies has been enormous, and both the physical remains and the written texts have had a contribution to make. The examination of the remains of the city has contributed toward the understanding of daily life in Syria-Palestine at approximately the time of Moses and the Hebrew judges. We know more about the kind of houses people lived in, the social structure, the system of taxation, the business dealings, international trade, and the regular routines of religious life than we did before. The remains of temples, together with the substance of the written texts, have illuminated for us the nature of the worship of Baal and other Canaanite gods referred to in the Bible. But what is even more significant, our knowledge of Hebrew language and literature has increased as a consequence of the rediscovery of ancient Ugarit. The Ugaritic language is a close linguistic relative of biblical Hebrew. The examination of Ugaritic words and grammatical forms has shed light on many formerly obscure portions of the biblical text; indeed, the rediscovery of the Ugaritic language is one of several external means which has contributed real improvements in the modern translation of the Old Testament. Among the Ugaritic texts there are many examples of poetry, as there are in the Old Testament. Some of the peculiarities of Hebrew poetry have been clarified by virtue of being compared to similar forms of Ugaritic poetry. Each particular instance in which a knowledge of Ugarit has contributed to a better understanding of the Old Testament may seem small, but taken together, the results of the excavations at Ras Shamra have been extremely important; the kind of information provided by this type of archaeological investigation helps bridge the gulf of time between our own world and that of the Old Testament.

(b) Tell Mardik: Ancient Ebla

Perhaps the most famous of recent archaeological discoveries in the Middle East is the recovery of the ancient city of Ebla from the mound of Tell Mardik in central Syria. In 1964 a team of Italian archaeologists from the University of Rome, led by Paulo Matthiae, began a series of excavations (which are still continuing on an annual basis) at the tell, which rises more than fifty feet above the surrounding plain and has a surface area of approximately one hundred forty acres. The potential area for excavation was huge, but the shape of the tell provided direction for Matthiae. The outer part of the tell was high and almost circular, suggesting that the earth covered the remains of a city wall. Within the circular heights was a flatter interior, where presumably the main portion of a city had once stood, and at the center of the inner portion was another high region, later called the acropolis.

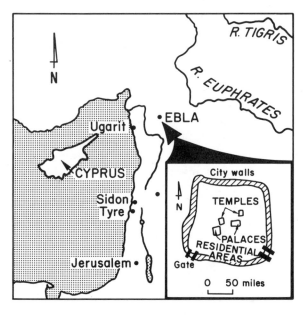

Figure 24. *Map of Ebla*

After a decade of excavations of Tell Mardik, Matthiae and his team had uncovered substantial portions of the ancient city once called Ebla. The roots of the settlement date back to the latter half of the fourth millennium B.C., but the settlement had grown to a great and powerful city which flourished initially from about 2400 B.C. to 2250 B.C. Evidence of invasion and destruction suggests that the city's power was undermined by about 2250 B.C.. It continued to be occupied, but regained some of its greatness after 2000 B.C. before being finally destroyed and abandoned around 1600 B.C. In both the earlier and later periods, Ebla had been a city with impressive palaces, fine temples, and strong military defenses; it had been a city of considerable wealth and importance, controlling a large portion of central Syria.

As with the discovery of ancient Ugarit, so also in the rediscovery of Ebla it was the finding of written texts that added considerably to the excitement and significance of the find. During the 1974 season of excavations, approximately forty clay tablets were found in the palace; this was a significant find, considerably supplementing the otherwise meager written resources that had been recovered during the first decade's work. As the excavation continued in the palace area in 1975, a phenomenal discovery was made—the Italian archaeologists uncovered the state archives of ancient Ebla. In that season alone, fifteen thousand clay tablets were added to the forty found the preceding year. More texts have been recovered in subsequent expeditions, bringing the total number of complete tablets and fragments to approximately seventeen thousand.

This huge collection of written texts from ancient Ebla came from the earlier period of the city's greatness, spanning the years 2450 to 2250 B.C. The texts are diverse in respect to content, providing information on the politics and history of the city, on administration and economic matters, and on religious life and faith in Ebla. Many of the texts were written in the Sumerian language, a non-Semitic language used in southern Mesopotamia (ancient Sumer) throughout the third millennium B.C. and afterward. As Sumerian was a language known well from the study of texts discovered at other archaeological sites in Mesopotamia, the Sumerian texts from Ebla can be read and understood immediately. But approximately one-fifth of the clay tablets recovered from the city's state archives are in a formerly unknown language, now called Eblaite after the city in which it was employed. The language of Ebla is Semitic, and although there is continuing debate over its precise classification, it seems to be a northwest Semitic language, making it an antecedent of later languages in the same group as Ugaritic and biblical Hebrew. The task of understanding this newly discovered language was considerably simplified by the discovery, in the state archives, of bilingual dictionaries, listing in parallel columns Eblaite words with their Sumerian equivalents.

What is the significance of the discoveries at Tell Mardik for the study of the Old Testament? There are both positive and negative comments to be said in response to this question. On the positive side, the rediscovery of Ebla and its archives makes possible a new and more detailed understanding of the emergence and spread of civilization in the ancient Near East, and particularly of the civilization and history of Syria from about 2500 B.C. to 1600 B.C. Indeed, the histories of Mesopotamia and of Syria will have to be radically rewritten as the results of these discoveries are gradually absorbed and better understood. This new understanding of the development of Mesopotamian and Syrian history and civilization, in turn, will increase our knowledge of the historical background and antecedents of the biblical world. We will be able to read the Old Testament text with a greater understanding of the background against which its story is set.

One must delay judgment before giving a firmer assessment of specific ways in which Old Testament studies may be illuminated by the discovery of Ebla. The texts from the archives are only just beginning to be published (the first volume appearing in 1980), and these texts must be carefully studied in their own right before comparative judgments of their value for the Old Testament can be ventured. It may take more than twenty years to publish the entire contents of the state archives—it is worth remembering that after fifty years there is still considerable debate among scholars as to the value of the Ugaritic texts for Old Testament studies. The much larger finds at Tell Mardik may have to wait even longer before all their wider implications are understood and developed. That the discoveries at Ebla will have much light to shed on the biblical text in the coming years seems indisputable, but it is too early to say precisely what that light will be.

The ballyhoo surrounding some of the initial announcements of the discovery of Eblaite texts contains a negative note of warning for all students of the Old Testament. As early as 1977, rash statements were made about the significance of the Ebla texts for the Bible (and especially for the study of Genesis). People who had never seen the written texts, or even set foot in Syria, made written claims that archaeology "proved the Bible true," and the debate continues, taking on both political and religious overtones. In matters such as this, it is best to be both cautious and conservative. The texts from Ebla need to be examined carefully and their substance weighed in the context of Eblaite history and civilization before any supplementary and specific relevance to Old Testament study can be discerned. For the moment, it is sufficient to know that as a result of the excavations at Tell Mardik the base of knowledge concerning the history and civilization of the ancient Near East has been considerably expanded. Patience (and perhaps long life) may enable us to appreciate more profoundly any wider significance of these discoveries for the Old Testament.

(c) Qumran: the Dead Sea Scrolls

The western shores of the Dead Sea, more than twelve hundred feet below sea level, are a barren and inhospitable land. The terrain rises sharply to the west in rocky slopes with cliffs and wadis. Apart from a few small areas blessed with springs, there is little natural vegetation in the region and negligible rainfall. In the winter months of 1946–47, some bedouins of the Ta'amireh tribe were pasturing their small herds of sheep and goats in the vicinity of Ain Feshkha, where a fresh water spring provided some food for the animals. One of the young men of the tribe, a teenager called Muhammed Ahmed el-Hamed (nicknamed "Muhammed the Wolf"), made a remarkable discovery during those winter months. In the cliffs above where the animals were grazing, he climbed through a small hole into a cave. Inside, he found a number of tall earthenware jars, and in some of them there were rolls of ancient leather—later identified as scrolls, the precursors of modern books. This chance discovery of ancient scrolls was to set off a flurry of exploration and a series of new discoveries during the next two decades.

The cave in which the first discovery had been made was in the vicinity of Qumran, and later exploration was to reveal eleven caves containing ancient manuscripts in the Qumran area. The initial searches of the bedouin were followed in the 1950s by the more technical explorations of scientists and archaeologists. In addition to the explorations of caves, the archaeologists extended their work in 1951 to the excavation of what seemed to be the remains of a human settlement on a plateau area called Khirbet Qumran. The ancient manuscripts hidden in the caves had to come from somewhere, and the remains at Khirbet Qumran seemed to offer possibilities.

The excavations in the settlement area revealed a number of large buildings forming the base of a Jewish community which had settled

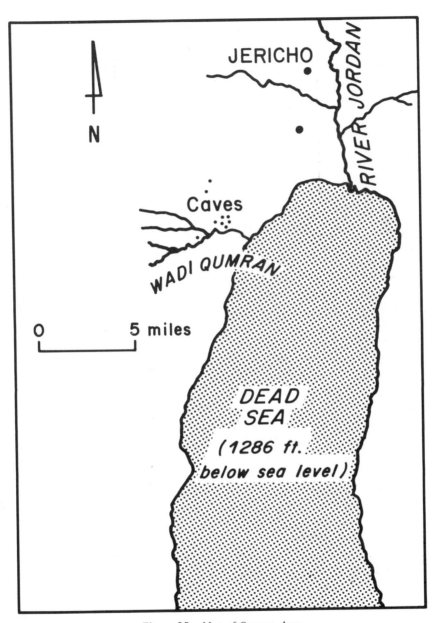

Figure 25. *Map of Qumran Area*

in that remote desert region around 135 B.C. These Jews were apparently a sectarian religious group, settling in the wilderness at Qumran in order to "prepare the way of the Lord" (Isaiah 40:3). They lived by their ancient Scriptures, engaged in daily worship, and prepared for the anticipated intervention of God in the world and the establishment of a new age. The devotion of this Jewish community was such that they had an extensive library, containing manuscripts of biblical books, commentaries, and other works. In 68 B.C., following a Jewish revolt, the Roman armies spread throughout the province of Judea, crushing all resistance before them. It seems that the Jews at Qumran, anticipating Roman attack, scrambled to hide their precious scrolls and manuscripts in the caves of the surrounding wilderness area, thereby saving them from falling into the possession of the Romans. The Jewish community perished at the hands of the Romans, but their manuscripts remained safe and hidden until the middle of the twentieth century. The remoteness of the caves, together with the virtual absence of humidity in the air at Qumran, made it possible for the ancient leather scrolls as well as numerous papyrus fragments to survive.

The examination of the substance of the various scrolls and manuscript fragments from the Qumran area reveals diverse subject matter. The majority of the manuscripts contain either biblical texts written in archaic Hebrew, or biblical texts with accompanying commentary. Many of the texts have survived in a bad state of preservation, but some scrolls have survived in excellent condition and can be read with ease. In the decades following the discovery of the Dead Sea Scrolls, the various texts have been published and made available for general scholarly examination.

This third example of archaeological discovery illustrates a quite different role from that of the discoveries at Ras Shamra and Tell Mardik. The first two discoveries illuminate the general background and culture of the biblical world—the context in which the Old Testament story is set. But the discoveries at Qumran illustrate the survival of the actual text of the Old Testament and the influence it had in later Jewish life and faith. Specifically, as noted in chapter 1, the Dead Sea Scrolls have provided the earliest extant manuscripts of the Old Testament. The evidence is not complete, nor does it include the full text of every Old Testament book, but the scrolls add enormously to the collection of evidence upon which all modern translations of the Old Testament are based.

4. The Physical Evidence of Archaeology

The excavation of archaeological sites in the Middle East may result in the procurement of various kinds of evidence; these may be divided, in general terms, into two categories: physical evidence and written texts. As we have seen in the preceding paragraphs, written texts more commonly catch the attention of the media and the general public, but physical evidence is equally important in the larger context of trying gradually to rebuild from the remains the nature and character of the ancient world.

Of principal importance in this category of evidence are buildings and conglomerations of buildings in towns or cities. Usually what remains of a building when it is rediscovered in archaeological exploration might include foundations, floors, and walls (often partially destroyed), but the actual remains frequently provide sufficient basis for the projection of what the total structure would have been like. In much archaeological work, the focus has been on major structures—temples, palaces, military fortifications, and the like. These large structures are of particular importance, for they usually represent a focal point of activity in the community of which they were a part. Humbler dwellings are also important if we are to recapture a cross section of daily life in the ancient world, and recently a number of archaeologists have devoted their energies to the examination of simple homes and their contents in an effort to catch the flavor of the daily life of the ordinary person.

In thinking about the ancient world, it is perhaps too easy to focus on kings in their palaces and priests in their temples; it is true that the kinds of events recorded in the annals of history tend to be associated with important persons and significant institutions. But in reading the Old Testament, we require not only this regal and religious background, but also the texture of actual life in the biblical world. This, too, can be captured by the work of archaeologists on the remains of physical structures. I recall once listening to a ninety-minute slide lecture on sewage systems in ancient Syria-Palestine. Not a very inspiring topic, one might think, yet, even as we reflect on our own daily existence, we know how important the removal of sewage and waste water is in our lives! Archaeological work has illuminated many such aspects of the biblical world—water supply, sewage disposal, the nature of furnishings, crockery and household utensils, tools, and a multitude of other aspects of daily life.

Art objects and paraphernalia of religious worship are also frequently recovered in the exploration of archaeologists. Splendid gold bowls, small idols plated in gold or silver, wall paintings from Egypt, and fine stone reliefs from Mesopotamia are among some of the treasures recovered from the biblical world. Idols of gods similar to those described and condemned in the Old Testament writings are found in the rubble of long-destroyed buildings. From objects of this kind, it is possible to partially reconstruct the artistic canons and the religious practices of the people who lived in biblical times.

When all is said and done, the physical evidence recovered by archaeologists is, by itself, insufficient for the reconstruction of life and society in the ancient world. It provides a knowledge of life in cities and in towns, the floor plans of public buildings and homes, the layout of streets and public concourses, the furnishings of temples and the places of business; it tells us much but not enough. From physical evidence alone, we can only guess at the real fabric of human life. We do not know of human hopes and fears, of political intrigue and the character of government, of love and hate in human relations, of education and training, and a multitude of other things that add texture to the experience of life. Many of these things can be guessed at from an imaginative interpretation of physical data—but ideally if a comprehensive picture of life in the biblical world is to be given, the physical evidence must be supplemented by literary evidence.

5. The Literary Evidence of Archaeology

We are fortunate in that various forms of writing were used throughout the ancient Near East for all of the Old Testament period. Simple forms of writing had been in use since before 3000 B.C., and complex writing systems of various kinds were a well-established part of ancient civilizations before the story of Israel begins. In archaeological excavations throughout the biblical world, therefore, there is always the possibility that the discovery of physical evidence might be supplemented by written evidence. Chance or luck have a role to play in such discoveries, but there are also certain physical factors which make the rediscovery of written texts more likely in some areas than in others.

Nowadays, paper is the primary substance on which we do our writing. The quality or type of paper we use will determine its life. On the shelves of my library I have several volumes printed in the seventeenth and eighteenth centuries, and their paper is still in excellent condition—there are also paperbacks, purchased new less than twenty years ago, in which the paper is rapidly yellowing and cracking. Good paper can survive a long time under suitable conditions, but obviously there are more durable substances; if your name is engraved deeply on a gold signet ring, the writing may survive as long as the ring. This general principle is amply illustrated from the ancient world, in which a number of different surfaces were used for writing.

In Mesopotamia and Syria, writing was frequently imprinted on soft clay, which was then baked hard—the baking giving the texts a remarkably long shelf-life under certain conditions. (There are also in my library one or two clay tablets from the second millennium B.C., and their condition is superior to that of the seventeenth- and eighteenth-century books!) In all areas of the Near East, one may find examples of inscriptions carved into various kinds of stone, and these forms of writing are also exceptionally durable. In other parts of the ancient Near East, especially Egypt and the southern area of Syria-Palestine, paper (papyrus) and parchment (leather) came into common use for writing purposes. These materials have obvious advantages over stone and clay in the short run, but texts written on paper or parchment do not survive very long, except under exceptional circumstances. The Dead Sea Scrolls survived by virtue of being hidden, in containers for the most part, in a region of virtually zero humidity. (Now, they must be kept with care in climate-controlled conditions.)

As a consequence of the use of different kinds of substances for writing in the ancient world, the amount of textual evidence that has survived differs considerably from one region to another. Massive textual resources have been recovered from excavations in Mesopotamia, southern Turkey, and Syria; the archives of Ugarit and Ebla, described above, are just two limited examples of a very much larger literary corpus. Extensive written resources have also been recovered from ancient Egypt—they include rock inscriptions, clay tablets, writings "painted" onto the walls of sealed tombs, and papyri (which survived under conditions of low humidity in various parts of Egypt). The area in which the fewest ancient writings have survived is the region of the Holy Land, in and around ancient Israel. Only a few ancient texts have been discovered, and these are for the most part very brief. The climate and conditions were such that material on parchment and papyrus perished. What survived included a few inscriptions in rock and stone, a few clay tablets, some pieces of pottery bearing writing, and various other inscribed odds and ends. We are fortunate in this case to have the Old Testament text to illuminate the physical remains recovered by archaeologists.

Various kinds of writing systems and scripts were employed in the biblical world. Cuneiform has already been briefly described (section 3a in this chapter). The symbols of the writing were formed by pressing a stylus into soft clay. The standard cuneiform, in common use in Mesopotamia and northern Syria since the third millennium B.C., was extraordinarily complex, employing hundreds of symbols to convey the substance of speech in writing (see figure 28). At about 1400 B.C., a vastly simplified form of alphabetic cuneiform was developed (possibly in ancient Ugarit), employing initially only twenty-seven symbols. The classical form of Egyptian writing has been called hieroglyphic—although developed according to similar principles as were used in Mesopotamian cuneiform, hieroglyphic writing retains a much clearer pictorial element.

Alphabetic forms of writing were developed in the region of Syria-Palestine in about the middle of the second millennium B.C.,

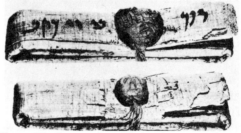

Figure 26. Papyrus from Elephantine, containing a marriage contract in Aramaic, tied, rolled, and sealed

9 8

Figure 27. *A clay tablet in its envelope*

with fundamental symbols developed initially from Egyptian writing. In addition to the cuneiform alphabet (above), developed in the north of the region, a different and distinct alphabet began to emerge in the south; evidence for this comes from the exploration of mines in the Sinai peninsula and from various other excavations in Syria-Palestine (notably Byblos). The development of alphabetic writing systems was to vastly simplify the arts of writing, which in Egypt and Mesopotamia required extensive education and training. More people could learn to write; therefore, literacy became more extensive (though literacy was still much more limited than in the modern world).

The texts that have been recovered by archaeologists from the ancient world differ enormously as to type and content. There are historical annals that record the military activities and campaigns of various kings and pharaohs; these are helpful in reconstructing the detailed sequence of historical events in the Near East as a whole and in correlating those events with the substance of the Old Testament. There are religious and literary texts that are particularly interesting for the student of the Old Testament, revealing, for example, the Babylonian version of the "flood" and Egyptian notions of creation.

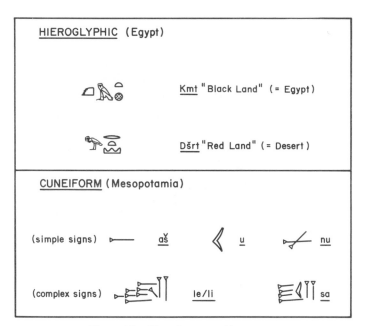

Figure 28. *Near Eastern writing systems*

There are political treaties, economic and administrative texts, census lists, and taxation documents which illustrate the way in which particular societies were managed. Love songs from Egypt and Assyria draw back the curtain on the world of romance and provide interesting background for the study of the Song of Solomon in the Old Testament. Letters, some of them personal and some pertaining to business, often reveal the hopes and fears of their senders.

It is the combined evidence of physical objects and written texts which makes biblical archaeology such a fascinating enterprise. The physical evidence, taken alone, provides as it were the skeleton of ancient civilizations; the written evidence clothes that skeleton with flesh and blood, bringing alive for us a world that has long since died. It is in our recapturing of this lost world, with the help of archaeology, that we prepare ourselves to read the Bible with greater understanding.

6. The Use and Abuse of Archaeology

The comments made so far indicate what is the primary use of the resources of archaeology for the study of the Old Testament. The results of archaeological work may illuminate for us the background of the biblical story, filling in the information and gaps that are not provided in the text as such. The word *background* may imply to some readers that this is not an important subject; the true task is to study the Old Testament *per se,* and everything else is marginal. Strictly speaking, this is an appropriate perspective, for the study of the text of the Old Testament must take pride of place, but those who downgrade the importance of background tend to underestimate their own ignorance, and they overestimate their capacity to understand the biblical text. It is worth repeating that the text of the Old Testament is not, for the most part, intrinsically difficult—the difficulty lies within ourselves and in our lack of knowledge about the world from which the text came. A personal reflection may illustrate the point. I have to admit that as an undergraduate student I found great chunks of the Old Testament to be either mystifying or boring. It was only later, as I began to read widely in archaeology and then study and travel in the Middle East, that the fascination of the text and its essential meaning became more clear. The text remained the same; it was the reader who changed. These chapters have barely filled in the background to the Old Testament. They have merely pointed to the importance of background knowledge; its positive use is to equip the reader with a better understanding of the substance of the Old Testament.

While archaeological results may be used to benefit the study of the Old Testament, they may also be abused. The common forms of abuse are committed by both religious and irreligious (or non-religious) persons. Many people would like to use archaeology to "prove the truth of the Bible," and there are probably as many who would use it in an attempt to disprove the Bible. The use of archaeology in proofs or disproofs of various kinds is extremely dangerous and usually veils a hidden motive. Those who seek to prove the Bible by means of archaeology are actually concerned with the proof of God's existence and the truth of God's word. They think that if they can prove historical statements in the Bible to be true, they will thereby have "proved God"—the disprovers attempt the same in reverse. There are fundamental logical flaws in either of these approaches to the Old Testament. More dangerous, though, is the pursuit of either approach in what amounts to a form of religious (or anti-religious) propaganda. People who write persuasive books and produce even more persuasive films, on the basis of exceptionally slender evidence, to show that Noah's Ark has been found are engaged in a kind of propaganda. The evidence is adapted, and the conclusion advocated rarely follows from the initial premise. From a religious perspective, the attempt to prove the Old Testament on the basis of archaeology tends to emerge, quite unconsciously, from a loss of faith. The crumbling faith is to be bolstered by the wobbly "facts" of archaeology.

It is true, in a thoroughly limited sense, that one can "prove" certain aspects of the biblical narrative by means of archaeology. It is also true that archaeology may require us to rethink carefully certain conclusions about the Bible. Perhaps many passages, which we always thought to be historical, when examined in the light of archaeological findings should be considered in a quite different light. The more important point, however, in studying a profoundly spiritual book such as the Old Testament, is the recognition of the necessary line that divides the realm of faith from that of archaeology and science. Archaeology may be of enormous assistance in studying the Bible at what might be called the mundane level. The religious level of study, however, requires a different kind of sensitivity and understanding. The Jews and Christians who believe in the God described in the pages of the Old Testament do so by an act of faith. Archaeology may inform, and even assist that faith, but it cannot replace it.

THE
BOOKS OF
THE
OLD TESTAMENT

THE LAW

T HE Old Testament canon, as we noted in chapter one, has three major divisions—the Law, the Prophets, and the Writings. The first of these divisions, the Law, consists of five books—Genesis, Exodus, Leviticus, Numbers, and Deuteronomy. We shall examine in this chapter the five books separately to gain some idea of each one in terms of its literary structure and subject matter. It will also be important to examine the five books as a whole; for all the independence of each volume, the five as a whole constitute a larger literary unit. This is not a haphazard collection of ancient works, but a carefully arranged narrative in which all five books have certain common goals.

From a strictly technical perspective, the five books of the Law are anonymous, with no explicit information being given as to the identity of their author or authors. Nor does the text provide us with clear information as to who may have edited the books or arranged them in their present sequence. We know that later in the history of Judaism the authorship of the books was traditionally ascribed to Moses, and Christianity followed Judaism in this view. But it should be emphasized that the texts themselves do not claim or identify any author, and it follows from the uncertainty as to authorship that there must also be uncertainty as to the time in which these books were written.

The title given to this first division of the canon, namely *The Law,* is an approximate rendition of the old Hebrew title, *Torah,* although the latter word can be translated more precisely as *instruction.* The Hebrew title was derived from expressions used within the Old Testament itself, such as "the book of the *law* of Moses" (II Kings 14:6). The first division of the canon is also frequently called the *Pentateuch,* an expression derived from Greek via Latin, meaning a five-part book—indicating once again that the five separate books must be seen as belonging to a larger whole.

1. The Five Books of the Law

We must begin by briefly reviewing the nature and character of each of the five component books of the Law; critical questions as to authorship, date, and literary structure will be held in abeyance until the character of the parts has been described.

(a) Genesis

The first book was traditionally named in Hebrew *Bereshith,* which is the opening word of the first verse, commonly translated "In the beginning"; the English title, *Genesis,* is from a Greek word meaning "origin." Its fifty chapters are written, for the most part, in prose, with only a few passages in poetic form. Most modern translations, such as the Revised Standard Version indicate poetic passages by the layout of the text (see, for example, Genesis 49:1-27, which is clearly rendered in English translation to show the poetic character of the text).

Genesis falls into two principal parts: (i) chapters 1–11 have a universal scope, moving from the creation of the world to the early generations of the human race (chapters 1:1–11:26); (ii) part II (chapters 11:27–50:26) has a more particular interest in the patriarchs, the ancestors of Israel. The book thus sets the stage for all that is to follow, with respect to both the human race in general and the people of Israel in particular.

From the opening verse, the author of Genesis has set the context: The key character in the book, from a literary perspective, is God.

Before anything else comes into being, God is; this is the writer's starting faith, presented without proof and without apology, but the existence of God is the foundation for all that is to follow. The opening words also provide an initial clue as to the perspective from which we may approach the understanding of Genesis—whatever else might be made of the book, it is clearly a religious work, penetrated throughout by belief in the existence of God.

The narrative, as it develops, broadens to include the physical world and, above all, human beings, whose existence in the physical world is believed to be an act of God. The story begins with broad sweeps of the pen, sketching in the creation of the natural world and of mankind. Then the focus narrows to the story of Adam and Eve, their creation, and the subsequent fall of mankind in the first act of sin. (*Note:* in this context, the substance of Genesis is discussed only in general terms; specific issues, such as *creation,* are examined in Part IV of this book.) The universal interest of Genesis 1–11 is maintained in an account of the first generations of the human race, amply illustrated in such stories as that of the flood and the tower of Babel.

We are presented in the first part of Genesis with a primeval history, an account of the origins of the world, of the human race, and of human evil. The story is told throughout from the perspective of religious faith, and insofar as it is a historical account, we must understand it as theological history. That is to say, one must be careful not to read back into the story the interests which the twentieth-century reader might have (prompted, for example, by science or modern historical method). Our initial guide to the literary genre of Genesis 1–11 should come from the world in which the Old Testament was written, and archaeological evidence may provide assistance. From various parts of the ancient Near East, creation stories have been recovered by archaeologists, providing some insight into the views of creation held by the Hebrews' neighbors. Of particular interest is a Babylonian text entitled *The Epic of Atra-hasis,* whose roots go back to before 1700 B.C. The epic describes the origin of the gods, the creation of the world and mankind, the growth of the human race, and finally the sending of a flood by the high god, Enlil, to wipe out the human race. One man, Atra-hasis, is warned of the coming flood, so he builds a large boat for his family and himself to escape. There are many differences between Genesis 1–11 and *The Epic of Atra-hasis* with respect to the details of the story, and the texts have totally different religious outlooks, but from a literary perspective, they are clearly parallel. We perceive that the primeval history was an established literary genre in the ancient Near East; its concern was to give expression to an understanding of the gods, of the nature of the world, and of the place of mankind in the world.

In the second major section of Genesis (12–50), the focus of the narrative is considerably narrowed; the created world and the human race now form the background for the story of one family over several generations. The unity in this portion of the book is provided by the overall perspective of family history—the story focuses initially on Abraham, then on his son Isaac, then on his grandchildren, Jacob and Esau, and finally on the family of Jacob. The overall unity has within it a patchwork quilt quality, sown together from incidents and stories about the several generations of the family. Genesis thus begins with creation and ends with a particular family. It starts at the beginning, but ends looking forward into a more distant future, for the family story has not yet reached its climax at the end of the book. Genesis ends with Abraham's descendants in Egypt.

(b) Exodus

The second book of the Law consciously resumes its story where Genesis left off, but after the opening verses linking the two books, it quickly becomes apparent that time has passed and the perspectives are different. The sense of family that permeates the latter part of Genesis is no longer possible; the descendants of Abraham have grown to vast numbers. With the passage of centuries separating the two books, circumstances have also changed; the hospitality of Egypt, with which Genesis closes, has become at the beginning of Exodus an unpleasant environment. The Hebrews are now aliens in a strange land, serving their masters as virtual slaves, and yet concurrently threatening the Egyptians by virtue of their number.

At the beginning of Exodus, we are introduced to Moses, who will be a key figure throughout this book and the remaining books of the Pentateuch. His birth and a few incidents from his early life are sketched in by the author, culminating in an account of Moses' vocation. In a profound religious experience, he senses God's call for him to serve as the person through whom the Hebrews would find liberation from their Egyptian slavery. The story then widens once again to incorporate not only the experience of Moses, but also that of the Hebrew people and their departure (which is the meaning of the word *exodus*) from Egypt. Following the miraculous escape from Egypt, under the leadership of Moses, the Hebrew slaves travel eastward in the Sinai peninsula, and at the Mountain of God, they establish a covenant, or contractual agreement, with the Lord who made possible their escape.

As the book continues, the narrative element is reduced and descriptive material is increased. There are detailed accounts of the making of the covenant with God and of the substance of the covenant law (chapters 19–24). These are followed by descriptions of a more religious character concerning the plan and building of the *tabernacle* (a kind of portable tent to serve as a temple), the role of priests, and the importance of the sabbath day. This descriptive material is interrupted only briefly by a further narrative of the story of the golden calf, and of the breaking and renewal of the recently established covenant (chapters 32–34).

From a literary perspective, the book of Exodus appears at first to be somewhat hodgepodge; it contains beautifully told stories that reveal remarkable insight into human nature, but alongside these are set law codes (including the Ten Commandments, or Decalogue— chapter 20) and intricate accounts of religious practice and the construction of movable marquees. In very general terms, the book can be divided into two parts: (i) the exodus (1–18) and (ii) the Covenant at Sinai (19–40). The structure is loose, and the book as a whole seems to be patched together from many different kinds of material, making it initially a somewhat disconcerting work to read. Though Exodus is not a literary masterpiece, it is nevertheless a foundational work for understanding the Old Testament as a whole. The exodus, the book's first major topic, establishes one of the major themes of the biblical message, namely *deliverance*. God, by virtue of his intervention in human history, delivered his people from bondage and led them to freedom. The formation of the covenant at Sinai, the book's second major theme, follows up the message of deliverance with that of *relationship*. God frees this group of people from human bondage in order that they might have a special relationship with him in covenant; by means of this relationship, the divine purpose for the world is to be worked out.

(c) Leviticus

The third book of the Law is perhaps one of the most difficult for the modern student of the Old Testament to read. Its title, Leviticus, suggests that a major part of its contents is concerned with the priests, the sons of *Levi* (from whence the name is derived). As one begins to read the book, it soon becomes evident that the movement of the larger story, which was clearly present in Genesis and Exodus, has now been more or less subsumed to another purpose. The book of Leviticus is a kind of handbook to religious life in ancient Israel.

The book begins by setting its entire content in the context of the covenant which was formed between God and Israel at Mount Sinai. All that the book contains is to be understood as a part of the divine law establishing the character of Israel's responsibilities toward God in this new relationship of covenant. The substance of the book falls into several clearly defined sections. First, the covenant involved formal religious activity to be conducted in the tabernacle; various kinds of sacrifices and offerings that the people were to make are specified (chapters 1–7). The opening section is followed by the only sustained narrative portion of the book, in which the inauguration of Israelite worship under the direction of Aaron, Moses' brother, is described (chapters 8–10). The next two sections of the book are concerned with holiness, from both a ritual and a moral perspective; laws specifying various kinds of impurities (chapters 11–16) are followed by a passage commonly called the "Holiness Code," which establishes the nature of holiness in persons with respect to both religious and ethical matters (chapters 17–26). The book concludes with a short appendix (chapter 27) concerning the making of vows and the offering of gifts in the sanctuary, or tabernacle.

There are at least two difficulties with which the modern reader of Leviticus must contend. The first lies somewhere between boredom and mystification—it is not easy for most of us to become enthralled by an account, for example, of the means by which animals were to be slaughtered for sacrifice. The second difficulty is that of coming to grips with the character of the religion of ancient Israel without projecting back into that religion our contemporary knowledge of religions such as Judaism and Christianity. The ancient religion resembled the modern in having clearly defined modes of worship, but the action of that worship, and especially the bloody practice of animal sacrifice, are not easy for the contemporary religious person to grasp. What we need to understand is that the relationship established between God and Israel at Mount Sinai was one which was accompanied by very specific religious responsibilities. What Leviticus makes clear is that underlying the specified religious responsibilities was the notion of *holiness,* both in formal religion and in personal morality. The covenant was with a divine being believed to be entirely holy; therefore, the partners to that covenant must also live according to the principles of holiness, which were to be reflected in both their religion and their daily lives.

(d) Numbers

The name of the fourth part of the Law is drawn from the ancient Greek translation of the book, in which it was called *Numbers* on the basis of the two accounts of census-taking (chapters 1 and 26). The content of the book is as diverse as that of Exodus, but after the lull in the story, which was suspended temporarily in Leviticus, the narrative now resumes from the point at which it ended in the book of Exodus. Numbers covers a period of approximately forty years in the history of the Israelite people; it begins with the people still camped at the foot of Mount Sinai, where the covenant was formed, and ends with them poised on the eastern banks of the Jordan River, preparing to cross over into the promised land. Although the book lacks a clear and coherent literary structure, it has a very general framework provided by geographical and chronological notes.

Although the narrative of Numbers covers a period of some forty years, it is not a systematic and carefully developed story; rather, the book contains a series of episodes arranged for the most part in chronological order, but interspersed from time to time with other material, such as quotations from ancient poetry (chapter 21) and what appear at first to be miscellaneous laws (chapters 15, 18, and 19). In the first major division of the book, the geographical setting is still that of Mount Sinai (1:1–10:10), but preparations are underway for the departure of this group of refugees from their temporary desert camp. They journey eastward on a relatively short trip to Kadesh Barnea in the eastern region of the Sinai wilderness, and from there they test out the approaches to the land in which they want to settle. But there is to be no immediate invasion of the promised land; the oasis region of Kadesh Barnea becomes a base camp for the refugee crowd for several years—eventually they set off again for the promised land. Moving into the Arabah, the great and barren depression extending south from the Dead Sea, the people are eventually led by Moses through the territory east of the Dead Sea until they come at last to the plains of Moab, just east of where the Jordan River runs into the Dead Sea.

In part, the narrative portion of Numbers fills the gap, in both geographical and chronological terms, between the departure from Mount Sinai (which is the focus of the latter part of Exodus and the whole of Leviticus) and the arrival of the people on the plains of Moab (which is to be the setting for the book of Deuteronomy). But it is clear that the author had additional purposes in mind beyond merely filling in the gaps of history. The book begins with the Israelites newly installed in a special relationship of covenant with their God, and they are well equipped with a detailed set of laws providing guidance for their worship and daily life. With such an ideal beginning, one might expect the book to develop a happy story of the spiritual growth and maturity of the Israelites, but such is far from reality. Numbers is a miserable book in many ways, partly because it recounts the constant complaining, rebellion, and ingratitude of the Israelites and partly because in so doing it puts its finger accurately on the pulse of all human perversity. Great privilege and a special knowledge of God do not guarantee growth and maturity. Thus, in some ways, the principles of holiness and morality that are spelled out in a formal fashion in Leviticus are developed and illustrated vividly in the narrative of Numbers. Sadly, the illustrations are for the most part negative; the story of the Israelites wandering in the wilderness on the borders of the promised land indicates a whole generation wasting its privilege and failing to recognize the moral and spiritual require-ments of the relationship of covenant with God. However, if the substance of Numbers is negative and miserable in respect to the light it sheds on human nature, it is entirely positive in respect to its theological perspectives. The picture of Israel's God that emerges in these chapters is of a being who is patient and long-suffering, firm in dealing with human evil, but able to forgive and to restore.

(e) Deuteronomy

The geographical setting of the final book of the Law is on the plains of Moab, the region east of the place where the Jordan River flows into the Dead Sea. The occasion presupposed by the entire book is a great religious ceremony in which the Israelites mark the time and place at which they have arrived. In time, they have come to a critical juncture in their history; after generations as foreigners in Egypt, and after forty years of wandering as refugees on the fringe of the desert, they have come at last to the time at which they are prepared to cross the Jordan River and enter the land they believe God is going to give them. They have also come to a turning point in leadership; Moses, who led them out of Egypt and through forty years of dangerous journeys, is on the verge of death, and Joshua is about to become their new leader. On this dramatic occasion, the people assemble for a ceremony in which their covenant with God is to be remembered and renewed, and in which they will commit themselves once again in faithfulness to God.

The book does not describe all the details of the religious assembly; rather, it is set out as a long speech, or series of speeches, delivered to the assembled congregation. Moses, in his last words to his people, seeks to prepare them for what lies in the future. The book has a clear literary structure, and the structure in turn may reflect the stages and movements in the ceremony presupposed by the book. The speech begins with a review of history (chapters 1–4), focusing on the preceding forty years and the events that had led to the present moment. Then the focus shifts to a review of the covenant law, reflecting first of all on the broad implications of the law and the Ten Commandments (chapters 5–11) and then on numerous detailed aspects of the law (chapters 12–26). Following the address on the law, there is an elaborate series of blessings and curses (chapters 27–28), which are related to the covenant renewal ceremony; obedience to the covenant law would result in blessings for Israel, but the consequence of disobedience would be the curse of God. The book ends with some concluding words of exhortation from Moses, including two long poems (chapters 32–33), some notes on the transition of the leadership of Israel from Moses to Joshua, and an account of the death of Moses (34:1-9).

The entire action presupposed by the book of Deuteronomy takes place in a very short period, perhaps only a few days; yet, the book serves to bring into focus the thrust of the story of the Hebrews from the beginning of the account of Abraham to the end of the life of Moses. But the book of Deuteronomy is much more focused than the other books of the Law; it has a clear overall structure and reflects a specified occasion. Although some of the sections within the book are difficult to read in a coherent fashion (notably the long sequence of apparently miscellaneous laws in chapters 12–26), the book as a whole is characterized by literary clarity and purpose that make it an appropriate conclusion to the Pentateuch.

2. The Pentateuch as a Whole

The five books of the Pentateuch are diverse with respect to individual character and subject matter; yet for all the diversity there is clear continuity among them. Although each book can be studied independently, clearly the five must be taken together if the thrust of the whole Law is to be determined.

One of the first lines of continuity linking the books is that of story and history. The story begins with creation and the development of the human race as a whole. It then shifts to focus on a single family, that of Abraham, and traces the development of that family over several centuries until the family has grown to have the potential for nationhood by the time of Moses' death. Yet, the story, for all its historical elements, is clearly a theological narrative. The interest of the Law is not merely ethnic—namely the origin of the Hebrew people and their early growth—but it has universal and theological dimensions to it. From this perspective, the Pentateuch can be divided into two parts: (i) the universal human condition (Genesis 1–11), and (ii) the beginning of God's response to the human condition (Genesis 12–Deuteronomy 34).

The first part of the Torah, thus divided, sets out the unhappy plight of human beings left to their own ends. Created for the knowledge of God, human beings nevertheless shun relationship with their Creator and go their own separate ways (Genesis 1–11). God, however, refuses to abandon the human race. Through a particular people, the Hebrews, God will set about the task of bringing back all human beings to a knowledge of their Creator (Genesis 12–Deuteronomy 34). Thus the Hebrews, in being bound to

God in a special relationship of covenant, were to be a "kingdom of priests and a holy nation" (Exodus 19:6); that is, as a nation, they were to represent all other human nations before God and to reveal the holiness of God to all nations. The Torah is a story of God and the divine will for human beings above anything else—for all its particular interest in Israel, the prologue of the entire Pentateuch (Genesis 1–11) establishes from the beginning an international concern and a universal vision.

The Pentateuch also establishes the foundations upon which all of the remainder of the Old Testament will be built. The principal foundations are those of *exodus* (deliverance) and *covenant* (relationship). In the exodus from Egypt, the chosen people are delivered from human bondage; in the covenant formed at Sinai, they are given a constitution to potentially become a nation. These two foundational events are in effect the "magna carta" of Israel—although both events are described in the setting of human history, in both the intervention and initiative of God are paramount. The focus of the narrative on exodus and covenant, however, also serves to remind the reader that the Pentateuch is an incomplete work. The patriarchs in Genesis had envisioned living in a land of their own; their descendants in Egypt were slaves in a foreign land. The deliverance from slavery and the leadership of Moses again held out the promise of a land. Indeed, the law given at Sinai was in effect a constitution for nationhood. Yet, the Pentateuch ends before the Israelites have entered a land. On the one hand, this abrupt ending requires that there be further books telling us what happened after the death of Moses: Did the Israelites eventually get a land of their own? On the other hand, the abrupt ending raises the question of the importance of the land: Was deliverance enough? Was it sufficient to have a special relationship with God, as symbolized in the Sinai covenant? These are some of the questions to be addressed from different perspectives in later books of the Old Testament.

Thus the Pentateuch contains five separate books, which are nevertheless inseparable. The inner structure and arrangement of each book make it a distinct entity with its own peculiarities and characteristics. The overall context of the five books, however, creates a larger whole out of the component parts. These general observations on the nature of the Pentateuch inevitably raise the critical questions, so central to scholarly interest, of authorship, date, origin, and editing.

3. Critical Issues in the Study of the Pentateuch

As has already been noted, none of the five books of the Law explicitly identifies an author in its introduction. They are technically anonymous works, and in this they are typical of many such writings that have survived from the civilizations of the ancient Near East. Despite the formal anonymity of the five books, however, an interest in their origin and authorship developed at an early date. Indeed, within the books of the Pentateuch there are a number of references to the writing and the authorship of particular sections. On occasion, Moses is described as being instructed to write something down (see Exodus 17:14; Deuteronomy 32:22). In other places, the text explicitly refers to some other ancient work that is being quoted (see Numbers 21:14), which is a biblical version of the footnote! But for all the occasional references to writing, the books, as a whole and individually, remain anonymous.

The early Jewish tradition that Moses wrote the Pentateuch was reasonable enough in its time, for clearly Moses was a key figure in four of the five books and, as noted, there were occasional references to his writing. Christianity generally followed the early Jewish tradition with respect to authorship, and it may be that in both Judaism and Christianity the identity of Moses as the author of the Pentateuch imparted authority to the substance of the five books. The tradition of the Mosaic authorship of the Pentateuch has continued to be held by some persons in the modern world, notably in conservative Jewish and Christian quarters, but it is not a view which reflects the consensus of scholarly opinion.

What kind of evidence does the reader have to examine in dealing with issues of origin, authorship, and date in the study of the Pentateuch? First, it is reasonable to suppose, both from the substance of the five books and from the evidence of other Near Eastern texts, that the matter of authorship was held to be less important in biblical times than it is in the modern world. It is natural enough that we should be concerned about determining the identity of the author, but we should not project our views backward in time and assume that the original author(s) shared our concern. What was written seems to have been considered more important than the identity of the writer.

Further, the subject matter of the five books of the Pentateuch is so diverse and the styles so different from one section to another that a single author for all the books, or even an individual author for each of the books, seems at the outset to be unlikely. Consider, for instance, some of the following examples of the kind of evidence that must be dealt with. (i) Of the various words for *god* in Hebrew, two are used with particular frequency: *Elohim,* which is translated *God,* and *Yahweh,* which is rendered in most English versions as LORD. Why is it that some sections of the Pentateuch seem to use *Yahweh* consistently, and others use *Elohim?* (ii) In two of the stories about Abraham in Genesis, the patriarch seeks to avoid trouble by claiming that his wife, Sarah, is actually his sister (see Genesis 12:10-16 and 20:1-7). The stories differ, but inevitably the question is raised whether these are two ancient versions of what was once a single story. (iii) There are two versions of the Ten Commandments (see Exodus 20 and Deuteronomy 5). Although the general substance is similar, there are differences in detail; different reasons are given, for example, for the observation of the Sabbath day. How are we to account for such differences? These are only a few examples from many that suggest more than one hand has been at work in the writing and compiling of the books of the Pentateuch.

The detailed examination of this kind of evidence has been pursued by biblical scholars for more than a century. The nature of the evidence is so elusive, and the scholarly task so complex, that it would be rash to claim that any overall consensus has been reached by Old Testament scholars. Nevertheless, there are a few points on which there is fairly wide agreement; they remain to a large extent hypothetical, but provide a general perspective for reading the Pentateuch.

(a) The Analysis of Sources

To some extent, the character of the books of the Pentateuch can be clarified by the hypothesis that they were compiled from a number of earlier sources. This hypothesis, in its classical form, was expressed as follows. Lying behind the Pentateuch in its present form, there were four principal sources; these are conventionally designated by the letters *J, E, D,* and *P.* (i) The letter *J* designates the "Yahwist Source," so named because one of its characteristics is the use of the divine name Yahweh (in German, *Jahweh*, hence *J*). This source was composed in Judah, perhaps in the vicinity of Jerusalem, as early as the tenth, or perhaps the early ninth century B.C. (ii) The letter *E* designates the "Elohist Source," named after the common use of the word *Elohim* for God, dated to a later period than *J* (ninth–eighth centuries B.C.); *E* is believed to have been compiled in the northern state of Israel. (iii) *D* designates Deuteronomy in the Pentateuch (and other material outside the Law) and is dated to the seventh century B.C. in Jerusalem or Judah. (iv) The final source, *P*, is the "Priestly Document," dating from perhaps the sixth or fifth centuries B.C., and as its name implies, it reflects priestly interests and concerns.

According to the hypothesis, the Pentateuch as we now have it was compiled from these various sources (although it should be added that none of the hypothetical source documents have survived). The process was a long and complex one; first the individual sources came into existence, and perhaps *J* and *E* were drawn together to form a single narrative at an early date. To the initial collection, or blending, of *J* and *E, D* was added, and eventually the portions of *P* were inserted by priestly editors who reworked the entire tradition, culminating at last in the creation of the text as we now have it.

The theory of sources is worthy of careful study and assessment, though there is not the space to undertake such an assessment in this context. The following points, nevertheless, will set the theory in context. (i) Most, but not all, modern Old Testament scholars work with some variation of the source hypothesis in the study of the Pentateuch. There is debate concerning which parts of the text belong to which source, and even about the identity of some of the sources, but that there are sources lying behind the present books of the Pentateuch is generally accepted. (ii) The subject matter of the sources is exceptionally hard to date; therefore, assessments of historical value are difficult to make. For example, while *P* has traditionally been dated as the latest source (sixth/fifth centuries B.C.), the date reflects the compilation of *P*. The actual substance of the source, the priestly legislation, is in all probability to be traced back to a much earlier date than that of the source. (iii) The identification of sources only partially resolves the problems which gave rise to the hypothesis in the first place. Even if the sources could be pinpointed with some accuracy in time and place, one would still have to press back behind the sources to find the origin of their contents. (iv) There is a certain danger in becoming too obsessed with sources. The scholarly investigation starts with the Pentateuch as it is and then seeks to trace its origins in the identification of antecedent sources. The danger of this pursuit is that the search for sources may blind us to the finished product that we now have and the collection of books as a whole. If we fail to see the overall structure of this finished product, then we will have missed the entire point of the Pentateuch.

(b) New Trends in the Study of the Pentateuch

In recent decades, new approaches have been taken to the study of the Pentateuch, most of them presupposing some form of the source hypothesis, but a few abandoning it in its generally stated form. One approach which has been fruitful is the study of oral tradition; that is, the examination of stories that are told, retold, sometimes developed, and then passed on perhaps for several generations before eventually being reduced to writing. For example, it is likely that the stories of Abraham and the patriarchs were passed on by word of mouth prior to being recorded in writing.

Another fruitful approach has been the study of the Pentateuchal literature in terms of its form and function. Nowadays, we tend to think of literature as being written in order to be read, but we can still recognize that different kinds of literature are written to serve particular functions. Hymnals and prayer books are designed for use in the worship rituals of synagogues or churches. College textbooks are written to be used in the context of a particular course of study. What function might the books of the Pentateuch, or parts of them, have served in ancient Israel? It is possible, to give one example, that Exodus 1–18, with its story of the Hebrews in Egypt and their great deliverance, was written in part for use in the later celebration of the Passover. And it is possible that Deuteronomy, which reflects a covenant renewal ceremony, was designed for use in just such a ceremony. This functional approach to the study of biblical texts can be conducted on a large scale (with an entire book) or on a small scale (with a particular passage), but it clearly has potential in the study of texts. At the moment, however, the functional approach has produced somewhat more assured results in the study of such books as the Psalms than it has in the study of the Pentateuch.

One of the most recent approaches to the Pentateuch is the study of it, or portions of it, from a strictly literary perspective, employing the same methods that might be employed, for example, in the study of English literature. Within this general approach, the study of the narratives of the Pentateuch has produced some valuable results. The examination of narrative involves the study of characterization, plot, voice, and point of view (the perspective of the narrator and that of persons in the story) as well as descriptive techniques and variations in style. Narrative study takes as its starting point the text as it is, without any initial recourse to the possible sources lying behind the finished text; what is interesting from preliminary studies, nevertheless, is that the integrity of many narrative units incorporates portions of some stories that formerly would have been assigned to different sources.

From this brief survey of just a few contemporary approaches to the study of the Pentateuch, it is evident on the one hand that there is no overall consensus on all matters pertaining to the study of the five books of the Law. On the other hand, the absence of consensus may be a good thing, for varieties of methods are now being applied to the study of the Pentateuch and older hypotheses are constantly being abandoned or refined. The state of flux in this field of study makes it difficult to provide any summary of the current state of scholarship. Nevertheless, we must attempt to form some overall view of how the Pentateuch came into being—not least because that summary will affect our whole understanding of the early history and religion of Israel.

4. The Formation of the Pentateuch

How did the books of the Pentateuch come to be written, and by whom? How did they come together in the five-volume collection? Do they contain genuine historical material, or are they more legendary in character? In dealing with such questions, one must make use of all the sources of information that are available, recognizing from the outset that there may be insufficient information to answer the questions completely. It is also important to recognize from the beginning that any answer to questions such a those posed above must necessarily be hypothetical.

The evidence for attempting to reconstruct the manner of the Pentateuch's formation is relatively limited. There is, on the one hand, the Old Testament literature as such; it contains a few clues to guide us in the reconstruction, but it contains no comprehensive information. On the other hand, there is the evidence provided by archaeology; this evidence, as we shall see, provides general background knowledge, but no specific help. From the extensive archaeological evidence, it is known that writing of various kinds was in common use throughout the ancient Near East during the whole Old Testament period. This information, in turn, leaves open the possibility that the books of the Pentateuch could have been written or compiled at either an early date (the age of Moses) or at a late date. It does not, however, indicate anything more specific. From the texts found in Mesopotamia, it is clear that types of literature parallel to what is in the Old Testament existed during the period from the third to the first millennia B.C. We know of law codes, creation stories, primeval histories, epic stories, and the like from various periods of Mesopotamian history; again, however, the parallel evidence leaves open various possibilities for dating the literature of the Law, but it does not indicate automatically which possibility is the most likely. A further possible source of help from archaeology is the general information it provides about Near Eastern civilizations at various points in history; these data may be employed as a yardstick for measuring the substance of the narratives of the Pentateuch and attempting to determine what period it reflects.

Archaeological information can be of assistance, but for more specific help we must turn to the biblical text itself. We may start with the endpoint, the stage at which it seems the Law came to approximately its present form.

(a) The Role of Ezra

Toward the end of the fifth century B.C., the Jewish people in the homeland formed a colonial community under Persian rule. Their religious life had come to a low ebb, but a reform of religion and government took place under the leadership of Ezra and Nehemiah. The details of this era will be examined in more detail in chapter 10 ("The History of Israel"). For the moment, it is sufficient to make a few observations on the person of Ezra, who played a part in this reform movement.

Ezra, who was of priestly background, is described as a "scribe skilled in the law of Moses" (Ezra 7:6) and as "the scribe of the Law of the God of heaven" (Ezra 7:21). During the course of the reform, Ezra read from the ancient scriptures to the assembled Jews—specifically, he is said to have read from the "book of the law of Moses" (Nehemiah 8:1). Now, inevitably there must be some uncertainty as to what book was intended by these various expressions. The implication may be simply that Ezra read from a book of law such as Exodus or Deuteronomy. On the other hand, it is quite possible that the entire Pentateuch is intended, and that it was from this that Ezra gave instructions to the Jews.

Ezra's professional status as a scribe (one who copied out and studied the law) and his influence as a reformer have suggested to many interpreters that he was more than just an expert teacher of the law. Perhaps, as later Jewish tradition suggests, Ezra was the one who collected together the ancient traditions of the Jews and formed them into something like the present Pentateuch; he was not an author, but an editor, and his role as teacher seems to have given considerable prominence to the role of Scripture in the Jewish religion. In summary, Ezra may have had a hand in the final shaping of the Pentateuch, but whether this was so, it seems to be the case that the Pentateuch was in existence at this time and came to be recognized as authoritative. The titles of the book associate the *law* with both God and Moses; the longer title associates Moses with the law, as is appropriate, rather than implying authorship ("the book of the law of Moses" Nehemiah 8:1).

(b) The Role of Moses

If Ezra provides a reasonably secure endpoint for the formation of the Pentateuch, what can be said about the starting point? As we have already noted, there are a number of references to Moses' writing within the books of the Law. Although the five books themselves do not contain any claims as to the identity of their author(s), they do contain a number of specific statements. Moses is instructed to record the defeat of enemies, namely a group of people called Amalekites (Exodus 17:14). He is told to write down the words of the divine law he proclaimed (Exodus 24:4 and 34:27). He is said to have recorded various stages of the travels of the Israelites through the desert regions (Numbers 33:2). And finally, Moses is said to have recorded the words of a song to be employed in the renewal of the covenant (Deuteronomy 31:22; the song is in chapter 32).

What are we to make of these references to Moses' writing? First, it is clear that whoever was responsible for writing (or editing) the five books clearly wanted to convey the impression to his readers (or audience) that Moses did write some things. Second, given that statements are made about the writing of Moses, it is interesting that no attempt was made, apparently, to identify Moses as the actual author of the five books. (To put it another way, if the traditional view of Moses as author of the Pentateuch were correct, it is curious that he refers to his writing of some things, but makes no initial claim to authorship of the whole.) The books of the Pentateuch, with the exception of Genesis, give Moses a key role in the origins of Israel and recognize him as one who wrote down certain things, though they do not claim him as author and they consistently refer to him in the third person.

Now from the perspective of contemporary biblical scholarship, it must be admitted that only a few scholars would take seriously the possibility of Moses as author of some of the material that is included in the Pentateuch. (Indeed, as we shall see in chapter 10, there are some scholars who doubt the real historical existence of Moses.) Yet, given the stature of Moses in the Hebrew tradition and the textual traditions concerning his writing, it would seem foolish, a priori, to deny the possibility that there may be a "Mosaic base" to the literature of the Pentateuch. Certainly it cannot be proved, by literary or historical means, that this or that passage was written by Moses. On the other hand, the possibility, indeed probability, that there is a solid Mosaic foundation for parts of the Pentateuch is not unreasonable. It is a difficult task, however, to be more specific with respect to particular passages; a reasonable degree of scholarly support may be found for the Mosaic origins of the Decalogue, but the agreement would not extend far beyond that.

(c) From Moses to Ezra

The period from Moses to Ezra, which provides tentative limits to our study of the formation of the Pentateuch, covers approximately eight hundred years. Within this period the books of the Pentateuch, and then the collection as a whole, came into being. Unfortunately it is extremely difficult to be precise in tracing the formation over this long period of time. As has already been noted, one inevitably must deal with hypotheses in attempting to fill in the process of the formation, and at present the formerly secure hypotheses are in a state of considerable flux. What can be done, nevertheless, is to approach the problem from a slightly different direction; the new direction may illuminate why the Pentateuch came into being, even if it does not establish the chronology of the process.

Why were the books of the Pentateuch written? One may propose several reasons, which are complementary rather than mutually exclusive. (i) *Religious reasons*—the ritual and forms of worship employed in the temple (and before that in the tabernacle) celebrated particular aspects of Israel's faith, such as the exodus and the covenant. (ii) *Legal reasons*—the government of the people and the administration of justice would have been best served by written law codes. (iii) *National reasons*—namely the recording of the national epic and history, which in turn were important to the nation's health and sense of identity. (iv) *Social reasons*—ranging from the role and classification of the priesthood to the nature of civic administrators, may also have required the writing down of traditions. These and many other reasons were no doubt among the stimuli that contributed to the writing of the books of the Pentateuch. Genesis establishes the foundations and traces the origin and calling of the chosen people. Exodus establishes the foundations of both religion and statehood, namely the deliverance from slavery and the entering into a covenant with God. Leviticus establishes the foundations of the forms of worship and the role of the priesthood. Numbers, in addition to adding to the national epic, presents both promise and threat in the light of past experiences and failures. Deuteronomy confirms the absolute importance of the covenant in Israel; the faith must be renewed from one generation to the next, if the blessing of God were to be experienced and disaster avoided.

There remain, however, almost insuperable problems in the study of the formation of the Pentateuch. While one can trace a variety of reasons as to *why* the books may have been written or compiled, it is much more difficult to say *when* those processes happened. On matters such as this, there is immense variety of opinion among biblical scholars, and that lack of agreement in turn has consequences for the way in which one reads and understands the Pentateuch.

(d) Problems of Interpretation

Let us take, by way of example, the book of Deuteronomy. If the book is taken at face value, it describes a renewal of the Sinai covenant during the last days of Moses on the plains of Moab; the date may be set tentatively in the middle of the thirteenth century B.C. What is the reader to make of the substance of the book? Is it to be understood as describing a historical event? Or is it some other kind of literature?

It is at this point that one's understanding of the formation of the Pentateuch comes into play. If, as I think, Deuteronomy were written down shortly after the event it describes (within a generation, let us say), that perspective will influence the way in which the book is read. But if, as in the classical expression of the source hypothesis, Deuteronomy is a product of the seventh century B.C., in its present form, that view will equally influence the manner in which the book is interpreted. (Indeed, regardless of which view one adopts, one is caught in the circle of interpretation. The hypothesis is formed by our reading of the evidence and then determines how we continue to read the evidence.) Those who date Deuteronomy in the seventh century may differ little from those who adhere to an early date; they may argue that the final form of the book merely codifies very ancient material. On the other hand, they may claim it was written essentially to meet the needs of the seventh century B.C. and that it is essentially legendary with respect to its purported history.

Problems of this kind can be duplicated for each book of the Pentateuch and there appears to be no end in sight to the varieties of opinion. Students faced with such a plethora of opinions may reasonably complain: "Who knows?" (and the more jaundiced may add: "Who cares?"). There is a purpose, nevertheless, in this illustration of problems in interpreting the Pentateuch. The opinions on the literature are so diverse that inevitably, as we shall see in chapter 10, there are enormous varieties of opinion as to the early history of Israel and the whole nature of Israel's religion. There is, unfortunately, no way of avoiding such problems; they are a concomitant part of studying ancient history and literature. For the reader's information, I should confess, as author, to being more conservative than many of my colleagues. My views on the Pentateuch are such that I take seriously their historical content, while recognizing that the documents were not written primarily to convey history. My confession of perspective, or perhaps prejudice, is simply a guide to the reader; my reconstruction of Israel's early history and literature is more positive than many would allow. Regardless of one's perspective, it is important to recognize the role of hypothesis in studying the five books of the Law. We cannot escape it, and, therefore, should regard all conclusions as being tentative.

There is a final word to be said on the Pentateuch that may be important for some readers. Those who have come to the academic study of the Pentateuch from a conservative Jewish or Christian background may be disconcerted to discover that so few scholars accept the traditional Mosaic authorship of the Pentateuch. In such a context, it is necessary to stress that ultimately the authority of the books of the Law is to be found in their source in God—that is, in their character as revelation. The view that the Pentateuch is a part of divine revelation is necessarily an article of faith; that faith, nevertheless in the divine authority of the books can be maintained, while concurrently one engages in the difficult questions of the human origins and forms of the Pentateuch.

THE
PROPHETS (I):
HISTORICAL BOOKS

THE second division of the Hebrew canon is entitled "The Prophets" (*Nebi'im*). From a modern perspective, this section appears to contain two different types of books, *historical* and *prophetic*. However, on further examination, the distinction is not so sharp as at first it might appear. The so-called historical books are four in number: Joshua, Judges, Samuel, and Kings—in most modern English Bibles the latter are subdivided into two volumes each: I and II Samuel and I and II Kings. This collection of books, however, does not include all the works of a historical character outside the Pentateuch; there are also works of a historical kind in the third division of the canon, the Writings (I–II Chronicles, Ezra, and Nehemiah). The reason for the distinction made between these various works of historical character will become evident later in the chapter. The traditional designations (dating from the early medieval period) for the two types of writings in the Prophets are the *Former Prophets* (the historical books) and the *Latter Prophets* (Isaiah, Jeremiah, Ezekiel, and the Book of the Twelve Prophets).

The four books of the Former Prophets, like those of the Pentateuch, are all technically anonymous works; their titles designate in very general terms the subject matter of the books. As with the Pentateuch, we shall have to survey first the four books as separate and independent works. Having done that, it will be important to review the books as a whole and to attempt to determine the significance of the fact that these four books constitute a single and distinct collection within the Prophets.

1. The Books of the Former Prophets

(a) Joshua

The first of the Former Prophets, the book of Joshua, is named after the person who plays a central role in its contents. Joshua is already known, from the Pentateuch, as a key figure in the early leadership of Israel. At the end of the Pentateuch, in the description of the last days of Moses, an account had been given of the transition of the leadership of Israel from Moses to Joshua. The book of Joshua quite consciously resumes the story of the Pentateuch from the point at which it terminated in Deuteronomy; the principal subject matter of the book extends over a single generation from the death of Moses to the death of Joshua.

In the ancient Jewish tradition, the view was maintained that Joshua was not only the key character, but also the author of the book named after him. This view was based on a reference within the book to Joshua's writing (Joshua 24:26), but the context of the statement does not clearly imply authorship of the book as a whole. The book begins in chapter 1 with words introducing the subject matter and date, but with no statement as to authorship. Indeed, within the last century even the more conservative scholars have for the most part abandoned the notion that Joshua was the author of the book; as with the books of the Pentateuch, we must content ourselves with the recognition that we are dealing once again with an anonymous work.

The book of Joshua falls into two major sections, to which a short appendix has been added:

(i) Chapters 1–12 describe the initial stages of Israel's conquest of the promised land under the leadership of Joshua. At the end of Deuteronomy, the Hebrew people had been gathered to the east of the Jordan River on the Plains of Moab; they had reached the end of a period of forty years during which they had wandered as refugees on the fringes of civilization and had now reached a point of new beginnings. Under Joshua's leadership, they were to cross the Jordan River and begin to take control of the land that would form the basis of their new nation. The opening chapters of Joshua describe the beginnings of the process: First, spies are sent across the river to prepare the way. Then the people follow, crossing the Jordan River in a miraculous fashion reminiscent of the crossing of the Red Sea. The narrative describes several military campaigns—first against the immediate settlements they faced on the west of the river at Jericho and Ai, and then the further campaigns extending to the north and south. The first part of the book concludes with a summary account of the military victories of Moses and Joshua (chapter 12).

(ii) The second principal section of the book (chapters 13–22) focuses on the allocation of the promised land to the various tribes that constituted the new nation of Israel. The section is introduced in such a fashion as to make it clear that the military conquest of the land was far from complete, but the foothold on the land was sufficiently secure to allow the allocation of various geographical regions to each of the tribal groups. The chapters that follow, with their designation of geographical regions and lists of villages and towns, are not the easiest to read; like many legal and administrative documents pertaining to the tenure of land, they are important, but make for dreary literature! In addition to referring to the territory and its subdivision in specific terms, this portion of the book describes the appointment of "cities of refuge" (cities in which persons charged with crimes could find sanctuary until their cases were considered) and cities for the priestly Levites. The section concludes with the tribes whose land lay eastward, in Transjordan, returning across the Jordan to consolidate their holdings, leaving their fellow Hebrews to the west of the river to consolidate their landholdings there.

(iii) The short and final section of the book (chapters 23–24) describes the last days of Joshua, his farewell address to the people he had led at a ceremony of covenant renewal, and finally his death.

The book of Joshua as a whole has a clear internal development and sense of continuity; yet, like many ancient works, it seems to have been compiled from various parts. The component parts of the book of Joshua are different in kind. The historical material includes both detailed stories of particular incidents or military campaigns, as well as summary accounts that sketch in less detail a series of events or activities. The second section of the book seems in places to have been compiled from ancient archives or administrative documents, with its detailed boundary lists and its description of administrative districts. The account of Joshua's final words at the end of the book (chapters 23–24) is reminiscent, from a literary perspective, of the book of Deuteronomy in which Moses' last words are given in the context of a covenant renewal ceremony. Indeed, in one instance the author or editor of the book cites his source; in the description of the famous incident of the sun's standing still, reference is made to the ancient and no longer extant book of Yashar (Joshua 10:13), which is referred to again later in the Former Prophets (II Samuel 1:18).

It seems probable that the book of Joshua has been edited or compiled from various ancient sources, as one would expect of a work having historical subject matter. The process of compilation, however, was not a simple scissors-and-paste task; the author (or editor) has carefully chosen data to communicate a particular message, and the message, in turn, though it is rooted in history, has much more to do with religion. The genius and purpose of the finished book of Joshua have more to do with the book as a whole than with the component parts—anyone can compile a collection of ancient documents, but it takes a more creative mind to weld the ancient sources into a coherent narrative with a distinctive message. What is the message and purpose of the book of Joshua?

From an initial perspective, the purpose of the book may be seen as the bringing to completion of the whole substance of the Pentateuch. The patriarchs had dreamed of a land of their own, as had their descendants in Egyptian slavery. The exodus from Egypt under Moses' leadership had brought the ancient dream closer to reality, but at the end of the Pentateuch, the Hebrews were still essentially refugees with no land of their own. Joshua moves the story forward, so that the hope which had survived for centuries comes closer to fulfillment. Under Joshua's leadership, the Hebrew people take preliminary control of the promised land. This initial perspective on the book is essentially historical in character. (*Note:* The historical problems pertaining to the book are examined in chapter 10.) The book of Joshua fills in some further chapters in the national epic of the Hebrew people and their passage to nationhood. Yet, a historical perspective alone is inadequate for the interpretation of Joshua; the book has also a powerfully religious character.

The author, or editor, of Joshua had more to communicate than simply a nation's story; the historical sources alone could have done that task. The deeper purpose of the book can be seen in the meaning attributed to the promised land and the relation between the possession of the land and the people's obedience to the law of God given in the time of Moses. The successes under Joshua's leadership could be attributed to the people's obedience to the divine law; failures, such as military defeats, were a consequence of disobedience. Therefore, it is not only the history of the Hebrews that is continued from the conclusion of Deuteronomy. The theology of Deuteronomy, with its focus on the promised land and its statements on blessings and curses (Deuteronomy 27–28), also penetrates the chapters of Joshua. This "Deuteronomic" character of the book, as we shall see, is pertinent not only to the interpretation of Joshua, but also to the other books comprising the Former Prophets.

(b) Judges

The book of Judges, like that of Joshua, is named after its principal subject matter; it contains stories about the *judges* (who were national heroes or military leaders, rather than officers of the court). Again, this is an anonymous work; there is a later tradition in Judaism that it was written by Samuel, but there is no internal evidence to this effect. Indeed, the internal evidence, such as it is, suggests a later date of writing in the time of the monarchy or even later. Judges differs from Joshua, however, in embracing a wider sweep history. Whereas the latter book focuses on a single generation, the time of Joshua, Judges is concerned with events over the passage of several centuries. The book begins quite deliberately with the concluding point of the preceding book—the death of Joshua—but from there it moves on to describe selected incidents from the following centuries.

The book contains one major section, preceded by a prologue and concluded with a kind of epilogue:

(i) The prologue (chapters 1:1–2:5) contains some concise and summary remarks about the conquest which was the subject matter of Joshua; as that book had already indicated, while the major campaign had been successfully completed, the detailed task of settling the land and conquering its inhabitants was far from complete. Pockets of resistance remained scattered through the hill country of the promised land; some of the successes and failures of the various Hebrew tribes in dealing with these Canaanite settlements are described in the prologue.

(ii) The main section of the book (chapters 2:6–16:31) contains a collection of stories about the various *judges* and their exploits in early Israel. Of the dozen judges mentioned, six are described only in a cursory fashion; these are referred to as the "minor judges," not because they were unimportant, but because of the paucity of information about them (they are Shamgar, Tola, Jair, Ibzan, Elon, and Abdon). The major judges, concerning whom we have a little more information, include Othniel, Ehud, Deborah (and Barak), Gideon, Jephthah, and Samson. Some of the major judges are described in considerable detail, so that something of their characters and significance can be determined (for example, Gideon, chapters 6–8; Samson, chapters 13–16). The stories about the judges reflect how quickly conditions had changed in early Israel after the demise of Joshua. Whereas in the time of Moses and Joshua the people had functioned for the most part as a single unit with a single goal, following the deaths of the pioneers the sense of unity in Israel quickly fell apart. The common task of forming a nation had been lost in the multitude of regional tasks as each tribe of Hebrews tried to secure some land and protection for itself.

The stories about each of the judges are set against this backdrop of a fragmented people lacking unity of purpose and becoming regional with respect to its interests and concerns. The judges are described as having authority in all Israel, but in reality Israel at this stage of its history was so broken up that the influence of the judges tended to be regional. Deborah and Barak were concerned with a military threat in the north of the promised land, but it is clear that they received little help from the tribes living in other regions (Judges 5:14-17). Samson was engaged with the threat posed by the Philistines in the southwest of the promised land. The stories about the judges are set in a chronological framework which, at first sight, seems to set the incidents in chronological sequence, the events as a whole covering a period of 410 years. But, in all probability, the chronological framework of Judges may describe overlapping periods, for the judges who are described operated in particular regions, rather than in the nation as a whole. So, in general terms, the subject matter of the book of Judges can be set approximately in the twelfth and eleventh centuries B.C.

(iii) The epilogue of the book (chapters 17–21) contains two stories which illustrate the conditions of life in early Israel, though they are not closely integrated with the preceding stories of the judges. The first story concerns a man called Micah who established a private sanctuary and hired a priest to serve in it (chapters 17–18). The second relates an incident of rape perpetrated by members of the tribe of Benjamin and the consequent action taken by other tribes against the tribe of Benjamin (chapters 19–21).

The author or editor of Judges has used various types of material in the compilation of the book. The principal source is the collection of stories about particular judges; these stories no doubt began life in oral form, being told and retold over several generations prior to being reduced to written form. Sometimes a particular incident may have survived in different sources—the story of Deborah and Barak is told both in prose form (chapter 4) and poetic form (chapter 5). The latter, called the "Song of Deborah," is a magnificent example of ancient Hebrew poetry, dramatic in its staccato style and evocative in its images of the battlefield.

The stories about the various judges may well have been brought together into a collection of "Tales about the Judges" before the book reached its present form. Each story is presented in a similar manner with a chronological introduction, a national setting, and a conclusion providing a religious interpretation of the event described. Then the prologue and epilogue were added to the collected stories about the judges, thereby linking the book thus created with the preceding book of Joshua and establishing the overall religious meaning of the book.

As with the book of Joshua, the overall character of the book of Judges can be described as "Deuteronomic." That is to say that its religious perspectives, as revealed in both the editorial comments and the overall structure, reflect aspects of the distinctive theology of Deuteronomy. The historical subject matter of the book describes several generations of social and religious chaos, mitigated only occasionally by the emergence of a judge who brought deliverance to the hard-pressed people. This setting of chaos, relieved only occasionally by order, is given religious meaning: Chaos was a natural outcome of Israel's failure to maintain the integrity of faith, but order was restored when the people were led back, by a judge, to their true commitment to God. The prologue and epilogue set the religious meaning of the book in context and indicate that the book's primary purpose is religious, not historical. The prologue is retrospective, establishing a good past in the time of Joshua, but reminding the reader of the failures that followed upon disobedience; in a sense, it introduces a period of chaos in Israel's history that will be in marked contrast to the preceding age of Joshua. The epilogue, at first sight merely an appendix containing two miscellaneous stories, serves to balance the theological tone of the introduction; Israel, when its people jettisoned the national faith, tended to become increasingly criminal in character. Thus the book ends on a bleak note, but it looks toward the future with elements of hope: "In those days there was no king in Israel; every man did what was right in his own eyes" (Judges 21:25).

(c) I–II Samuel

The two books of Samuel, which originally constituted a single work, are named after the first of several key figures described within the books. Samuel's life and ministry, although they occupy less than a quarter of the chapters in I–II Samuel, nevertheless precipitated the key figures and events in the texts as a whole. Again, we are dealing with an anonymous work; despite an ancient tradition attributing authorship to Samuel, the events described within the book extend well past the time of his death. Nevertheless, the chronological scope of I–II Samuel is more restricted than that of Judges; the period reflected within the book is approximately 1050–960 B.C.

The subject matter of the book, although it is characterized by considerable diversity with respect to its sources, focuses essentially on three persons—Samuel, Saul, and David. Given the nature of the history, the narratives describing these three key figures inevitably overlap, but in terms of content the substance of the book divides loosely into three sections.

(i) The first key figure is Samuel (I Samuel 1–12), whose story begins before his birth. He combines in his person three roles—that of priest, of prophet, and he was the last of the judges in Israel. The narrative of this first unit is at first sight choppy and disconnected. After the account of Samuel's birth and early years, the narrative then switches to the political conditions of Samuel's time (around 1050

B.C.). The dominant military power of the time, threatening the very survival of Israel, was a coalition of Philistine states. The Philistines were a people who had come to that part of the world from southeastern Europe and the Aegean area and had settled in the vicinity of Gaza along the Mediterranean coast. They were competitors, along with the Hebrews, for the promised land. During Samuel's time as a judge, a degree of temporary success was gained against the Philistines, but the survival of the Hebrew tribes continued to be a matter of uncertainty. Hence, a significant part of Samuel's work was to prepare the people for a monarchy; perhaps with a king and a united government, a centralized and more powerful response to the Philistines threat could be established. Saul was singled out for elevation to the role of Israel's first king.

(ii) Although Saul has already figured in the opening chapters with respect to his coronation, the narrative begins to focus primarily on Saul in the second section (I Samuel 13–31). The new passage is introduced by a formula indicating Saul's age and the length of his reign (I Samuel 13:1). Saul quickly assumes the role of king, interpreted primarily in the sense of the nation's military leader. He engages in various military campaigns with the Philistines, winning some victories, but also being defeated on several occasions. Saul's story is a sad one; for all his military strength, he has not fully grasped the religious foundations of his nation. Samuel is critical of him, despite the fact that Saul was in some ways Samuel's protégé. Even while the narrative recounts the exploits of Saul, another character is introduced—David is marked by Samuel as the young man who will succeed to the kingship following Saul's death.

(iii) Saul's death is described at the end of I Samuel so that the focus of the entire book of II Samuel is on David. The narrative describes the establishment of the monarchy under David, his capture of Jerusalem, which was to serve as his capital city, and his defeat of the Philistine threat. A major portion of the book (II Samuel 9–20) contains an account of the events taking place in David's royal court, ranging from military exploits to more personal events. The book concludes with a series of chapters (21–24) which appear at first to form an appendix, but which (as we shall see) provide a theological perspective from which to view the books of Samuel as a whole. (The details of the establishment of the monarchy in Israel and of the reigns of Saul and David are examined in chapter 10).

As was the case with the book of Joshua, I–II Samuel draw on various ancient sources. On the one hand, the book is a collection of writings compiled from earlier sources; but on the other hand, the way in which the sources have been employed conveys the overall intent of the author or editor. There are numerous sources lying behind the present form of the book, although only a few are explicitly mentioned. There is a reference to the book of Yashar, from which an ancient poem has been quoted (II Samuel 1:18) and which we have already noted as an ancient, but no longer extant source (see Joshua 10:13). Again, it is said that Samuel himself recorded the responsibilities of the king in a book (I Samuel 10:25).

Apart from such explicit references, variations in subject matter and style suggest other ancient sources: (1) *Cycles of stories*—In I Samuel 1–7 there appear to be at least two cycles of stories, one forming a partial biography of Samuel, the other concerning the fate of the ark (the container in which, according to tradition, the tablets of the Law were kept). (2) *Larger literary units*—II Samuel 9–20 and I Kings 1–2 contain coherent and beautifully written accounts of life in David's court and of some of the incidents preparing the way for Solomon's succession to David's throne. (3) *Poetic passages*—There are a number of poetic passages, apparently drawn from early sources, which have been integrated within the book in its present form. For example, "Hannah's Song" (I Samuel 2:1-10), celebrating the birth of a boy, has been smoothly integrated into the story of Samuel's birth and early life. Again, David's great hymn of thanksgiving (II Samuel 22) can be found duplicated in the Psalter (Psalm 18). From sources of this kind, which existed before the book as we now have it came into being, I–II Samuel was brought into its present form.

For all the importance of recognizing the place of sources in a historical text, the sources must not detract us from the overall purpose of the finished product. In I–II Samuel, the sources have been woven into a skillful narrative by means of their arrangement and sequence, but the editor has allowed the sources to speak for themselves with very little editorial comment. While the general Deuteronomic character that has already been noted in Joshua and Judges continues in Samuel, it is much more subdued and rarely explicit. The sources speak for themselves of the importance of abiding by the divine law and of the consequent blessings or curses. By the skillful use of sources, the editor has developed Israel's story from the chaotic days that marked the end of the time of the judges to the point at which David's great kingdom is soundly established. Joshua and Judges had brought to fulfillment the thrust of the Pentateuch by recounting how at last the Hebrews had come to possess a land of their own, but the possession of land does not make for a great nation, as is clear at the end of the Book of Judges. The story progresses from mere possession of land to the establishment of a powerful nation in I–II Samuel.

The development of the narrative in the books of Samuel also illustrates two other significant parts of the books' message. First, human history is not an accidental or random process; rather, it develops within the framework of God's overall purpose. Inevitably, this notion of history somehow reflecting God's purpose is expressed in elusive terms. Some of the historical sources employed in Samuel are remarkable for their objective character and their dispassionate recording of events (see the so-called Court History, II Samuel 9–20). Nevertheless, the introductory "Song of Hannah" (I Samuel 2:1-10) and David's great concluding psalm (II Samuel 22) set the whole historical narrative in a theological context—God is at work in and through the lives of his people. The second point of significance in these books is the growing focus on the office of the king. In part, it is simply a consequence of the development of history; the office of *judge* gave way to that of *king*. But the books of Samuel reflect more than just the changes in history; they present David, for all his flaws, as an ideal king. The notion of ideal Davidic kingship, as we shall see, penetrates many of the later books of the Old Testament.

(d) I–II Kings

The anonymous books of Kings continue directly with the narrative from the point at which it concluded in II Samuel. Indeed, I Kings 1–2 seems to have been drawn from the same source that had formed a central part of the preceding book (II Samuel 9–20 in which life in David's court had been described, together with the events leading gradually to the end of David's reign and the succession of the monarchy).

The books of Kings (originally a single book), though they are approximately the same length as those of Samuel, contain a review of a far more extensive historical period (from about 960 B.C. to 560 B.C.).

As in the preceding books, there is a chronological structure to the whole work, even though the primary purpose of the books is not in a strict sense historical. The subject matter falls into three distinctive periods.

(i) The reign of Solomon (I Kings 1–11). The narrative begins with the end of David's reign and the establishment of Solomon in the office of king. As the narrative progresses, however, it is clear that the author is concerned not simply with giving an account of Solomon's reign, but also with highlighting what was most important in that reign, namely the building of a temple in Jerusalem. The establishment of the temple and proper worship is seen as the focal point in Solomon's story (chapters 5–9), and around that a number of other stories about Solomon's wisdom as well as his folly have been gathered.

(ii) The Two Kingdoms (I Kings 12–II Kings 17). Following Solomon's death, the originally united kingdom split into two separate states—Israel to the north, and Judah, with its capital in Jerusalem, in the south. The history of both kingdoms is traced by means of accounts of the successive kings who ruled in them. Nevertheless, the narratives describing the two monarchies are incomplete when viewed from the perspective of modern history. The author is not particularly concerned with giving an adequate account of events in the successive reigns, but is interested rather in the faithfulness of the various kings when viewed from the perspective of Israel's religion. The focus of the narrative is not limited to the lives of kings, however, for interspersed at various points there are detailed descriptions of the lives and ministries of various prophets. The principal prophetic narratives are those concerning Elijah (I Kings 17:1–19:21 and II Kings 1) and Elisha (interspersed throughout II Kings 2–13). The stories of these and other prophets serve once again to highlight the author's concern with the religion of Israel.

(iii) The Kingdom of Judah (II Kings 18–25). In 722 B.C., the northern kingdom of Israel was defeatd in war and ceased to exist as an independent state; this last section of Kings recounts the history of the southern state of Judah down to its destruction and defeat in 586 B.C., and the exile that followed. It concludes with a short note on the fate of Jehoiachin, the penultimate king of Judah.

In compiling this sweeping panorama of four centuries of history, the author or editor has obviously drawn on a variety of ancient sources. To a greater extent than in the preceding works of the Former Prophets, the antecedent sources are referred to explicitly by name. There are, for example, seventeen references to the book of the Chronicles of the Kings of Israel (for example, I Kings 14:19) and fifteen references to the book of the Chronicles of the Kings of Judah (for example, I Kings 14:29). These ancient texts have not survived independently, though we may speculate that they contained more detailed historical records of the reigns of the various kings than have survived in the books of Kings. Other sources are implied rather than identified. It is possible that the collections of stories about the prophets Elijah and Elisha initially circulated independently prior to being incorporated in I–II Kings.

As with the other books of the Former Prophets, it is the skillful welding of the sources into a total package that has created the books of Kings as they have survived, and it is in the total package that the purpose of the author/editor can be seen. The influence of Deuteronomy is clearly evident in the final form of the books, most notably in the religious assessment which is given of the reigns of respective kings. Those kings who did not observe the divine law experienced the curse of God, as reflected so clearly in the blessing-cursing section of Deuteronomy (chapters 27–28). The failure of the kings to act properly is frequently identified quite explicitly as a failure to observe what was written in the "book of the law of Moses" (see II Kings 14:6 which cites Deuteronomy 24:16). Thus the books of Kings do not attempt to write a secular history of the Hebrew kingdoms; rather, they contain a reflection of that history when viewed from the perspective of the Mosaic law, particularly as it is presented in Deuteronomy. It is not an objective history, but a judgmental and moral one. The author does not spare those who have failed in their responsibility before God, but occasionally praises those few who fulfilled the law.

There has been considerable debate as to what was the overall purpose of I–II Kings, and it is probable that no single answer will suffice. In part, the books provide an understanding of why it was that first Israel and then Judah were defeated in war and lost their status as independent nations. In neither case was it the mere accident of history or the consequence of fluctuating conditions in international affairs. Instead, the collapse of the nations is traced to their failure to

139

abide by the Mosaic law, and that failure in turn is located primarily in the men who ruled as kings. The books have something positive to say, in addition to this rather bleak understanding of past history. The positive message perceives history as a paradigm. Sin, as is so evident from the past, must culminate in judgment. Repentance, that is turning from evil and back to God, offers prospects of hope. Thus the reader of I–II Kings can learn from history; the past clearly reveals what will be the culmination of a life lived in disregard of the ancient Mosaic law, but turning back to God's will, as expressed in the law, offers prospects of blessing.

There is also a strong prophetic thread running through the books of Kings. Whereas (as we shall see) the prophetic books focus primarily on the Word of God, amplifying it from time to time with historical material, the Former Prophets focus primarily on history, amplifying it with references to the Prophets. Although the reigns of successive kings dominate the narrative of I–II Kings as a whole, there are frequent references to prophets—in addition to Elijah and Elisha, already mentioned, prophets such as Nathan (I Kings 1:45), Ahijah (I Kings 11:29-40), Shemaiah (I Kings 12:21-24), and many others have a significant role to play. These prophetic figures are not players of minor roles in the narrative, but signify the deeper religious meaning underlying the whole story.

2. The Former Prophets as a Collection

It makes a difference when you begin to read a book to know before hand whether you are opening a separate and self-contained volume, or whether, for example, you are beginning to read volume three of a four-volume set. If you are beginning to read the latter, then you will recognize that although the book may make sense in and of itself, nevertheless it is a part of a larger whole. That larger whole will bear on the interpretation of the particular volume. Are the Former Prophets parts of an integrated whole? Or are they merely four, originally independent volumes which happen to have been brought together and have survived from Israel's antiquity?

The overall evidence strongly suggests that the four books, in their present form, have been deliberately brought together to form a four-volume series; they follow one another in chronological sequence. Although they are relatively self-contained, they are nevertheless interdependent. Solomon is introduced in II Samuel, but his reign is described in I Kings. David is the central figure in II Samuel, but the story is not completed until I Kings. In these and numerous other ways, the divisions between the four books seem somewhat artificial; taken together, they tell a wide-ranging story, spanning more than half a millennium from Israel's entry into the promised land to the later expulsion of the people from that land. For all the continuity between the four books, each volume can stand on its own as an independent work. The editorial framework of each and the arrangement of the sources lend not only continuity between the volumes, but also a sense of wholeness in each volume. They are part of a larger epic; yet, each has a distinctive story to tell and a particular emphasis to make.

One of the lines of continuity running through the four volumes has been called *Deuteronomic;* that is, the underlying philosophy of the author(s) and/or editor(s) is rooted in the fundamental notions of the Book of Deuteronomy. The importance of the written law of God as the basis of covenant life, the sense that obedience leads to blessing and disobedience to the divine curse, the role of a single sanctuary in which Israel was to worship—these and related themes in Deuteronomy can be seen constantly recurring in the Former Prophets. Sometimes this Deuteronomic material is explicit and dominant, influencing each step of the narrative—as in Judges and I–II Kings. In other places it is implicit rather than explicit (II Samuel), reflected in the choice and arrangement of ancient material, but maintaining a lower profile.

Once one recognizes the generally Deuteronomic character of the Former Prophets, the problem then emerges as to whether one can specify authors and dates for the individual books and collections. A classical hypothesis in this connection is that of a distinguished German scholar, Martin Noth. He proposed that the whole "Deuteronomistic history" was the work of a single writer, a Judean historian of the sixth century B.C. This hypothesis, first proposed in 1943, has much to recommend it, though with the passing of time it has been subjected to considerable modification. If indeed a single author, unknown but entitled the "Deuteronomist," is responsible for the Former Prophets in their final form, then it must also be recognized that the four books were subjected to a degree of Deuteronomic editing prior to the sixth century B.C. That much most scholars can agree on, but to go any farther one inevitably becomes enmeshed in the complex arguments of the continuing scholarly debate. Were the four books originally quite independent, Joshua and Judges being early works and Samuel and Kings being later works? If such were the case, then the final Deuteronomic edition of the four volumes is merely the end stage in a very long process. It should be noted that the Deuteronomist would almost certainly not be a single person, but a group or school in ancient Israel that functioned over several centuries. On the other hand, it is equally possible to see a shorter process in the formation of the books; perhaps they reached their penultimate form in the seventh century B.C.—the last days of the kingdom of Judah—and were only slightly revised in the late sixth century, sometime after 561 B.C., which is the last date implied by the content of the final chapter of II Kings.

If scholars have not been able to agree on the exact process by which the books came into being, it should also be said that they have not reached any agreement on the identity of the elusive Deuteronomist (in a singular or plural sense). Some have argued that the Deuteronomic perspective reflects the particular interests of the servants of the temple, perhaps priests or Levites serving in the Jerusalem temple, but there are serious objections to this view. Others have claimed that the Deuteronomistic writings were produced by the "wise men," in effect professional civil servants engaged in the government in Jerusalem. As we shall see (chapter 8), the "wise men" were indeed responsible for producing literary works in ancient Israel, but the argument that they were responsible for the Former Prophets is not entirely persuasive, though it remains a possibility. Perhaps the strongest probability is that the prophets themselves, or persons associated with the prophets, were responsible for the final production of these four historical books.

Although the identity of the person or persons who produced the Former Prophets cannot be pinned down with any certainty, the overall purpose of the books can be stated in general terms. Though superficially they are works of history, these books contain a very distinctive kind of history. Ordinary history was already available in ancient Israel in books like the Chronicles of the Kings of Israel, to which reference has already been made. These books, although they have not survived, presumably contained records of kings and historical events. The Former Prophets, on the other hand, contain what might be called a "history of the prophetic word." The *prophetic word* is the law of God, particularly as it is given expression in Deuteronomy. It is in one sense law, but it is also prophecy, being the Word of God given through the prophet Moses. The historian in the Former Prophets is not content to tell Israel's story in a dry and objective fashion; he interprets his nation's history through the prism of the law, or the prophetic word. These books do not simply record the ebb and flow of Israel's fortunes in the world of international affairs, but understand that ebb and flow in direct relationship to the nation's obedience or disobedience to the divine law. In times of obedience, though they were rare, the nation prospered. In times of disobedience it experienced calamity. This principle of interpretation provided the basis for selection from the sources available to the author. For example, Omri, one of the greatest and most powerful kings in the northern state of Israel (who reigned around 876–869 B.C.) can be disposed of in a few lines, for his reign did not fit clearly within the didactic and theological purpose of the author. But Josiah, who led a great reformation in Judah during the latter quarter of the seventh century B.C., deserves much more space, for his importance lay as a religious reformer who was apparently influenced by the book of Deuteronomy (II Kings 22–23). The theology and substance of Deuteronomy, in other words, seems to have provided the basis for the interpretation of Israel's history. As we shall see in a later chapter, this theological perspective introduces problems for the modern historian, whose goal may be simply the reconstruction of the history of ancient Israel "as it actually happened." For all the importance of modern methods of historical study, we must not let it distract us from the purpose of the ancient author(s) of the Former Prophets. They told not only the story of a nation, but also of a nation's relationship with its God. Such a task is by definition suprahistorical, but we shall miss the point of these four books unless we attempt, in reading them, to share the writer's perspective.

3. Summary: The Value of Former Prophets

The preceding sections of this chapter may seem to some readers to be unnecessarily complex and obscure. All the comments about sources, editing, and the role of the elusive Deuteronomist, may seem to cast a pall of suspicion on books which otherwise seemed straightforward and interesting. It will be of little comfort to most readers to learn that the scholarly debate over the nature and formation of these four ancient books has been considerably simplified, if not grossly oversimplified. For more than a century now, the Former Prophets have been the subject of scholarly debate, and though a few points of consensus are emerging, total agreement remains an elusive goal.

In part, the complexity of studying the Former Prophets is integral to the subject matter. Together they form a large literary corpus, and it is not an easy task to determine the meaning and message of the whole. Scholarly discussion of the ancient sources drawn on by the historian, while sometimes it may seem to roam randomly in the wide fields of hypothesis, is for all that not a scholarly invention. It is the books themselves that raise the issue of sources by referring to other ancient writings. For those of a scholarly disposition, the study of the origins and development of the Former Prophets may contain all the fascination of a detective story; for others, it may be less interesting than the solemn reading of a telephone directory. But is there a more universal importance in these ancient books, an insight which we would not easily gain if we did not read them?

For most readers in the modern Western world, the Former Prophets post the challenge of viewing human life and history from a different perspective. We are conditioned by our culture to view everything from the perspective of reason. Even religious persons— Christians and Jews, for example—are thoroughly conditioned by the pervasiveness of reason in our society. Reason lies behind modern science as much as it does behind modern history. Reason is the lens through which we view all forms of reality. Reason is one of the principal means by which we know and understand our world, but we may also be seduced into thinking it is the only way of knowing and understanding. We may forget, for example, that reason does not easily explain the mysteries of human love or the beauty of great music, and that if reason becomes the only lens through which we view life and history we may be restricting our vision.

The substance of the Former Prophets challenges us to entertain alternative visions, to see what a different lens might reveal to us about reality. It does not abandon reason; indeed, David's Court History (II Samuel 9–20) is as fine a piece of objective historical writing as could be found in the twentieth century. The Former Prophets as a whole challenge the reader to view human history not only through the lens of reason, but also through that of faith. This alternative vision of history, viewed from the stance of faith, casts things in a different light. Perhaps there is more to human history than either cause and effect or random process. Perhaps there is indeed a moral component to history. How one behaves may indeed profoundly affect what happens. For the Christian or the Jew, there is the challenge to think through the meaning of God's involvement and human responsibility in the movement of history.

It is true, of course, that the attempt to share in the vision of the Former Prophets will vary from one person to another. The religious person may interpret and understand these ancient books in a very different fashion from the atheist or agnostic. My point is that the attempt to share the vision of the Former Prophets is not an exclusively religious task. The person or persons who wrote these books had an extraordinary insight that is not common in the history of human thought—therein lies their greatness. The reader who sees no more in the Former Prophets than the annals of ancient Israel's history has totally missed the point; they offer for consideration an alternative vision of history and a profound wisdom that is worthy of careful reflection.

THE
PROPHETS (II):
MAJOR PROPHETS

T HE second division of the Old Testament canon, the Prophets, contains not only the historical books designated Former Prophets, but also a series of volumes entitled the Latter Prophets, which are more directly related to particular persons. These Latter Prophets comprise four volumes, three of which (Isaiah, Jeremiah, and Ezekiel) are frequently called *Major Prophets*, while the fourth, the Book of the Twelve, is an anthology of twelve smaller books, the so-called *Minor Prophets*. The *major/minor* distinction is not an altogether satisfactory one; it refers only to the length of the respective volumes, implying nothing with respect to the significance or importance of the prophets as such.

The first three volumes in the Latter Prophets are each approximately equivalent in length to a modern book; whereas, the Book of the Twelve is a collection of much shorter works. Each of the four volumes may originally have been written on a single scroll, all four being of generally the same length. Unlike the Former Prophets, in which the successive volumes succeed each other chronologically and develop a historical theme, the Latter Prophets are more independent works. They appear in various sequences in the ancient manuscripts, and each can be read without reference to the others. There are few signs of any editorial hand that might have provided links between the volumes. What holds the volumes together is their common prophetic character, rather than any consistent development of a story or theme. (In this chapter and the following one, the focus is on the prophetic literature as such; prophecy and the nature of the prophet are examined in chapter 11.)

It must be admitted from the outset that the prophetic books are not easy to read; indeed, it can be helpful to begin by not thinking of them as books in the modern sense. A few words of explanation may clarify the issues. First, in the majority of cases, the *books* of the prophets were not designed to be books; that is, their subject matter was not created specifically for the purpose of being written down. The prophets were, for the most part, activists rather than authors, more engaged in preaching than in the activity of writing. Thus, although a few of the prophetic books may have been specifically created as written works, the majority of them preserve a deposit of the ministries and messages of the various prophets. A modern analogy might be provided by imagining a volume containing the collected speeches of a famous political figure, to which a few elements of history and biography have been added. The speeches were not written to form the basis of a book, but have been incorporated into a volume to serve a secondary purpose. The analogy will have to be modified somewhat in the examination of particular prophetic writings, but it is generally the case that the words of the prophets that have been preserved were originally *spoken words*. They were addressed to a particular group of people on a particular occasion; only later were they incorporated into the book in which they have survived. The analogy may also help to explain some of the difficulty of reading the prophetic books. A speech delivered on a particular occasion to a select group of people might be easily understood, but when that speech is later read in a book by a reader unfamiliar with the original occasion, the meaning may be less clear. To a large extent, such is the difficulty in reading parts of the prophetic books.

In a limited sense, therefore, the books of the prophets can be viewed as anthologies, collections in written form of words which started in a living and oral context. To the words and speeches have been added fragments of historical records, scraps of biography and autobiography, and perhaps summaries of earlier speeches. There are certain dangers in viewing the prophetic books simply as anthologies. In most cases, there are two creative processes that have been at work, both of which can be traced in the surviving books. One is the original creative process in the ministry of the prophet—for example, the delivery of a speech or sermon. The second is the creative process that went into the production of the book; though it may be in part an anthology, the material has usually been carefully arranged and structured so that in its literary form it conveys its own distinctive message. The books of the prophets, though they are rooted in the ministries and words of the prophets, are thus more than simple records of prophetic preaching; they convey a prophetic message in their own right.

The difficulty in reading the prophetic books is paralleled by the difficulty in studying their form and background. It is extremely difficult, for example, to reconstruct the process involved from the time that a prophet spoke certain words to the stage at which those words, or a summary of them, were committed to writing. The words of some prophets may have been committed to memory and passed on by word of mouth before being set down in written form. In other instances, the spoken word may have been immediately recorded for some reason. The actual production of the books that have survived, whether by a prophet or a prophet's disciples or followers, introduces the issues and complexities of editing and arranging. The best way to illustrate the difficulties in reading and studying the prophetic books is to turn to a study of the volumes themselves. As will soon become clear, there is enormous variety of opinion among scholars as to the meaning and interpretation of the particular prophetic books. The slender and often ambiguous nature of the surviving evidence is such that the academic debate on the prophetic books is unlikely to abate. An awareness of the issues, nevertheless, may be helpful in setting a context for reading the Major Prophets.

1. The Book of Isaiah

Perhaps none of the prophetic books has evoked more debate and interest among scholars and readers than that of Isaiah. It is, on the one hand, a magnificent book in terms of its substance, its fine poetry, and its religious insight. On the other hand, its sixty-six chapters pose seemingly intractable problems to the scholarly investigator.

The book is named after Isaiah ben Amoz, who is specified in the title verse (1:1) as a citizen of Jerusalem in the state of Judah. His prophetic ministry in the eighth century B.C. was a long one, extending from approximately 740 to 700 B.C. He was a married man with two children, at least, and from the substance of the book we can infer that he was a man of some influence in the royal court of Jerusalem. He lived in a momentous period in Judah's history when the nation was constantly threatened by external enemies, but was equally threatened by the internal decline of religious and communal life in Judah. It was during Isaiah's ministry, in 722 B.C., that the neighboring state of Israel was defeated in war by the Assyrians and its history brought to an end.

The book of Isaiah, though it contains portions of prose, is written for the most part in poetry. It is magnificent poetry, the vigor and force of it surviving clearly in English translation. In many places, the poetic language may reflect an original oral proclamation, for poetic language could be employed on occasion to assist an audience in remembering the substance of a message. In other cases the poetry in Isaiah may reflect an original literary creation of certain passages. The contents of the book fall into three main sections: (a) chapters 1–39; (b) chapters 40–55; (c) chapters 56–66.

(a) The Contents of Isaiah

(i) **Chapters 1–39.** After the opening verse (1:1), the equivalent of a title page in a modern work, the book launches immediately into a prophetic *oracle* in poetic form. (The word *oracle* is used to designate a prophet's message or speech, that speech in turn being a declaration of words whose source is believed to be God. Thus in 1:2a the *prophet* says, "the Lord has spoken"; immediately following, in verse 2b, the words which the prophet speaks are declared as *God's* words.) The first section of the book principally contains prophetic oracles to which has been added some historical material (notably chapters 36–39). In addition, we are given a moving account of the prophet's vocation of divine service and his commissioning (chapter 6).

The substance of the particular messages that constitute the first section of the book varies widely in content, though there are certain overarching themes linking the whole together. Isaiah is concerned with the religion and faith of Israel, but these themes, in turn, are so integrally related to the national life that politics and religion, as we would describe them today, frequently intertwine in his words. On the one hand, he addresses the sin and evil rampant in his society and its inevitable consequence in divine judgment; on the other hand, he addresses such matters as foreign policy, for a nation's political decisions cannot be entirely separated from its spiritual health. What dominates Isaiah's whole perspective is his faith in God, whom he refers to frequently as the "Holy One of Israel" (1:4; although this title is relatively rare in the Old Testament as a whole, it is used some twenty-six times in Isaiah). The holiness of Isaiah's God is in such sharp contrast to unholy Israel that inevitably God's message through his prophet to the chosen people is penetrated with condemnation and judgment.

(ii) *Chapters 40–55.* There are subtle changes in both the literary style and the perspective of the second major portion of the book of Isaiah. This section continues to be principally poetic in form, but the poetry is now more distinctly literary than oral; that is, the impression of these chapters is that they were designed as literature, rather than being rooted in public ministry. The perspective is different; whereas the first thirty-nine chapters are clearly rooted in the history of the eighth century B.C., anticipating future judgment, now it seems that the judgment has come. The section opens with a message of comfort: Those who are in exile can anticipate a restoration of their homeland through an act of God's grace. What is even more startling than the message of restoration from exile is the means by which it was to be achieved. The Hebrew people would be restored from their exile in Babylon through the actions of Cyrus in conquering the Hebrew's captors (44:28 and 45:1). Now as we have seen, Isaiah of Jerusalem lived in the eighth century B.C., whereas Cyrus did not conquer the Babylonians until the sixth century B.C. Hence the setting of exile and the reference to Cyrus set off chapters 40–55 very sharply from the opening section of the book.

The message concerning the end of exile is rounded out through the anticipation of the renewal of national life in the promised land. In this whole process, indications are given that the "servant of the

Lord" would be instrumental in the restoration. This "servant," whose identity is elusive, is referred to in a series of songs or poems—42:1-4; 49:1-6; 50:4-9; and 52:13–53:12. The *Servant Songs,* which have been the focus of extensive scholarly investigation, indicate that the servant's suffering would have an extensive role in the redemption of the chosen people. Whether an individual was intended by the servant figure (as in early Christian interpretation, for example, where the servant was identified with the Messiah), or whether the servant was the personification of suffering Israel as a whole remains a matter of debate.

The theological perspective remains similar to that of 1–39, with its emphasis on the "Holy One of Israel"; the expression is used eleven times. But the poetry is notable for its expression of a rigorously *monotheistic* viewpoint—the total denial of the reality of gods other than the Lord of Israel. The monotheistic perspective is reinforced by both a profound creation theology, in which God's mastery of history and nature are stressed, and by a thorough critique of all forms of idolatry and false worship.

(iii) *Chapters 56–66.* The third and final section of the book is at first appearance a less unified and coherent passage than chapters 40–55. It contains a series of oracles, or messages, in which various topics are addressed—the observation of the sabbath day, a critique of bad government, a denunciation of false worship and various types of evil, and a promise of future deliverance and the happy estate of the faithful. The perspective, for the most part, is no longer that of exile, but that of the homeland. However, as in the second section, the messages seem less directly related to the eighth century B.C. than are those in chapters 1–39.

In summary, the substance of Isaiah falls into three principal sections. While there are common themes running through all three sections—and a generally common theology and notion of God pervades the whole—style, perspective, and subject matter suggest the threefold division. It should be noted that there are no explicit divisions or markers in the text to separate the three parts; chapters 40–55, for example, do not have a new heading similar to that contained in 1:1. The general analysis of the book, however, brings us to the point at which we must turn to the difficulties faced in the academic study of Isaiah.

(b) Critical Problems in the Study of Isaiah

Since the eighteenth century, Isaiah and the Pentateuch have provided major focal points for biblical scholarship. The issues they raise invite the kind of critical investigation which is central to the scholarly enterprise.

With respect to Isaiah, one of the first major conclusions at which biblical scholars arrived was that Isaiah could not be considered a single work, as had been traditionally supposed. The differences between chapters 1–39 and 40–66 were so striking that the hypothesis of two "Isaiahs" was proposed—Isaiah of Jerusalem, who was responsible for chapters 1–39, and Second Isaiah (or Deutero-Isaiah), who was the author of chapters 40-66. (The differences within chapters 40-66 also attracted attention, so that many scholars preferred to think of Second Isaiah, chapters 40–55, and Third [Trito-] Isaiah, chapters 56–66.) Isaiah of Jerusalem was the traditional eighth-century author; Second Isaiah was an otherwise unknown prophet of the sixth century B.C.; and Trito-Isaiah may have lived after the exile.

Whether the hypothesis of the multiple authorship is correct, there were reasonable grounds giving rise to its formation. From a historical perspective, there are sharp differences between the major sections of the book. Chapters 1–39 are filled with historical statements or allusions that set them clearly in the eighth century B.C.. Chapters 40–66, although they are more vague in historical terms, seem to presuppose the time of the exile which occurred in the sixth century B.C. Whereas specific persons of the eighth century are referred to in the first part (for example, King Uzziah, 6:1), there are two specific references to Cyrus, a citizen of the sixth century, in the second part. These different historical perspectives have suggested to many scholars that we are in fact dealing with two quite distinct works, separated in time by almost two centuries, which have been somewhat artificially joined together.

There are also differences in the literary styles employed in the major sections of the book, although these are not always easy to detect in English translation. The principal focus of the subject matter changes between the two sections, judgment being the more dominant theme in chapters 1–39, whereas promise and restoration are more prominent in the second major portion of the book. These

changes in focus, in turn, have led some scholars to suppose a quite
different theological viewpoint to lie behind the main sections of the
book.

As has been indicated, the unity of the second major portion of the
book (chapters 40–66) has also been the subject of debate, but here
less agreement between scholars has been achieved. Although most
scholars would agree on the division separating the work of Isaiah of
Jerusalem and Deutero-Isaiah, the analysis of chapters 56–66 has
been less susceptible to consensus and Trito-Isaiah remains a more
elusive figure than Deutero-Isaiah. Whereas the background to
chapters 40–55 seems to be that of exile, chapters 56–66 reflect life in
the promised land. Some scholars argue that the conditions of life
reflected there were those which pertained after the exile. Others
claim that chapters 56–66 are a more miscellaneous collection of
oracles in which it is not possible to discern the work of a single hand.

This summary of the critical examination of Isaiah does not do
justice to the complexity of the various hypotheses that have been
proposed. Thus 1–39 have been described as constituting the work of
Isaiah of Jerusalem, but many scholars would argue that a closer
analysis would indicate only some of the material in these chapters is
authentically Isaianic; several sections of 1–39 have been added by a
later hand and reflect a later period. This much is clear at least from
the summary provided above, that the appearance of unity provided
by a superficial reading of Isaiah has been severely fragmented as a
consequence of modern study.

Every action, of course, elicits a reaction, and the critical analysis of
Isaiah into two or more works has not gone unchallenged. The more
conservative tradition in biblical scholarship has argued that the data
giving rise to multiple-authorship hypotheses are open to alternative
interpretation. The historical perspective of chapters 40–55, while
admittedly that of exile, need not actually presuppose the exile. That
is, if the author of these chapters were indeed Isaiah of Jerusalem (the
same author of chapters 1–39), he writes *as if* in exile, anticipating the
exile as a future judgment of God. The references to Cyrus are
interpreted either as predictions or as *glosses*—explanatory comments
added by a later hand to indicate how and by whom the prophecies
were fulfilled. The differences in style between the two sections are
claimed to be particularly fragile. While the differences can be
admitted, there are also similarities, for example, the common

references to the "Holy One of Israel" which penetrate both sections. The differences may be explained in various ways: Perhaps chapters 1–39 reflect the prophet's early ministry, while chapters 40–66 contain the prophet's reflections from the later and more mature perspectives of old age. Or chapters 1–39 may record the prophet's active ministry, whereas chapters 40–66 may have been from the beginning a literary creation, thus different somewhat in style and structure. Those who have reacted to the fragmentation of the book have noted that it is astonishing that nothing is known of "Second Isaiah" outside the book. If the hypotheses are correct, he must have been one of the towering intellectual and spiritual figures of the sixth century B.C., but the historical sources of the period have not a word to say about him. The implication, many conservative scholars suggest, is that there was never such a person as Second Isaiah.

In these and other ways, a conservative reaction to the consensus of mainstream biblical scholarship has sought to preserve the integrity and unity of a single book of Isaiah. Their arguments are not without weight, but it would be fair to say that they represent a minority position within biblical scholarship as a whole. The generally accepted view is that in the book of Isaiah we are dealing with the work of at least two, and probably more, "Isaiahs." The issue is not simply one of sources, but, according to the hypothesis, of distinct and major works.

Now when a degree of consensus is reached in biblical scholarship, as in the analysis of Isaiah, there is considerable danger that the subject upon which agreement has been achieved may shift from the realm of hypothesis to established fact. This has already happened, to some extent, in the study of Isaiah; there are now books written on Second Isaiah which accept the unknown prophet's existence as more or less self-evident truth. For all the strength of the critical perspectives on the book of Isaiah, there are also several severe limitations inherent in them.

(c) Isaiah: Perspectives for Reading

In the detailed study of trees and shrubs, there is a certain danger of losing sight of the forest. In the detailed analysis of the book of Isaiah, with its consequent fragmentation of the unity of the book, it has been difficult to retain a vision of the whole book. Therefore, if one accepts the hypothesis that there were at least two "Isaiahs," it is important to recognize that the author or editor of the book that has survived has done nothing explicit to confirm that view. For all the changes in style and subject matter that begin in chapter 40, there is no heading to indicate that a new work is beginning, as there is in every other prophetic book that has survived in the Old Testament. This is an important observation. Setting aside for the moment the correctness or otherwise of hypotheses concerning multiple authorship, it is essential to recognize that the book of Isaiah in its present form is presented, apparently deliberately, as a single and unified work. The editor(s) who was responsible for the book's final form wanted to convey to the reader the impression of a single work. He did not explicitly distinguish between chapters 1–39 and 40–66.

Now this observation on the character of the extant book of Isaiah neither proves nor disproves the hypothesis of multiple authorship. But it does set an overall perspective within which to read the book; it should be read as a whole, if we are to grasp the editor's overall intent. The questions of authorship and background, fascinating as they may be to the scholarly investigator, should be recognized as secondary questions. They concern the pre-history of the book, not its final form. The final form of the book indicates that to grasp the whole message of *Isaiah*, we must take into account all sixty-six chapters. The book as a whole is concerned with *both* judgment *and* deliverance, with *both* promise *and* fulfillment. To separate the substance of 1–39 and 40–66 and reconstruct two distinct and different prophetic messages is to do a severe disservice to the intent and form of the book as it has survived.

Thus whatever the date and authorship of the parts of Isaiah, they have only survived in the present book as a whole. The parts have been deliberately linked together by an author or editor, and the meaning implied by that author or editor is the overall perspective within which to read the book. These observations are not intended to deny the validity, or even correctness, of the analysis of the book in contemporary scholarship and the hypotheses concerning the various "Isaiahs"; they simply stress the initial perspective within which the book should be read. Is it possible to go further? Is it possible to reconstruct the process by which the book reached its final form?

It has already been suggested that we should not think of the prophets primarily as *authors;* rather, their first responsibility was their involvement in prophetic ministry, which involved both speech and actions. Prophets may be the authors of the books named after them insofar as the books contain a record and an account of their word and ministries. They were not necessarily the persons who sat down and put pen to parchment; that more mundane task may have been undertaken by friends or disciples of the prophets.

Now it is clear that during his lifetime, Isaiah of Jerusalem had a group of disciples (8:16); how many there were and how long they continued to function after his death cannot be determined. Nevertheless, it is not unreasonable to suppose that the disciples of Isaiah were largely responsible for leaving us the book that has survived in the prophet's name. Beyond this general hypothesis, it is extremely difficult, if not impossible, to reconstruct the detailed process by which the book of Isaiah came to exist in its present form. Those of a more conservative persuasion would suggest that the book was compiled, or edited, in the seventh century B.C. by Isaiah's disciples, perhaps in the years following his death; additional editorial comments (such as the reference to Cyrus) may have been appended at a later date. Other scholars might propose a major Isaianic tradition, initiated by Isaiah of Jerusalem but perpetuated at a later date by Second Isaiah and perhaps even Third Isaiah. Eventually, perhaps in the sixth or fifth centuries B.C., the works of the various "Isaiahs" were brought together into a single volume, which would be, in effect, the *book of the Isaiah Tradition*. These alternative views, and others like them, must necessarily remain in the realm of hypothesis. But in the last resort, the value and message of the book of Isaiah do not have as a prerequisite the resolution of all difficulties and the establishment of one hypothesis over and against another. The message of the book, with its remarkable balance of judgment and mercy, of promise and fulfillment, and its extraordinary insight into the nature and grace of God, ultimately transcends the critical questions that emerge from the study of this ancient and remarkable text.

2. The Book of Jeremiah

The second of the Major Prophets—and the longest of them in total number of verses—is the book of Jeremiah, named after a prophet in Judah who ministered during the seventh and sixth centuries B.C. Jeremiah was born shortly before 640 B.C., probably during the last years of the reign of King Manasseh. Jeremiah came from a long line of priests and was brought up in the village of Anathoth, just a few miles northeast of Jerusalem. He did not follow his family's tradition into the priesthood; rather, Jeremiah became a prophet, sensing his vocation to this particular ministry in about 626 B.C.. He continued to serve as a prophet for more than four decades, dying (the exact date is unknown) some years after the fall of Jerusalem in 586 B.C.

Jeremiah's ministry was undertaken during the last and most crucial years of the history of Judah. He preached and served during the reigns of Judah's last five kings, and even when he was exiled to Egypt, following Judah's defeat in war he did not cease to engage in his prophetic ministry (see figure 14). The years of his life and ministry ranged from the high point of national hope during Josiah's great reform (around 622 B.C.) to the lowest ebb of the nation's spirit prior to the fall of Judah and destruction of Jerusalem (596–586 B.C.). Throughout the decades leading up to his nation's demise, and indeed even after the end, Jeremiah was actively engaged both as a preacher and as an activist in the life of his nation—in the political events and in the religious aspects. He was first and foremost a man of his own times, but his message was such that it has long outlived the era of his ministry.

Figure 29. JEREMIAH'S MINISTRY

Dates	Judah's History	Jeremiah's Ministry	
687–642	King Manasseh	circa 642 B.C.	Birth
642–640	King Amon		
640–609	King Josiah		
622	Reform	circa 626 B.C.	Vocation
609	Josiah's death		(ministry)
609	King Jehoahaz		
609–598	King Jehoiakim	604	Jeremiah's scroll
598–597	King Jehoiachin		
597–587	King Zedekiah		(ministry)
586	Fall of Jerusalem		
586	Beginning of exile		
586–?	Governor Gedaliah	586	Exiled to Egypt

(a) The Contents of Jeremiah

The book named after this extraordinary prophet is in certain ways similar to Isaiah; it is in part an anthology of materials pertaining to the life and ministry of Jeremiah. But the general difficulty of reading prophetic books is exacerbated in the case of Jeremiah by the apparent absence of any strict chronological sequence in which the material is presented. It is possible, nevertheless, to delineate certain chunks of material that are linked together by common themes or subject matter.

(i) **Chapters 1–25.** These chapters are largely poetic in form and principally contain a collection of the prophet's oracles from the first two decades of his ministry. His preaching focused upon the sin of Israel and the nation's failure to maintain the ancient covenant faith in matters both religious and moral. This national evil, Jeremiah affirmed, must inevitably result in divine judgment, and he proclaimed impending disaster and the fall of the holy city of Jerusalem. Interspersed throughout the prophetic messages to the people as a whole are a number of more personal passages, such as an account of Jeremiah's vocation to the prophetic ministry (chapter 1) and the intensely personal "Confessions of Jeremiah," in which are laid bare the inner struggles of the prophet in the context of his suffering and uncertainty (see 15:10-12 and 20:10-18).

(ii) **Chapters 26–45.** This section is dominated by prose material rather than by poetry, and focuses much more on a series of historical incidents in the prophet's life, into which have been inserted some prose summaries of his preaching. These chapters are fascinating for the insight they give concerning the prophet's ministry in general, and in particular concerning the continuing opposition he evoked along with its hardship and persecution. There are references to Baruch, Jeremiah's companion and scribe; these references (as we shall see) may provide some understanding of the process by which Jeremiah's book came into existence.

(iii) **Chapters 45–51.** This section contains a series of oracles or messages addressed to foreign nations, which find their parallels in Isaiah, Ezekiel, and other prophetic books. They are indicative of the fact that Jeremiah's ministry had an international dimension to it; although he addressed primarily his fellow citizens in Judah, his understanding of God was such that it could not be constricted by national boundaries.

(iv) **Chapter 52.** This chapter, which is closely parallel to II Kings 24:18–25:30, concludes the book as a kind of historical appendix. It indicates to the reader the eventual outcome of all that has preceded, for the words of Jeremiah are explicitly said to terminate at the end of chapter 51 (verse 64).

(b) Critical Problems in the Study of Jeremiah

The character of Jeremiah is in part that of an anthology, or perhaps an anthology of anthologies. Some of the major chunks of material that have already been identified may first have existed as relatively independent collections of Jeremiah's sayings. Thus Jeremiah 25:1-14 has the character of a summary and conclusion; it is probably designed to complete and round out the substance of the material in the first twenty-five chapters. Chapter 30:1-2 appears to introduce a new book or collection of sayings—probably the various messages of comfort contained in chapters 30–33, the so-called *Book of Consolation*. Also, 46:1 seems to serve quite consciously as an introduction to a further anthology, namely the collection of oracles concerning foreign nations in chapters 46–51. In part, therefore, the finished book of Jeremiah can be seen as a collection of anthologies which have been brought together to form a more comprehensive anthology of material pertaining to Jeremiah.

The study of particular passages reveals that the processes lying behind the formation of the book are still more complex. For example, chapters 2–6 contain a series of messages from the prophet's early ministry pertaining to sin, the necessity of repentance, and the coming of judgment. In their present form the chapters constitute a systematic literary unit, developing smoothly their inner theme. But a detailed examination of their substance indicates that the chapters have been compiled from a variety of shorter sayings, or perhaps extracts from longer messages. In other words, chapters 2–6 form a coherent literary unit in their present form, but they have drawn on a variety of sermons and messages delivered originally by the prophet on different occasions. They are not so much a record of particular sermons as a summary anthology drawing on many sermons. Thus four short chapters in the book of Jeremiah may veil many months and years of the prophet's actual preaching.

One of the most useful approaches to the study of the literary components of Jeremiah's book is to be found in the recognition of different types of material that have been employed. There are three general types, which encompass the majority (though not all) of the substance of the book. *Type A* material is poetic in form and contains for the most part Jeremiah's oracles (for example, chapters 2–6, just noted, are *Type A* material). *Type B* is in prose form and consists of narratives that are primarily historical and biographical in character. *Type C* has certain similarities to *Type A* in substance, but differs in form; *Type C* texts contain what purport to be the prophet's sermons and discourses, but they are written in prose and appear in summary form. A few portions of the book cannot be fit satisfactorily into any of these categories. Jeremiah's so-called Confessions, although they are sometimes classified as *Type A* material, should probably be viewed as an independent and distinct category of texts.

While most scholars accept the general threefold classification of the components of Jeremiah, considerable debate emerges in the interpretation of each type. There is a fair degree of agreement that *Type A* material is authentic; that is, that it contains an accurate record of the prophet's poetic pronouncements. *Type B* material is subject to more debate, referring as it does to Jeremiah in the third person. Some would ascribe it to Baruch, Jeremiah's companion and scribe; others would attribute it to later tradition and would therefore maintain considerable doubts as to the authenticity of its record. *Type C* material has been the focus of considerable debate. If, as in *Type A*, the prophet employed poetry as the medium of his message, why are the sermons in *Type C* recorded in prose form? Did Jeremiah use both poetic and prosaic language in his delivery? Or is the *Type C* material merely a later record, or synopsis, of his speech compiled perhaps by Baruch? Indeed, many scholars would argue that *Type C* material is not Jeremianic at all, but reflects the thought and preaching of persons at a later date who stood in the tradition of the prophet.

The debate as to the proper interpretation of the different types of material in Jeremiah has had certain significant conclusions for the understanding of the prophet and his book. Thus those who are fairly conservative in their interpretation of the texts, especially in the treatment of *Type B* and *Type C* material, have reasonably been able to reconstruct a fairly comprehensive portrait of Jeremiah's life and ministry. While there is certainly not a complete biography in the book of Jeremiah, a positive interpretation of the substance of the texts provides a more comprehensive insight into prophecy than is available in any other book.

On the other hand, those scholars who have ascribed much of the material (especially *Types B* and *C*) to the development of later schools of tradition have concurrently had to limit any possibility of knowing about the prophet *per se*. Indeed, some of the most recent work on Jeremiah attributes so much of his book to the work of later tradition that the prophet himself has virtually become lost in the mists of history. The apparently historical material concerning Jeremiah is said to be essentially the legendary production of later generations. Such an approach is surely too skeptical, and while it may be admitted that there are severe difficulties in the recapturing of a "historical Jeremiah," the so-called traditionalists who are said to have left us this extraordinary book are even more elusive figures on the stage of ancient history.

A more constructive approach toward understanding the text is provided within the book itself, specifically in the narrative contained in chapter 36. Jeremiah was instructed to record in a book (or scroll) the substance of the messages he had proclaimed to Judah. The prophet dictated them, and they were copied down by his scribe, Baruch. When the finished work was destroyed by the king, the prophet compiled yet another scroll, this time with additional material in it. Now the story is beautifully told. The year is about 605 B.C., and the king, Jehoiakim, is reading the scroll during the months of winter. After reading a few pages of the manuscript he casts them on the fire to keep the blaze bright, and then reads a few more pages destined for a similar fate! It is not so much the incident as the implications that are of interest to the biblical scholar. Here we have evidence that the prophet employed two forms of communication—the spoken word and the written word. We also have insight into the process—the prophet dictated words, presumably from memory, and they were copied down by his scribe, Baruch.

The incident of the burning of the scroll suggests at least general directions in which a reconstruction of the formation of the book of Jeremiah might be pursued. Over a period of time, beginning quite early during the lifetime of the prophet, collections of the prophet's sayings were brought together. For example, the scroll referred to in chapter 36 chronologically represents approximately the mid-point in the prophet's ministry. (The attempts to identify the substance of the scroll have not been entirely successful, although it may have contained the substance of chapters 2:1–25:14, or at least parts thereof.) Presumably later in the prophet's life, and eventually perhaps after his death, further collections were compiled and to them various other elements were added, such as the prophet's brief autobiographical writings. The book in its present form with its historical appendix (chapter 52) may have been compiled within a decade or so of the prophet's death although it should be noted that the final form of the book may have remained fluid for some time. The Greek translation of Jeremiah not only is shorter than the principal Hebrew texts that have survived, but also presents the material in a somewhat different sequence. It seems likely that several slightly different editions of Jeremiah co-existed for several centuries after the prophet's death.)

(c) Jeremiah: Perspectives for Reading

Although it has not been possible to reconstruct in detail the process by which the book of Jeremiah reached its present form, the general clues within the book provide an appropriate perspective from which to read it. The starting point is the life and ministry of the prophet as such; it is clear from the surviving book that both his *words* and his *experiences* were part and parcel of his message. What we have in the book is a general account of these words and experiences, whose preservation began in the prophet's lifetime and concluded shortly after his death. The record of the words may be in some instances verbatim (especially in the poetic sections) and in some instances in summary form (the prose sections), with the usual editorial and reflective touches appended by the hands of those who compiled the book. The record of experiences may go back in part to the prophet, in part to Baruch, and in part to the prophet's disciples or editors. The historical narratives in no sense provide a comprehensive biography, but convey only those incidents in the prophet's life that are pertinent to his preaching and significant for conveying the force of his message.

What has survived for us, then, is a deposit of the life and ministry of one of ancient Judah's most remarkable prophets. We are provided in the chapters of this book with a series of glimpses into the last years of Judah and the proclamations of a man who saw all too clearly the meaning of the events through which he lived. The calamities of history, as Jeremiah perceived them, were not simply the unkind twists of fate; they were the consequences of national evil pursued to its ultimate consequences. The conquest of Judah and destruction of Jerusalem, anticipated in the prophet's preaching and then experienced in his lifetime, were to be understood as acts of divine judgment. In a very real sense, Jeremiah foresaw and lived through the end of the ancient covenant, whose roots stretched back to the time of Moses. Yet, doom and the end of the covenant were not the entire substance of the prophet's message; he also perceived beyond the immediate horizon of history a future age in which God would form a new covenant with his people (Jeremiah 31:31). Thus, although the English language has been given the word *jeremiad* (meaning "lamentation, doleful complaint") from this prophet in ancient Judah, he was not entirely a prophet of doom. He had a message of hope that pertained to a future age. The stark realism and horror of the message he declared to his contemporaries was balanced by a vision of a new and better world, which has continued to offer hope in both Judaism and Christianity into the twentieth century.

3. The Book of Ezekiel

The third of the Major Prophets, the book of Ezekiel, is named after a man who was a younger contemporary of Jeremiah. Born about 623 B.C., when Jeremiah was already active as a prophet, Ezekiel grew up in Jerusalem where his father, Buzi, served as a priest in the temple. As the priesthood was a traditional office, passed on from one generation to the next, we may suppose that Ezekiel in his early life was educated for service as a priest.

However, as we have seen already in the summary of Jeremiah's life and work, Ezekiel was born in tumultuous times in Judah's history. At the time of his birth, Josiah's great reformation was being undertaken in Jerusalem, but by the time Ezekiel was a young man the survival of Jerusalem and Judah was in grave doubt. In 597 B.C., when Ezekiel was about twenty-six years old, Jerusalem was attacked and defeated by Nebuchadnezzar, the Babylonian Emperor. The city itself survived, but many of its leading families and citizens, Ezekiel among them, were deported to Babylon. The young man who was educated for service as a priest in Jerusalem's temple found himself resident in an alien land where there was no temple of his faith. He lived, along with other exiles, in a settlement called Tel Abib, situated by the Chebar Canal, not far from the great city of Babylon.

It was in Tel Abib a few years later (about 593 B.C.) that Ezekiel, who had been trained for the office of priest, was called to serve in the role of prophet. He was about thirty years of age at the time, the point in his life at which, under normal circumstances, he would have assumed the full responsibilities of priesthood. Instead, he began a long ministry as a prophet, having responsibility for declaring the prophetic word to those who were in exile with him. From the dates provided in the book, we know that his ministry continued for at least twenty years (until around 571 B.C.). We do not know with any certainty where and when Ezekiel died, but even today a shrine survives in Iraq at a place called al-Kifl, not far from the ruins of Babylon, which ancient tradition had identified as the tomb of Ezekiel.

(a) The Contents of Ezekiel

Unlike the books of the other Major Prophets, that of Ezekiel appears from the beginning to have been arranged in a more orderly and systematic fashion. Its major sections have common subject matter, and the frequent statements of date provide an orderly and sequential chronological structure to the book as a whole. Like the other prophetic books, the characteristics of an anthology continue to pervade Ezekiel, but the substance of the anthology has been carefully and systematically arranged. The book falls into two major sections of approximately equal length, within which a number of shorter sections can be clearly distinguished.

(i) **Chapters 1–24.** These chapters have as their major theme the proclamation of judgment and the anticipation of the defeat and destruction of the city of Jerusalem. The chapters reflect for the most part the early period of the prophet's ministry, the years 593–586 B.C., when those in exile wondered about the ultimate fate of Jerusalem and whether it would survive. Ezekiel declared that Jerusalem would not survive and that its destruction would be an act of divine judgment. His message was hardly designed to cheer his companions in exile, whose principal hope for the future lay in the survival of a homeland to which eventually they might return.

The substance of this first major section of the book indicates the diversity of Ezekiel's ministry and message. His call and commissioning as a prophet (chapters 1–3) are set in the context of a visionary experience, and a vision was to play an important part in his ministry. Later, in vision, Ezekiel "visits" Jerusalem (chapters 8–11) and is given insight into the spiritual life and fate of the city. In addition to the importance of visionary experience, we may note the considerable diversity employed by the prophet in the communication of his message to his fellow citizens in exile. Sometimes he used symbolic actions; his enacted scenes required of his audience that they think out for themselves the meaning and symbolism of what they were seeing. In speech, he used parables, allegories, and riddles in addition to the more conventional modes of prophetic address. In chapter 16, for example, he tells a simple and beautiful love story (verses 1-14), which turns suddenly into a story of love gone astray and perverted (verses 15-52); the story illustrates the life of the chosen people, beginning in God's love, but eventually terminating in the rejection of love by an ungrateful people.

The thrust of the first twenty-four chapters relates directly to the plight of Jerusalem, whose fate seems to draw constantly closer as the chapters progress. In the last chapter of the first section (24:15-17), a remarkable incident is described. Ezekiel is informed by God that his wife is about to die and that he is to inform his companions of her coming death. When she dies, he is not to mourn her passing in the conventional fashion. In the evening, following the announcement of the coming death, Ezekiel's wife, "the delight of (his) eyes" (verse 16), dies, and the prophet refrains from the customs of mourning. The incident has symbolic meaning—the death of the wife, loved so dearly by the prophet, was an anticipation of the coming destruction of Jerusalem's temple, so beloved by those in exile. The event took place in the summer month of 587 B.C.; within a few months of that incident, the temple in Jerusalem was detroyed by Babylonian armies.

(ii) *Chapters 25–48.* The second major part of the book reflects a distinct change in the emphases of the prophet's ministry. Whereas judgment and doom penetrate the first half of the book, hope and restoration are predominant in the second half. The historical event lying behind this radical transition is the destruction of Jerusalem and its temple (586 B.C.). In the early years of exile, the prophet's companions still harbored hope for Jerusalem's survival; Ezekiel's task was to destroy that hope and make clear the necessity of God's judgment falling on Jerusalem as a consequence of the sin of the chosen people. When the city and its temple were destroyed and all natural hopes entertained by those in exile went with them, then the roles were reversed. Instead of preaching doom to a people who lived on hollow hopes, Ezekiel now preached hope to a people who felt they were doomed.

Although the second part of the book focuses on hope and restoration, it begins nevertheless in a strange fashion. Chapters 25–32 contain a series of oracles addressed to various foreign nations—Moab, Edom, Philistia, Tyre, Sidon, and Egypt. Just when the reader expects, after the death of Ezekiel's wife, to learn of the fate of the temple, there is this long delay in which doom is proclaimed against the various enemies of Judah. From a literary perspective, the positioning of the foreign nation oracles serves to delay the climax and heighten the tension. But from a theological perspective, the foreign nation oracles illustrate the power of God over all nations, without which no restoration would be possible. Thus the second half of the book begins with a demonstration. The prophet demonstrates in his preaching that Judah was not alone in punishment for its evil, but all nations must answer to God and be judged for their crimes against humanity. This demonstration indicates in turn that God was indeed sovereign in human history; only a deity with power over all nations would be able to restore the chosen people to a new national life in the future.

The prophet's hope for his people's future is elaborated in some detail in chapters 33–37; he proclaims the ultimate restoration to new life of a people in exile who seemed to be cut off from their former freedom and vitality. The book concludes, as it began, with a visionary account; in chapters 40–48, the prophet recounts his vision of a new temple, a restored land, and a splendid city of God, in which God's presence would be experienced once again among his people.

(b) Critical Problems in the Study of Ezekiel

At the beginning of the twentieth century, it seemed that the book of Ezekiel was to be spared from the more radical criticism that had been attracted by Isaiah and Jeremiah. Scholars admitted for the most part that the forty-eight chapters of the book bore the marks of a single mind and seemed to reflect the work of a single author. The uniform structure of the book, together with the orderly sequence of messages and events indicated by the book's internal dating, seemed to secure for this work some protection against the apparently reductionist consequences of scholarly investigation. But the placidity that characterized the study of Ezekiel was not to last for long. In 1924, a study of Ezekiel, published in Germany, concluded that only about 13 percent of the verses in the book could be considered the authentic work of Ezekiel; the remaining 87 percent must be considered a secondary development from later hands.

Following 1924, almost every aspect of the book came under close examination and a multitude of hypotheses were proposed, many of them mutually contradictory. Although the setting of the book purports to be that of the exiles in Babylon, it was proposed by some scholars that a Palestinian setting best explained the original and authentic work. Although the dates within the book specified its period as approximately 593–571 B.C., some scholars moved it to an earlier date and some to a later date. These and many other hypotheses were proposed concerning the form, substance, and background of the book of Ezekiel, but few of them won any large degree of support in the scholarly community as a whole. After more than half a century of massive investigation and widely differing theories, the scholarly consensus, insofar as it exists at all, is returning to the position it held before 1924.

This is not to say that there are no difficulties or disagreements in the study of Ezekiel—far from it. Nevertheless, it is reasonable to affirm that the book does contain an essentially authentic deposit of a remarkable Hebrew prophet of the exile. The continuing difficulties lie in the understanding of Ezekiel as a prophet and in trying to determine how the book reached its present form. As in the other prophetic books, one must distinguish between at least two stages of development in the earliest period. First, a prophetic message was delivered "live" to a specific audience in a particular place, and later a record or summary of it was put down in writing. At presumably a still later stage, the written materials were compiled gradually into the book that has survived; the process of compilation involved not only the arrangement of material, but also in some cases the addition of material—sometimes simple editorial notes and sometimes more reflective comments on the substance of the original message in the light of later experiences.

Some of the stages of development may be inferred from a careful reading of Ezekiel, but the book does not contain sufficiently explicit data from the formulation of precise hypotheses. Whether the formation of the book into its present shape was undertaken by Ezekiel himself, perhaps in his later life (after 571 B.C.), or whether it was done by his disciples is not known with any certainty. But the sense of uniformity arising from the book as a whole is far more striking in this than in the other major prophets. It may not be too rash to think of Ezekiel himself compiling the book in old age, adding to the account of his earlier ministry the wisdom and insightful observations that came from reflection on bygone years.

(c) Ezekiel: Perspectives for Reading

At the outset, it should be remembered that in reading the book of Ezekiel, we are reading one of the most creative, individual, and artistic minds in the tradition of Hebrew prophecy. Ezekiel could preach a conventional sermon, but he could also tell a story or propound a parable. Although he was engaged in public speaking, he was equally likely to publicly enact his messages. Although he was a rational man, he did not hesitate to recount in glorious detail the fantastic substance of his visions. He could write splendid poetry, but he could also write rather dreary prose (unless the latter be the work of a later hand). Ezekiel, in other words, was apparently a man of many talents, and it follows that in reading his work, we must call upon various sensitivities within ourselves. The rational, analytical approach will always be helpful in studying ancient texts, but unless we are also able to be sensitive to symbol, allegory, and imagination in our reading of visionary accounts, we will inevitably miss some of the power of Ezekiel's book.

We must also keep in mind while reading this book the prophet's historical setting. He lived and ministered during critical years in the history of the chosen people, and the crises of the age raised for many some of the most fundamental questions of life and religion. For example, did the divine punishment for evil mean that there could be no hope for the future? For those in exile, there seemed to be little foundation upon which to build hope. Putting the question another way, did the destruction of Jerusalem and its temple mark the end of the religion of the Hebrews? After all, that religion had been built upon the possession of the promised land and the worship of God in Jerusalem's temple. The exile and the disastrous events of 587-586 B.C. must have seemed to many to toll the knell of death for a religion extending back to the time of Moses and earlier.

It is in the context of questions such as these that Ezekiel's combined message of judgment and hope takes on its full significance. On the one hand, he is a man gripped by a profound sense of God's holiness, precipitated no doubt by the visionary experience of God with which his ministry began. Such a holy God could not ignore human evil, the abandonment of responsibility, and the refusal to love. Thus, as Ezekiel saw it, God must act in judgment. Not only the legacy of past generations, but also the evil acts of the current generation invited God's judgment, for if God were truly holy he could not ignore evil. The consequence of this kind of thinking, carried to its logical end, was that the religion of the Hebrews must come to an end. Ezekiel's vision of God's holiness is balanced by his perception of the divine mercy and love. The loving kindness of God and the capacity for forgiveness could not ultimately be exhausted; there must, therefore, be hope beyond the cataclysm—a new world lying somewhere beyond the devastation of Jerusalem and its temple.

This, then, is a part of the perspective for reading Ezekiel. To those who held on grimly in hard times to hollow and false hope, the prophet felt compelled to announce judgment and to annihilate every aspiration. But to those who eventually reached the point of despair, precipitated by the calamities of the world around them, Ezekiel had a message of hope. It was not a message that could be established empirically in the changing scenes of history, but one which required of his people faith in the ultimate purpose of God for the world. Ezekiel was thus both a hard-nosed realist in the midst of a world caught in chaos, and also a visionary who glimpsed a different world beyond. We begin to grasp the perpetual pertinence of this remarkable book when we perceive the power of Ezekiel's delicate balance of realism and vision.

THE
PROPHETS (III):
MINOR PROPHETS

T HE three major prophetic books are followed in the Hebrew Bible by the Book of the Twelve, which is a collection of various shorter prophetic books that have been frequently called, on the basis of their brevity, the Minor Prophets. These books, though they vary in length from a few verses (Obadiah) to several chapters (fourteen chapters in Zechariah), are all considerably shorter than those of the Major Prophets. Although the Minor Prophets have left behind them less extensive evidence of their ministries, it is important to bear in mind that several of them in their own time and place may have been at least as important and influential as Isaiah, Jeremiah, or Ezekiel.

The order in which the books occur in the ancient manuscripts and versions differs somewhat, and the reasons lying behind the present sequence of the books cannot be determined with certainty. Nevertheless, this lack of knowledge is not important; the books can be read quite independently standing in their own right. The twelve books differ enormously with respect to their dates, ranging approximately from the eighth century B.C. to as late as the fifth century B.C. Nevertheless, from a reference to the "twelve prophets" in a post-biblical book (Ecclesiasticus 49:10), we can be reasonably

1 7 3

sure that the twelve-volume collection was already complete by the third century B.C. The disparity in dates is matched by a disparity in geographical and national settings—some books reflect national life in Israel, some reflect Judah, and others come from the colonial period following the Babylonian exile (see figure 30). The differences are such that the books must each be examined separately and independently. It is impossible to do justice to the separate volumes within the space of a few paragraphs, but the observations that follow will at least provide some overall perspective on both the diversity and the commonality of the Book of the Twelve.

1. The Book of Hosea

The ministry of the prophet Hosea occurred in the eighth century B.C. between the years 750 and 722 B.C. He was a prophet in the northern kingdom of Israel which, in the latter half of the eighth century, was living through the final decades of its historical existence. In 722 B.C., Israel was defeated by the Assyrians and ceased to exist as a nation. The nation, during Hosea's ministry, was not only in a dangerous situation in terms of political and international affairs, but it was also in a state of religious and spiritual decline. The integrity and purity of the ancient faith had been largely lost; in their place, a new syncretistic form of religion had emerged, in which the faith of Israel had become penetrated by elements of the pagan religion of the Canaanites—*Baalism*. The *Baal* religion was essentially an agricultural cult, its worship of Baal and other deities designed to secure the fertility of the land, hence abundant crops and cattle. It was a kind of religion in which sexuality was emphasized. The fertility (or otherwise) of the gods would be reflected in the fertility of the land. Thus the worship of Baal (whose name means literally "husband, master") frequently involved sexual practices and had a certain basic appeal to human nature.

It was in this context of tense international affairs and a declining state of religion that Hosea ministered. We know very little of the man himself beyond the fragments of biography (and autobiography) that have survived in the opening chapters of his book. It is reasonable to suppose that the fourteen chapters of his book contain only a small reflection of his total ministry, but enough has survived to provide

Figure 30. THE MINOR PROPHETS

Prophet/Book	Approximate Time Period	National/Geographic Setting
1. Hosea	740–722 B.C.	Israel
2. Joel	sixth century B.C. (?)	Judah
3. Amos	circa 746 B.C.	Israel
4. Obadiah	sixth century B.C. (?)	Judah (Edom)
5. Jonah	sixth century (eighth century?)	Judah (Nineveh)
6. Micah	730–690 B.C.	Judah
7. Nahum	circa 615 B.C.	Judah (Nineveh)
8. Habakkuk	circa 610–605 B.C.(?)	Judah
9. Zephaniah	630–625 B.C.	Judah
10. Haggai	August–December, 520 B.C.	Jerusalem (Judah)
11. Zechariah	520–518 B.C.	Jerusalem (Judah)
12. Malachi	circa 460 B.C.	Judah

some insight into the substance of his preaching and the goals of his prophetic activity. His primary focus was on the decline of religion in Israel and the sad syncretistic estate to which it had sunk. Although he worked toward achieving a change of heart among his people, his preaching is dominated by the proclamation of the coming doom and judgment. The fundamental abuses of the ancient faith of Israel were so deep-seated, that Hosea was compelled to announce the coming of judgment and the end of God's covenant.

The book of Hosea is largely an anthology of sayings and proclamations from the prophet's ministry. It falls into two principal sections.

(a) Chapters 1–3

These chapters form a relatively coherent unit focusing on the marriage and family life of the prophet. They are very difficult to interpret for various reasons. The difficulty lies, in part, in the proper translation of these chapters, for the Hebrew text of Hosea has not been well preserved. A further difficulty lies in the present form of the chapters, for original events and subsequent interpretations have been so tightly intertwined that it is no longer easy to distinguish the events from interpretation.

A tentative reconstruction (though subject to considerable debate) of the events lying behind the chapters would go as follows: Hosea's call to prophetic ministry takes the peculiar form of an injunction to marry a "wife of prostitution" (1:2), presumably a woman who had been involved in the sexual activities associated with the fertility cult of Baal. Hosea marries Gomer and they have three children, each of whom is given a curious name which is a message to Israel of God's coming judgment. Later, Gomer is unfaithful to Hosea and he divorces her; after the divorce, she either remarries someone else or returns to her life as a "sacred prostitute" in the religion of Baal (the text is unclear). Still later (chapter 3), Hosea is instructed to love Gomer again and bring her back into the relationship of marriage. The details of the reconstruction of Hosea's marital experiences are debated, given the difficulty of translating the Hebrew text, but it is at least clear that the prophet's life served as both a sign and as an allegory of God's relationship to Israel. The covenant between God and Israel, which was a covenant like that of marriage, marked the originally intimate relationship between God and his people. Israel's unfaithfulness, however, must inevitably culminate in "divorce," or an end to the covenant—this was the prophet's message of judgment. Beyond the divorce, Hosea saw a time of new marriage when God would renew once again his relationship with the chosen people. Thus the prophet's message of judgment is balanced by his insight concerning the nature of divine love.

(b) *Chapters 4–14*

The second part of the book has far less inner coherence than the first. It contains extracts and summaries from the prophet's preaching ministry over many years, but it is extremely difficult to discern any particular order or sequence in the arrangement of the texts. The themes of the first half of the book continue in the second; the coming judgment predominates, but occasionally there is an insight concerning the love of God that dispells the general gloom of these chapters.

The nature of the evidence is such that it is virtually impossible to reconstruct the manner in which the book reached its present form. We may suppose that at least a draft of the book had been formed, either by the prophet or his disciples, prior to the collapse and defeat of Israel in 722 B.C. In that critical year, or afterwards, presumably some refugee took the book south to Judah, for that state survived the calamities of that year. In Judah, the book reached its present form, as indicated throughout its chapters by a number of editorial comments which seem to be designed to relate the northern prophet's preaching in its new southern context. (The bad state of the Hebrew text may be explained either as a consequence of damage suffered to an original manuscript in its journey from Israel to Judah, or perhaps as a reflection of the northern dialect of Hebrew, which had some differences from the language employed in Jerusalem.)

The major theme of the book, on first reading, seems to be that of judgment. Hosea proclaims that Israel's prostitution of its ancient faith and its eager embrace of pagan religion must inevitably culminate in judgment. That judgment came in 722 B.C. in the nation's collapse, though we do not know whether Hosea lived to see it. The greatness of the book of Hosea lies not only in its judgmental theme, but also in its exposition of human and divine love. The pathos of the prophet's own marital experiences illuminates the divine agony—judgment is not simply the wrath of God, but a reflection of the pain of God. Hosea reveals to us some of the many faces of love, both human and divine, its brief joy, and its enduring grief.

2. The Book of Joel

The second of the Twelve Prophets immediately introduces a set of difficulties that cannot be easily resolved. It is named after "Joel, son of Pethuel," but he is unknown outside the book and virtually nothing of biographical interest remains within the book. Whereas many of the prophetic books (for example, Hosea) specify a date in the opening verses, such as referring to the current kings, the book of Joel gives no clear indication of its date. This book concerns the ministry of a virtually unknown prophet who functioned in an undetermined century. Speculation concerning the date of the book of Joel has ranged from the ninth to the fourth centuries B.C., which simply confirms the inadequacy of the facts for dating purposes! One might tentatively propose a date for the book in the latter decades of the sixth century B.C., after the exile, but such a hypothesis is clearly a fragile one.

If the key character and the date of the book are uncertain, there can nevertheless be a degree of certainty about the geographical setting and the events giving rise to its writing. The general setting of the work is that of Jerusalem and Judah. The principal event giving rise to the writing of the book was the experience of a terrible locust plague. Locust (or grasshopper) plagues have occurred in the biblical world many times over the centuries. In the twentieth century, for example, a terrible outbreak of locusts occurred in the spring of 1915 and was vividly recorded in the pages of the *National Geographic Magazine* (December, 1915). At the end of February, enormous numbers of locusts flew into Syria and Palestine from a northeasterly direction, settling on the hills and fields and laying vast numbers of eggs. The eggs hatched a few months later—as many as sixty thousand per thirty-nine square inches of soil. The new brood began to crawl across the land—about six hundred feet per day—devouring every scrap of living vegetation that lay in its path. (Lest a locust plague should sound too "biblical," it is worth recalling that such events are not unknown to North America. In the summer of 1984, while these pages are being written, in rural Alberta the fields outside my window are swarming with grasshoppers; children can catch hundreds of them in a matter of minutes. The crops of some farmers have been totally devastated by the grasshopper plague.)

In Joel's time, the plague had terrible effects on the land, destroying crops and demolishing the food supply for both human beings and cattle. The prophet, however, perceived the plague not simply as a natural disaster, but as a harbinger of divine judgment. It was a sign of the "Day of the Lord," the day of coming judgment which is the principal theme of Joel's book. Thus, although the book is rooted in a particular historical event, that event in turn becomes the launching pad for the presentation of a message concerning divine judgment.

There are two principal sections in this short book. (a) Chapters 1:1–2:27 (chapters 1–2 in the Hebrew text) deal with the plague as such and its role in the prophet's preaching. Because Joel perceived the plague to be not merely an actual disaster, but also a forewarning of further potential disaster, it became the focal point of his ministry. He sees such national and natural disasters as more than the flukes of the cycle of nature—they are signs from God. He preaches a message of the threat of further judgment and the necessity of national repentance, if further disasters are to be avoided. It seems, from reading between the lines of the text, that the prophet's preaching is heeded; a national assembly is called, the people turn from their evil ways, and further disaster is averted. (b) Chapters 2:28–3:21 (chapters 3 and 4 in the Hebrew text) focus on a more distant future. The themes still include judgment and the "day of the Lord," but the prophet's eyes are fixed on a more distant age and God's action in that age in judging the world's nations and establishing his people in security.

The evidence of this short book is too slender for the formulation of hypotheses concerning its formation. Attempts have been made to separate the two parts, (a) and (b) above, and attribute them to different authors, but the criteria for such hypotheses are exceptionally fragile. If we are to understand why the book of Joel has survived at all, we must retain its two sections together. The first section, with its focus on locusts, takes on significance only when balanced by the second section, in which a particular event is given more universal significance.

What is most remarkable about the book of Joel is the prophet's elastic conception of time and the relationship between the experience of the present and the anticipation of the future. Joel's ministry is initiated by a particular crisis, the locust swarms. That crisis evokes not simply dismay, as it does for his fellow citizens, but an understanding of the hand of God in the world of nature. His nation, in its pursuit of evil, had become immoral; God was moral. The crises of the natural world received, in Joel's thought, a moral and religious interpretation. Disaster was averted, or perhaps postponed, by his nation's act of repentance, but Joel clearly perceived that the "Day of the Lord" must always hover on the horizon of human history. Therefore, his message is explicitly didactic; it is to be passed on from parents to children over the generations that follow (1:3).

Joel's preaching moves from the time in which he lives, in which it has very immediate relevance, to address the future in an eschatological fashion. The shaping of the future lies always in the hands of the present generation. They may invite by the perpetuation of evil the "locusts" which destroy all basis of human life, or they may shape the future to a more positive end. Joel does not see himself as a predictor indicating what must come to pass. Rather, he sees within himself and his people the capacity to shape the future for good or ill. The human capacity for evil is such that it always has within it the ability to launch the apocalypse. Repentance can always lead to a brighter prospect. Ultimately Joel's hope lies in God, not the human capacity for good or evil. It is the work of God in the human world, in both present and future, which lends this book some elements of brightness amid its darker themes.

3. The Book of Amos

Amos was a contemporary of Hosea, ministering in the northern state of Israel in the mid-eighth century B.C. Though his prophetic activity can no longer be pinpointed precisely, it can be set somewhere in the general period of 760 to 746 B.C.

Although Amos undertook his prophetic responsibilities in Israel, he was actually a citizen of the southern state of Judah. His home was the village of Tekoa (nowadays called Tekua). It is a dozen miles south of Jerusalem and lies in an elevation of some twenty-seven hundred feet above sea level. The wilderness of Tekoa is a barren area lying to the east of the village, dropping some four thousand feet in twenty miles to the shores of the Dead Sea. It was in this semi-wilderness area that Amos lived and worked. From two references in the book (1:1 and 7:14), we know that he was engaged in farming sheep and cattle, apparently being the owner or manager of herds, and was also engaged in the production of fruit for the market. Amos, in other words, was a business man, involved primarily in agri-business. It was probably his business interests that took him beyond his native Judah from time to time; he may have visited the northern markets in Israel to sell his products. From a religious point of view, Amos was a layman. His call to serve as a prophet may have been limited to a short period of his life; estimates of the length of his ministry have ranged from a few weeks to a couple of years. But there is nothing in his book to suggest that he was either a professional prophet or a perpetual prophet, as were some of those whose books have survived. Amos was a layman who combined, for a while, his business interests with his prophetic vocation.

Although Amos served as a prophet in the same general period as did Hosea, there are several striking differences between these two remarkable men. Whereas Hosea appears to have been a native of Israel, Amos was a visitor or foreigner in the northern state. On the one hand, his alien status must have made it more difficult for him to function as a prophet, and Amos seems to have been a man of considerable personal courage. On the other hand, perhaps as a foreigner in Israel, he was able to see more clearly than the citizens of the state what was its true moral and spiritual condition. A further contrast between Hosea and Amos appears in the substance of their preaching. Whereas Hosea's message is most sensitive to the decline of spiritual life in Israel, Amos sees more clearly the moral collapse. Whereas Hosea is appalled by the syncretism in Israel's religion, Amos condemns the collapse of justice and the preponderance of social evil and exploitation. These two prophets have different perspectives and distinct emphases in their prophetic declarations, but they share common ground. Both perceive clearly that the moral and spiritual corruption in the life of the nation must inevitably culminate in divine judgment.

The book of Amos can be divided into three fairly distinct portions. (a) Chapters 1–2 contain a series of messages addressed to various foreign nations. The nations are singled out for judgment by the

Universal God, no doubt to the delight of a partisan audience, but the section concludes with an oracle of judgment addressed to Israel (2:6-16). These two chapters seem to form a coherent unit, reflecting initially a single address to an Israelite audience, though the occasion of the address can no longer be determined. (b) Chapters 3–6 are a more heterogeneous collection of sayings and sermons, but from this collection some of the prophet's principal concerns become clear. He condemns the rampant social evils of Israelite society—the exploitation of the poor by the wealthy, the dishonest business practices of the merchants, the corruption of law and the courts, and a multitude of other sins. He perceives that all the religious activities in the nation are but a veneer which hides beneath its surface a massive hypocrisy and loss of true faith. (c) Chapters 7–9 contain a series of visions, five in all, which also become a part of the prophet's spoken ministry. Inserted between the visions are further oracles and a fascinating historical section (7:10-17) recounting Amos' clash with the priest Amaziah, a representative of the northern religious establishment. Amaziah tries to curtail the prophet's ministry and to silence him, but Amos is not an easy man to stop; he seems to have continued courageously despite all efforts to make him cease and desist. The book concludes with a short section (9:11-15, or perhaps 8-15), which most scholars consider to be secondary. Its more positive tone and message of hope are in such contrast to the preceding threats of judgment that the passage is thought to have been added by an editorial hand.

The formation of the book of Amos and the reasons for its preservation can only be determined in a limited fashion. The book is characterized by the diversity of its subject matter: It contains the typical poetic oracles which may have been preserved initially in oral form; it contains some historical narrative (7:10-17) in which Amos' activities are described in the third person; it contains autobiographical material, principally in the five vision accounts; and it contains the usual signs of editorial process in the opening verse (1:1), perhaps in the concluding verses (9:11-15), and at various other points within the text itself. Thus it is a collection or anthology of material pertaining to Amos, similar in general form to the other prophetic books with occasional traces of the mature reflection involved in the editorial process. Who it was that compiled the book (whether Amos, his friends, or unknown persons at a later date) is not known. The substance of the book and the professional (secular) background of its key figure suggest that Amos was a man of some education and verbal (or literary) talent. Much of the book may, therefore, have been written in Amos' lifetime. But the preservation of the book may be due to other causes. The destruction of Israel in 722 B.C. would indicate all too clearly the authenticity of the prophet's message; the judgment of which he had spoken had come to pass. From the authenticity of the original message, perhaps its eternal value had been perceived; what Amos had said of Israel held true also for Judah. Thus in Judah, it seems the book was preserved and treasured as an authentic record of the prophetic voice.

Amos has not left us a cheerful book to read. The clouds of judgment are thick in his words, and they are rarely, if ever, penetrated by the sunlight of hope. He declares that social evil and the exploitation of fellow human beings must culminate in disaster and judgment, but he does not waste much time in calling for repentance; it is as if things were too far gone for that. If the book seems a bleak one because of the predominance of its message of judgment, its real gloom is to be found in the terrible social conditions which called forth such a message. Amos took sin seriously. Exploitation, injustice, poverty, pride, and the corruption of courts and places of worship were grave matters and must be addressed with gravity. It is precisely this gravity of the book of Amos which makes it, sadly, a book for all seasons.

4. The Book of Obadiah

The shortest book in the Old Testament is that of Obadiah; its single chapter contains only twenty-one verses. Unfortunately, the brevity of this little book does not make it the easiest to interpret.

In a very brief introduction (verse 1), we are told that the book contains "Obadiah's vision," but the identity of Obadiah (other than his name) remains a mystery, and even the time in which he lived is far from certain. Speculations on the date of the prophet, based upon the contents of the book, have ranged from the ninth to the fifth centuries B.C. The most probable hypothesis is that the book is to be dated in the decades following 586 B.C., for it seems to contain fairly vivid reflections of the events associated with Jerusalem's destruction.

The central subject matter of the book is focused upon the foreign state of Edom, which was one of the small states lying adjacent to the territory of Judah. In modern geographical terms, Edom lies within the area that is now a part of the kingdom of Jordan. Its territories flanked the southeastern shores of the Dead Sea, extending south from there along the barren rift valley, the Arabah, and eastwards toward the great Arabian desert. Edom was a state which achieved for a while in the biblical world a relative degree of prosperity, in part, as a consequence of its control of major trading routes (see figure 31) and, in part, because the mountainous terrain of its territories enabled them to be protected against foreign enemies.

Despite Edom's proximity to Judah, relations between the two nations had rarely been happy, even though (according to Hebrew tradition) the Edomites and the Israelites were distantly related through their ancestors, Esau and Jacob. In King David's time, Edom had become an Israelite colony, and though later it regained independence, there was little love lost between the Edomites and the Hebrews. Following the collapse of Judah and the destruction of Jerusalem in 586 B.C., it seems that the Edomites grasped the advantage of their neighbor's calamity by taking for themselves territory belonging formerly to Judah and by showing no mercy to the Judean suvivors of the war with Babylon. It was probably these specific circumstances, early in the sixth century B.C., which precipitated the prophecy of Obadiah.

The first part of the book, verses 1-9, anticipates the coming judgment of the state of Edom, and immediately a difficulty emerges in the interpretation of the book. The opening verses, especially 1-5, are virtually identical to a passage in Jeremiah (49:9, 14-16); whether the passages are in some fashion inter-dependent, or whether they both go back to an earlier source, cannot be determined with certainty. Following the declaration of Edom's coming doom, some of the reasons giving rise to the anticipated judgment are specified in detail (verses 10-14). The reasons are all related directly to Edom's past actions toward Jerusalem and the Judeans. By their cruelty, gloating, pride, and exploitation of a neighbor's calamity, they had exemplified in their actions mankind's potential inhumanity toward fellow human beings.

In the final section of the book (verses 15-21), the horizons of the prophecy are expanded somewhat. The focus on Edom gradually fades and the future fortunes of Jerusalem and the chosen people

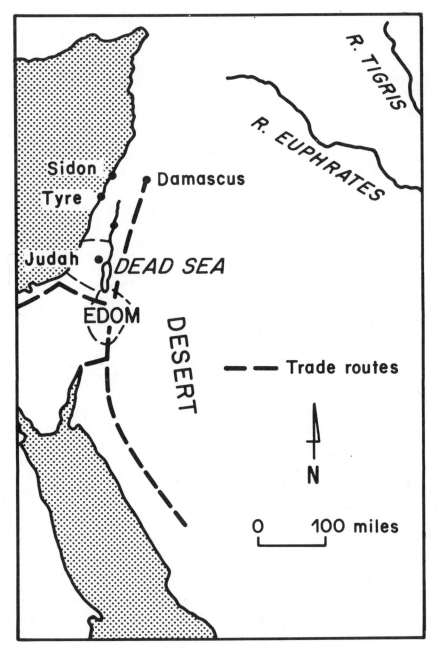

Figure 31. *Map of Edom*

come to the forefront. The theme of the last section is the *Day of the Lord*, a theme already noted in the book of Joel. It will be a day of judgment for foreign nations, such as Edom, but a day of restoration for the chosen people.

The book of Obadiah is not a pleasant book to read, with its scathing denunciation of Edom's evil and its proclamation of that nation's coming downfall. It is, nevertheless, an instructive book with respect to understanding the Hebrew notions of history and theology. If at first the verses of this book appear to be stained by the spirit of vindictiveness, it must be recalled that the announcement of Edom's judgment seems to be proclaimed by one who has already experienced divine judgment. That is, Obadiah writes as one who has already known the divine judgment in the destruction of his native land; he perceives in Edom the same (and worse) evils that culminated in Judah's collapse. And Obadiah perceives a moral principle to be operative in human history: "As you have done, it shall be done to you" (verse 15). Judgment is not a random act of God; rather it is an inevitable consequence of evil returning eventually on the perpetrator of evil. Edom's coming judgment, just as Judah's past judgment, was of its own making.

This short and gloomy book ends on a slightly more positive note. Obadiah concludes that eventually, beyond the immediate crises of history, "the kingdom shall be the Lord's" (verse 21). His immediate reference is to the restoration of the chosen people and the return of exiles from the distant points of the earth. There is a visionary quality to the concluding verses of Obadiah; the immediate situation giving rise to the prophecy has faded and a more distant world has come into view. The bitterness and despair of the opening verses has given way to a gleam of hope, and it is this concluding hope which probably led to the preservation and survival of the book.

5. The Book of Jonah

If Obadiah is the shortest of the biblical books, then the book of Jonah must be considered one of the most curious at first reading. Though it is grouped in the canon with the prophetic books, it is totally different in form and contents from the books of the other prophets. As we have seen, the prophetic books, although they may contain portions of biography and history, focus for the most part on the proclamation of the prophetic word. In the book of Jonah, however, the record of the prophetic word occupies only a very minor position in the book as a whole. The principal subject matter is a story concerning the prophet Jonah, his disobedience to God and its consequences, and his ultimate obedience in undertaking a prophetic mission to pagan Nineveh.

Thus the initial difficulty facing the reader of Jonah is that of determining how to read the book and how to interpret its substance. One approach is to interpret the book simply as a historical narrative—a story of a series of events in the life of the prophet Jonah. This approach to the interpretation is rooted in the observation that Jonah was a real historical person, a prophet who ministered in the northern state of Israel early in the eighth century B.C. Outside the book of Jonah, brief reference is made to this figure in the historical writings (II Kings 14:25); the external reference, however, adds very little to our knowledge of Jonah and says nothing of a mission to Nineveh. The relative lack of external information about Jonah, together with the peculiar substance of the book, has led numerous interpreters to the view that it must be interpreted as something other than historical prophetic literature.

The form and substance of the book have suggested to many that it should be read as a parable, or perhaps (though this is less likely) as an allegory. The parable has taken as its starting point a real human figure from history, one whose name would have been known to the initial audience, and then has developed a story around that figure to convey an important theological and moral message. Like other parables, for example that of the Good Samaritan in the New Testament, Jonah ends with a question designed to provoke the book's audience to reflect on its meaning (Jonah 4:11; compare Luke 10:36). As an extended parable, the book of Jonah has both a central message to convey concerning God, and a series of minor messages of a moral and didactic nature which emerge in the course of the story.

The story is a fascinating one, beautifully told, and drawing upon humor and caricature to convey its message. Jonah, in a conventional manner, receives the divine call to embark upon a prophetic mission. But after the opening words, all conventions are abandoned. Jonah is not called, as are other prophets, to minister to the chosen people. He is sent to Nineveh, a gentile city in Assyria renowned in the pagan world for its evil. Jonah, upon receiving his vocation, immediately sets off in the opposite direction; rather than heading northeast toward Nineveh, he promptly buys a ticket for the boat to Tarshish, somewhere to the west of the promised land in the Mediterranean. Jonah, unlike the other prophets, is disobedient to the divine call.

The prophet's journey away from God is destined for disaster. The ship on which he sails is caught in a great storm; the crew, on learning that Jonah is the cause of their crisis, cast the unhappy prophet overboard, thus saving the ship from wreck. Jonah's journey down into the depths is arrested by a great fish who swallows the prophet and becomes his home for three days, before eventually vomiting his belly-aching burden upon the beach. Jonah, who upon this beachhead of his life has finally learned the folly of disobedience, sets out at last upon his prophetic mission to the great city of Nineveh.

The prophet arrives at last at Nineveh, the city embodying paganism and evil, and begins to proclaim his message—unless the citizens of that city should repent, they must soon experience the judgment and destruction of God. To Jonah's astonishment, and indeed horror, his preaching immediately precipitates a great religious and moral revolution. Throughout the kingdom, from the common folks to the members of the establishment, there is a general turning from evil and a national act of repentance, as the people of Nineveh sought God's mercy. In theory, one might suppose Jonah would have been delighted, but he was not; he did not particularly like these pagans to whom he preached. He had been obedient in proclaiming his message, but secretly harbored the hope that as they refused to repent there would be released by God the spectacular display of judgment of which he had spoken. The final scenes of the book, in which Jonah's perversity and inconsistency are comically revealed, bring home the central message: Surely God, whose nature it was to be merciful, could have compassion on the citizens of Nineveh?

The incidental moral themes of the story emerge along the way. Thus the account of the prophet's response to the divine vocation contains a clear anatomy of disobedience and the consequences of departing from the divine will. But the real thrust of the story concerns the gentiles and their status in relation to God. Jonah embodies in his attitudes and actions the Israelite people, or more precisely the book's audience. They have a particularistic notion of God, whose mercy has been extended to them in the relationship of covenant, but they cannot conceive of that divine mercy being extended to the gentiles, least of all to Nineveh which was the pagan center of the gentile world. The peevish and petulant prophet, Jonah, has become in the story a caricature of Israel, perhaps overdrawn in the dimensions of his perversity, yet conveying accurately enough the popular and widespread attitudes toward the gentiles.

From a certain perspective, the theme of Jonah is mission. It is not mission in the sense of proselytizing, of making the citizens of Nineveh convert to Judaism. It is a mission in the more general sense of creating an awareness of God, together with God's hatred of evil, but character of mercy, in a world ignorant of God. Yet the mission of the book is not in the last resort Nineveh, but Israel; the faith of the chosen people, as a result of bitter historical exprience, had developed a shrunken notion of God. The Lord of Israel was *their own* God, and though his power might extend over all nations, his compassion surely did not. But to those who heard the story of Jonah, and who at last perceived in Jonah's perversity a reflection of themselves, the message would become clear. The mercy of God could not be confined to Israel; it knew no bounds and extended to all living creatures.

Although it is not possible to pin down precisely the details of the formation of the book of Jonah, the substance and interpretation of the book suggest some general guidelines. The real historical Jonah lived in Israel during the eighth century B.C., but if it is correct to interpret the book as a parable, it may have been composed in Judah at some point after the exile (during or after the sixth century B.C.). Its purpose was to combat the particularism and narrowness of faith that had emerged as a consequence of exile and harsh treatment at the hands of gentile nations. Its goal was to re-establish a greater notion of God and to restore to the chosen people one of the reasons for their election to a place of privilege, namely that they should reveal the light of God's mercy to all nations.

6. The Book of Micah

The latter half of the eighth century B.C. was one of the great ages of prophecy in the biblical world. In the northern kingdom of Israel, it was the time during which Hosea and Amos ministered. In Judah, it was the age of Isaiah and Micah. While a certain amount of information has survived about the lives and work of Hosea, Amos, and Isaiah, very little is known of Micah beyond the brief summaries of his public proclamations that are contained in the book named after him. We should be careful, nevertheless, not to let the lack of extant information about the prophet lead us to assume he was a minor figure in his own time and place. We know from other sources that his work was remembered clearly in Jerusalem almost a century after his time. When Jeremiah, almost a century later, had spoken of the coming destruction of the temple, there were those in Judah who wanted his execution on the grounds of his statements about the temple. Jeremiah's death was averted when some of his allies reminded the prophet's enemies that Micah had preached the same message concerning Jerusalem and its temple (Jeremiah 26:1-19). Not many preachers can hope to have their sermons recalled a century later; Micah appears to have been a man of considerable fame.

The prophet is called "Micah of Moresheth"; Moresheth was a small country town some twenty miles southwest of Jerusalem. Whether the prophet lived in this town or whether he lived in Jerusalem and was named after the town from which he came, is uncertain, though the latter is more likely. In any event, Jerusalem appears to have been the context of his prophetic ministry, though he brought into many of his public statements the concerns of the country folk, a reflection no doubt of his background. The general period of his ministry, indicated by the reference to kings in the book's opening verse, was the end of the eighth century and the beginning of the seventh century B.C., though we do not know precisely the time of his death. His public proclamations probably began before the fall of Israel and destruction of its capital city, Samaria (in 722 B.C.), for his message in part embraces both the nations of the chosen people. Hence the general limits of his activity would be approximately 730–690 B.C.

The seven chapters of Micah may be subdivided into three principal sections. (a) In the first section (chapters 1–3), we perceive some of the main themes of the prophet's message. He is outspoken against the various forms of evil prevalent in his society and announces that their consequence will be divine judgment. Both Samaria, in the north, and Jerusalem in Judah must be punished because of the injustice and oppression that flourished within their boundaries. (b) In the second section (chapters 4–5), the judgmental themes of the first section are contrasted with various prophecies of a more positive nature; Jerusalem (Zion) would be restored beyond its time of judgment and would become the focal point of a new world in the divine scheme of things. (c) The third section (chapters 6–7) blends the contrasts of the two initial sections, containing both announcements of coming judgment and words anticipating a more distant experience of the blessing of God.

The book of Micah, despite its relative brevity, has caused enormous debate amongst biblical scholars with respect to its form and structure and the authenticity of its contents. There is general agreement that the book, in its present form, reflects a distinctive and carefully planned structure in which the themes of judgment and promise are balanced and contrasted. From this literary perspective, the book has two principal sections, though they are uneven in length. Part one (1–5) begins with judgment (1–3) and follows that with promise (4–5). The same balance of judgment and promise recurs in chapters 6–7. But the agreement over the general literary character of the work is not matched by agreement over the authenticity of its subject matter. Thus while many scholars would accept chapters 1–3 (judgment) as the authentic proclamation of Micah, they would also interpret most of chapters 4–7 as secondary material coming from a later age.

The argument in simplified form is that Micah was a prophet of judgment, not of hope, and that the more hopeful themes of chapters 4–7 reflect a later age than that of the prophet. Whatever their merits, there has emerged no consensus in the arguments pertaining to the substance of chapters 4–7. Although a few clues have survived as to how the book was formed, the data are insufficient for the formation of firm hypotheses. But it seems unwise to deny to Micah the origin of all elements of hope and future restoration that have survived in his book. He saw in his lifetime the destruction of the northern kingdom, Israel, and the destruction of Judah must have seemed to him to be equally inevitable. The prophet's view of the inevitability of judgment may well have evoked the pronouncements of a more distant hope; beyond the disaster there remained a future in the divine scheme of things.

Thus the grounds for denying the authenticity of more than half of the book are not sound, and it is not too rash to claim that the book as a whole reflects the ministry of Micah in Judah. But there are a number of secondary elements in the book. The beautiful prophecy of a future time of peace (4:1-5) is duplicated in a slightly abbreviated form in Isaiah 2:2-4. Whether one prophet drew upon the words of the other or whether both drew upon a more ancient source cannot be determined with certainty, but the duplicate passage indicates a degree of commonality between the two great eighth century prophets in Judah. Another passage that may be secondary is the concluding portion of the book as a whole, chapter 7:8-20. It is in the form of a liturgical psalm and seems to reflect in its substance the later period of which Micah spoke. It may have been added to the book by those faithful followers of Micah who preserved his message through subsequent centuries.

Micah has been called the "conscience of Israel," and certainly the substance of his message was designed to prick the conscience of those who had long since abandoned the integrity of Israel's faith. He condemns the exploitation of the poor by the rich, the corruption of the law courts, and the abdication of moral and spiritual responsibility by secular and religious leaders alike. His condemnation of social ills is not an abstract notion, but is intimately tied to the conviction that such evil actions demand a divine response; hence the preponderance of the theme of judgment in Micah's words is a reflection in turn of the corrupt nature of the society to which he belonged. If it is correct to take the book of Micah as an authentic record of the prophet's ministry, then we can see throughout how his bleak words to his own age are balanced by brighter words to future generations. His message of hope presupposes the inevitability of disaster, but sees beyond the judgment to a new world. Micah's words and vision have a messianic character (which were taken up and developed later in both Judaism and Christianity). One day there would be a new king of David's line and a world characterized by order, in which the weapons of war would be transformed into the implements of peace. It is this dual character of the prophet's message which gives it perpetual significance. He viewed the present with hard-nosed realism, but refused to despair of the future; his knowledge of God was such that he could only view the distant future as an age in which a better world would dawn.

7. The Book of Nahum

The prophet Nahum was a citizen of Elkosh, but we know virtually nothing of Nahum and even the location of Elkosh cannot be determined. Proposals as to the location of Elkosh have ranged from a site in Iraq north of Mosul (Al-Kush) to a settlement in Galilee, but it is perhaps best to think of Elkosh as a small town in Judah whose location has long since been forgotten. The Book of Nahum retains a sample of the prophet's dramatic and vigorous poetry, but tells us nothing of the man himself.

The subject matter of the three short chapters that constitute this book is Nineveh, one of the greatest of the Assyrian cities which, in the seventh century B.C., became for a while the Assyrian capital. The remains of the city of Nineveh can still be seen in Iraq, bordering the eastern banks of the Tigris where the city of Mosul now stands. Despite the shattered nature of the ruins that have survived, it is still possible to recapture something of the physical splendor of the city of Nineveh as it was in Nahum's time. Nahum's theme is not a cheerful one; the whole purpose of his book is to announce the imminent collapse of Nineveh as an act of divine judgment. The collapse of Assyrian Nineveh would be like that of the Egyptian city Thebes, which the Assyrians themselves had destroyed in 663 B.C. (Thebes, or No-Amon, is referred to in 3:8). The reference to the destruction of Thebes and the fulfillment of the prophetic anticipation in Nineveh's collapse in 612 B.C. establish the chronological perspectives of the book; it must have been written shortly before 612 B.C., perhaps around 615 B.C.

The book begins with a poem describing God's character in the dual roles of judge and liberator. The poem is terrifying in its portrayal of the power of God, who can draw upon all the forces of nature to execute his wrath against his enemies. The focus of the Divine Warrior's wrath is Nineveh, a city that has embodied in its history both human evil and cruelty. Nahum's theme is that the day of Nineveh's judgment is about to dawn. In chapter 2, there is described in the terse and dramatic lines of war poetry the siege of Nineveh and its ultimate collapse. The third and final chapter elaborates still further on Nineveh's destruction, comparing it to that of Thebes (a former victim of Assyria's power), and concludes with an epitaph on a ruined people (3:18-19). The chaos and warlike atmosphere of this short book are only briefly penetrated by a more cheerful note, as the prophet indicates that Nineveh's downfall would be an act of liberation for Judah, hence a source of good news (1:15).

The process by which this short book was formed remains obscure. Much of the chapter 1 seems to be a partial acrostic poem (that is, a poem in which the succeeding verses begin with the successive letters of the Hebrew alphabet), which has been abbreviated and adapted to its present context; thus many scholars consider it to be secondary material. Whether the opening chapter is an authentic composition of Nahum, its location in the literary structure is essential in defining the character of God as judge. It is possible that the prophet took a familiar (or popular) acrostic poem and adapted it to his prophetic purpose. Though the background of chapter 1 is debated, few have doubted the authenticity of chapters 2–3. What occasion gave rise to the proclamation of these oracles is not known. They may originally have been proclaimed in some national act of worship in Judah, but their original setting in some specific situation in Judah remains obscure.

The book of Nahum is not at first a pleasant or uplifting one to read. It seems to relish the anticipated outpouring of the divine wrath upon Nineveh, and it is in stark contrast to the more compassionate tone toward Nineveh which is expressed in the book of Jonah. In order to grasp the force and intensity of Nahum, we must read it in the light of Judah's long history of oppression at the hands of Assyria. Nineveh in the seventh century B.C. had come to embody in its history and actions the worst forms of human terror and evil. Nineveh (representing Assyria as a whole) attained none of its imperial expansion by the limits of human decency; human lives could be casually thrown away in the pursuit of power and territory. While earlier prophets, Isaiah and Micah among them, had been able to affirm that Assyria was an instrument of God's judgment on the chosen people, later generations had raised the question of justice. Granted that the chosen people deserved the punishment they had received from God through the instrumentality of Assyria, where lay the justice of an even more evil nation, Assyria, apparently escaping judgment? Nahum affirms that the instrument of judgment would itself be judged. The Assyrians, perpetrators of some of the worst atrocities in human history, would eventually fall victim to their own kind of evil.

The book of Nahum is thus an early kind of "holocaust literature." If we find its tones of wrath and vengeance distasteful, we must remember that we have not experienced the atrocities of Nahum's world. While in our comfort we may dislike Nahum's tone, we should not blind ourselves to the fact that human evil in its grossest forms cries out for justice and retribution. Nahum has as its counterpart in our own century the literature that emerged after the holocaust; that literature raises not only the agonized question of how such evil can arise, but also expresses loathing of mankind's inhumanity toward fellow human beings. Nahum is a harsh book because it emerges from a harsh world, but it expresses something that is not always evident to survivors of cruelty—that ultimately the justice of God will prevail.

8. The Book of Habakkuk

The three short chapters of the book of Habakkuk are thoroughly imprecise with respect to the book's background and chronological context. The prophet is named in the introductory verses of the two main sections of the book (1:1 and 3:1), but no explicit historical information is given. Inferences drawn from the book have suggested to many scholars that the prophet ministered around 610–605 B.C., whereas others would set the book a little later, perhaps between 597 and 586 B.C. It is reasonable to suppose that Habakkuk was a contemporary of Jeremiah, but very little is known of his life and ministry compared to those of Jeremiah. The subject matter of the book may indicate that Habakkuk was a professional prophet, one who followed his vocation on a full-time basis in the context of the worship of the temple in Jerusalem. But his book, as we shall see, reveals both the private and the public lives of the prophet, though no detailed information of his ministry as a whole has survived.

The first main part of the book (chapters 1–2) introduces the subject matter as an "oracle of God" which the prophet "saw," but the two chapters break down into two quite distinct sections. (a) The first section is in the form of a dialogue between Habakkuk and God, and is characterized by the alternation between prophetic and divine speech. Habakkuk begins by asking how long violence and evil will continue unchecked (1:2-4), and he is told in response that a day of reckoning is coming (verses 6-11). God will use the Chaldeans (verse 6, namely the Babylonians) to execute his judgment on evil persons.

The divine response to the initial questions raises more difficulties than it solves; so the prophet resumes his dialogue with God by asking how a holy God can use a most unholy nation to execute his judgment and purpose (1:12–2:1). The Lord's response to Habakkuk is that an answer to his dilemma will be given to him in vision, but that he must be patient in waiting for the vision to come.

(b) The second section of the two opening chapters (2:5-20) is exceptionally difficult to interpret, in part because the opening verses (2:5-6) are difficult to translate. It may be that the Hebrew text has become damaged in the course of transmission, hence is difficult to understand, but it is more probable that the verses are deliberately obscure. If the five messages of "woe" that constitute the section as a whole were addressed to the Babylonian emperor (or the "arrogant man" of verse 5), common sense and consideration of personal safety may have prompted the prophet to write obliquely. In any case, the five messages of "woe" that follow seem to be addressed to the Babylonians (or Chaldeans), who have already been referred to earlier in the book as the instruments of God's judgment.

The second main section of the book (chapter 3) has its own heading (3:1), introducing the chapter as a prayer, or psalm, of Habakkuk. The prayer has many of the characteristics of the biblical psalms, including a concluding statement (3:19) concerning its musical performance. With respect to substance, the psalm seems to reflect the prophet's reaction to the experience of *theophany,* that is a vision of God. The vision in turn may be that which was anticipated at the end of the dialogue (2:2).

Despite the disparate nature of the contents, there need be few doubts as to the unity of the book and its origin in the life of an obscure prophet who ministered late in the seventh century B.C., or perhaps early in the sixth century B.C. In its present form, the book appears to be a literary work, but the prophet (or his disciple) has drawn upon various sources in the compilation of the book—the autobiographical material of the dialogue, the "woe oracles" which may have formed part of his public ministry, and the concluding psalm. The principal academic difficulty in the study of the book pertains to the identity of the "wicked" who are referred to in 1:2-4. Some have supposed them to be the Assyrians, who in the last quarter of the seventh century B.C., were in the final state of decline. When the prophet asks how long they will continue, he is told that their days are numbered and that the "Chaldeans" (Babylonians) will be the instruments of their final demise. But this interpretation is not altogether probable, and it is more likely that the "wicked" are the prophet's fellow citizens in Judah. When he inquires about their fate and learns that they will be dealt with by the Babylonians, the prophet's initial problem is aggravated. His fellow citizens might be wicked, but the Babylonians were surely worse. How could a holy God use them to achieve his goal?

The fascination and perpetual value of the book of Habakkuk emerge from an understanding of its place in the history of Hebrew (and human) thought. Habakkuk, the professional prophet, is a man of faith, but also a man who refuses to abdicate the responsibilities of reason. His dialogue with God is a bold enterprise, an attempt to pry from God some rationale for the apparently inexplicable manner of God's work in the world. He was a man who recognized the necessity of evil in his own nation being brought to justice, but he could not easily accept that there was any justice in the Chaldeans' executing God's judgment. As they were more reprehensible in moral terms than those whom they judged, inevitably the moral integrity of God in employing such an instrument of judgment must be called into question. So Habakkuk, in his dialogue, presses the questions and pursues the elusive answers. In part, a solution to his dilemma is to be found in his own public preaching; the "woes" he proclaimed against Babylon indicated that the instrument of judgment would also be judged.

In the last resort, nevertheless, no rational answer or systematic theological response is given to Habakkuk's plea. Instead he has a religious experience in which he encounters the Living God. We are not given an account of the vision as such, only of the prophet's response to the vision in the psalm of chapter 3. But we begin to perceive how in ancient Israel the questions of *reason* and *theology* (as we would call them today) are dealt with in part by religious experience. (The book of Job, examined in the next chapter, will provide a further illustration of the theme.) The difficult questions of human life are raised boldly by the prophet, but they are not explicitly answered; perhaps they can never be answered in a rational or theological fashion. Despite the lack of specific answers, the Book of Habakkuk does not terminate in a *cul-de-sac;* it suggests that a kind of answer may be achieved in the experience of theophany, the religious awareness of the nature of the living God.

9. The Book of Zephaniah

The three chapters of the book of Zephaniah are named after a man who ministered in the latter half of the seventh century B.C. We are informed in the introduction to the book (1:1) that Zephaniah served during the reign of King Josiah of Judah (640–609 B.C.). During that king's reign a great religious reformation was under-taken (around 622 B.C.), but the substance of Zephaniah suggests that the prophet's preaching was from a period prior to the reformation, approximately 630-625 B.C. The book's introduction also says something of the family background of Zephaniah, specifying his parental origins through four generations. The length of Zephan-iah's genealogy is unusual, for where such information is given in other prophetic books, usually one generation is sufficient. Hosea, for example, is called "son of Beeri," and Joel is "son of Pethuel." So why is it that Zephaniah is described as "son of Cushi, son of Gedaliah, son of Amariah, son of Hezekiah" (1:1)? Various suggestions have been proposed. His father's name, Cushi, means "Ethiopian, African"; perhaps the fuller genealogy is given simply to clarify his Hebrew descent. On the other hand, perhaps Zephaniah was of royal descent, if the ancestor Hezekiah was the king of that name. Or perhaps the prophet was simply a man with an awareness of his roots and preserved the family tradition in the book named after him. In any case, despite the long genealogy, very little is known of Zephaniah beyond the record of his words contained in this short book.

Zephaniah lived and worked in a difficult time in Judah's history, and it was an age in which the prophetic voice seemed long to have been silent. The end of the eighth century B.C. had been a great age of prophecy, with the work of Amos and Hosea in Israel, and Micah and Isaiah in Judah. But during the first half of the seventh century, there seems to have been a hiatus in the prophetic tradition, until the voice of Zephaniah was raised once again in prophetic proclamation. The years of prophetic silence had seen a sad decline in the moral and spiritual life of Judah. King Josiah's predecessors, Manasseh (687 to 642 B.C.) and Amon (642 to 640 B.C.), had reduced Judah to the status of little more than an Assyrian colony and had squandered the nation's spiritual resources in the pursuit of pagan traditions. In Josiah's time, a reformation was to come, but early in the reign the age of decadence continued, and to this unhappy nation Zephaniah brought his message from God.

The book of Zephaniah has the threefold division that is quite common in the prophetic collections. (a) The book begins (1:2–2:3) with words of judgment; the prophet anticipates a coming cataclysm embracing both nature and the world of human affairs, which would be a consequence of Judah's sin and corruption. (b) In the second section (2:4–3:8), the prophet declares that God's coming judgment would include various foreign nations as well as Jerusalem. (c) The concluding portion of the book (3:9–20) introduces a more cheerful note of hope, though it is thoroughly qualified hope. Beyond the coming cataclysm, there would be a future for the remnant of the chosen people and the other survivors of the disaster.

The academic study of Zephaniah has resulted, for the most part, in a general acceptance of the authenticity of the prophetic oracles stemming from the prophet's ministry. The principal debate focuses on the concluding verses (3:14–20), which seem to be a quotation from an ancient hymn and may have been added by the book's editor or compiler. The secondary nature of the concluding verses is by no means certain, and a proper appreciation of the setting of the prophet's ministry may indicate their original nature and purpose.

The prophet's principal theme is the "Day of the Lord" (see, for example, 1:7, 10, 14–16), a theme which has already been present in the preaching of earlier prophets, such as Amos. Although the "Day of the Lord" takes on special significance in Zephaniah's message, in the immediate context of ancient Judah the "Day of the Lord" was probably the focus of a great annual festival celebrating both God's acts in creation and his future purpose for his people and his world. A number of clues in the book (see especially 2:1) suggest that this festival, in which the "Day of the Lord" was cheerfully celebrated, was the setting for Zephaniah's delivery of his message. To the festal crowds gathered in Jerusalem to celebrate the day, Zephaniah declares that the day would not be a cheerful one, but a "Day of Wrath" (1:15). He converts the theme of national rejoicing to one of foreboding doom. The concluding verses (3:14–20), which some scholars have taken to be secondary material, may be an authentic part of the prophet's message to the festival crowds; he takes an ancient hymn employed in the festival, familiar to his audience, and adapts it to convey a part of his message.

If it is correct to interpret the substance of this little book against the background of a great festival held in Jerusalem, then it follows that we are provided here with only a tiny glimpse into Zephaniah's ministry as a whole. For how many years he worked, and with what success, we do not know. It may be that these portions of his message were preserved because they expressed so succinctly and powerfully the prophetic word in the language of the religious festivals which all the people understood.

The prophet's actual message, as we have seen, is a bleak one; he puts little emphasis on the call to repentance and sees little hope of the judgment's being averted. He is not so much a reformer as a visionary; the faith of Israel has been made to become so desperately corrupt that judgment seems to Zephaniah to be inevitable and hope can only be found beyond the judgment. His declaration of the inevitability of the coming cataclysm, for all its future dimensions, is rooted in a contemporary realism. He specifies the grounds of punishment, which include the miserable failure of the nation's leaders, the exploitation of the weak, and above all the apathy of the masses who think that God will do nothing at all, either for good or ill (1:12). It was national apathy which had allowed Judah to slip into anarchy and chaos, but the coming of judgment would indicate clearly enough to the apathetic that God was not otiose.

Thus Zephaniah is on the one hand a book rooted in the sad conditions of its own age, but the time-conditioned message has broken out of the boundaries of time and borders on the apocalyptic. The apocalyptic aspects of the prophet's message are not so much predictions of what must happen in a future world as they are a projection into the future of the potential that lies always within the human race. Insofar as Zephaniah is one of the pioneers of apocalyptic thought, we can learn from his writings. He was not, as are some modern representatives of the apocalyptic tradition, one who sat back waiting for the divine pattern of the future to unroll in a pre-ordained fashion. He perceived that the future was shaped in the present, that the horrors of apocalyptic dimensions that seem always to hover on the horizon of human history lay within the ever-present human capacity for evil, pursued to its ultimate climax. Zephaniah balanced this bleak view of human nature with a faith in God's love

(3:17), by which he was able to affirm a future of hope beyond the cataclysm.

10. The Book of Haggai

With the last three books in the collection of the Twelve Prophets, we shift to a different age in the history of the Hebrew people. Judah collapsed in 586 B.C., and there followed a time in which many of the nation's leading citizens were in exile. Beginning about 538 B.C., some of the exiles began to return to the homeland, there to join those who had remained after Judah's defeat. But in the years following 538 B.C., it was a distressed and despondent community that lived in and around Jerusalem. The people were poor; they tried with little success to rebuild the city that had been destroyed by the Babylonians and they sought to re-establish a once-flourishing agricultural industry. By 520 B.C., the community had achieved little growth. The sense of economic stagnation and despair spread to the religious life of the community, which was equally dispirited.

It was to this unhappy society that the prophet Haggai ministered. The two chapters of the book named after this prophet give only a very limited insight into the man's work; everything described within the book took place during the months from August to December, 520 B.C. The structure of the book is unusual in being defined very closely by a series of chronological statements. Five precise dates are given (1:1, 15 and 2:1, 10, 20), beginning with August 29, 520 B.C. (when the ancient dates were converted to modern equivalents) and extending to December 18 of the same year. The dates in turn subdivide the book into five sections (although some scholars, suspicious of the incomplete date formula in 1:15, divide the book into four sections).

In the book of Haggai, the prophet is consistently described in third person; it is reasonable to assume, therefore, that the work was compiled by one of the prophet's friends or successors. It comprises the prophetic oracles as such, together with some narrative account of the historical circumstances and the actual activities of Haggai. The five prophetic oracles are tied to specific dates, and thus to specific circumstances in the history of the post-exilic community in Jerusalem. These circumstances shed some light on the substance of Haggai's message and its enduring significance.

The prophet's ministry began in August of 520 B.C. with a call for the community to initiate the work of rebuilding the temple in Jerusalem, which had been destroyed in 586 B.C. The message is addressed primarily to the leaders in Jerusalem, Zerubbabel the governor, and Joshua the High Priest, though it clearly had implications for the people as a whole. The subsequent messages are related to the initiation of work on the temple in September, to the dispelling of criticism and discouragment in October, and to dealing with further difficulties (of an unspecified kind) which arose in December of that year. The book of Haggai, though, does not cover the entire period of temple restoration, for the work was not completed until about 516 B.C.

The substance of the prophet's oracles indicates something of the dual character of his message and ministry. On the one hand, Haggai was what would be called nowadays a political activist; by his public speaking and active engagement in political affairs, he was able to set in motion events that would lead to the rebuilding of a ruined temple. It is clear from his speeches that he saw no hope of his people's climbing out of their despondency and despair while the temple, the symbol of God's presence, lay in ruins. On the other hand common sense directed against his proposal; therefore, he had difficulty in persuading the community's leaders of the necessity of initiating the task. The community was poor, its crops were constantly failing, and what little activity there was in the construction industry was aimed at building and restoring family residences. In strictly economic terms it was no time to start expending time and money on the restoration of a temple.

A part of Haggai's significance, therefore, is to be found in his remarkable activities as both visionary and activist. In a visionary sense, he perceived that there was little hope of the restoration of his community's pride and faith while the symbol of God's presence among them lay in ruins. As an activist, Haggai was able to persuade his leaders and his fellow citizens to convert that vision into reality; as a result of his actions and speech, the ancient temple was restored and continued to function for many centuries.

Nevertheless, for all the significance of Haggai's ministry in the last months of the year 520 B.C., it is probable that his book was compiled and preserved for a quite different reason. Haggai prophesied that only when the temple had been rebuilt could the chosen people expect the restoration of Israel. Just as Ezekiel had foreseen a restored temple and a new Jerusalem (Ezekiel 40–48), so too did Haggai. His words have an immediacy which has suggested to many scholars that Haggai actually believed a new world would dawn from the moment the work of reconstruction was complete; of this we cannot be certain, but he did clearly see the reconstruction of the temple as a prerequisite for God's renewed work among his people. The preservation of the book was probably due to the recognition by later generations of Haggai's unquenchable hope. He had a vision of a world transformed by God and of a renewed Israel. He did not simply sit down and wait for that world to dawn, but set about the task of building it. The more lasting message emerging from his book is tied to the balance between vision and action, between hope for the future and the active commitment toward its realization.

11. The Book of Zechariah

Zechariah was a contemporary of Haggai. The ministries of the two prophets in Jerusalem not only overlapped, but shared to some extent a common interest, namely the building and restoration of the temple. We know that Zechariah was the "son of Berechiah, son of Iddo" (1:1), but very little is known of his life beyond the sparse and indirect information that has survived in his book. A number of dates are given in the first part of the book (1:1,7 and 7:1) which indicate at least one period of his ministry, 520–518 B.C., but probably do not include the whole.

There are numerous difficult problems attached to the study of Zechariah; they pertain both to the interpretation of the detailed substance of the book and to the literary analysis of the work as a whole. Most scholars have recognized that chapters 1–8 are marked by a unity of thought and structure, but the latter part of the book (chapters 9–14) is quite different in substance and tone. In part one there are three references to Zechariah in conjunction with the dates given, which clearly link the prophet's activities to the rebuilding of the temple. But in part two the prophet is not named nor are dates given; the literary form is that of poetry, rather than the prose which is predominant in chapters 1–8.

The range of differences between the major sections of the book (1–8 and 9–14) is so striking that many scholars have attributed the book to two quite distinct authors (or more, for chapters 9–14 are sometimes broken down into two further sections). That chapters 1–8 reflect the words and visions of the Zechariah who was Haggai's contemporary is not seriously doubted, but in modern scholarship (since at least the seventeenth century) chapters 9–14 have been attributed to "Deutero-Zechariah," whose work may be dated to the fifth or even the fourth centuries B.C. Nevertheless, although the majority of scholars have recognized the distinctive character of chapters 9–14, no scholarly consensus has emerged as yet with respect to the identity and date of Deutero-Zechariah (or Trito-Zechariah). Indeed, a few modern scholars are now returning to a long discarded possibility, namely that the whole book may indeed be the work of a single Zechariah, but that chapters 9–14 reflect a later period in his ministry, perhaps having been compiled several decades after the opening chapters. Whatever the differences between the two sections of the book, there are common themes linking them.

As no consensus has emerged—or is likely to emerge in the foreseeable future—concerning the literary structure of Zechariah, it is best to adopt a cautious approach toward the interpretation of the book. Whether the two parts of the book come from one or several authors, it is important to recognize the differences between them (The second section seems to reflect a different time period and more mature theological reflection.) If the two parts stem from different authors, then it must be noted that the editorial work of the book gives no clue to this fact; in other words, we may miss the point of the whole book in its extant form if we simply divide it into two and examine the parts separately.

Not only the literary structure, but also the substance of the book has given rise to difficulty in interpretation. Chapters 1–8 contain a summary account of the prophet's call of his people to repentance, which is followed in turn by an account of eight visions (1:7–6:8) which the prophet experienced "in the night." The interpretation of the visions and their significance in Zechariah's time is a complex task. The visionary accounts are followed by examples of the prophet's preaching (chapters 7–8). Chapters 9–14 are commonly divided into two further sub-sections, each introduced as an "oracle" or "burden" (chapters 9–11 and 12–14), in a fashion similar to the following book of Malachi.

Taken as a whole, the fourteen chapters of Zechariah convey a message that is at once rooted in its own time (especially chapters 1–8) and also breaks out of the constraints of time altogether in an apocalyptic fashion (chapters 9–14). The opening chapters are clearly linked to the task at hand, namely the rebuilding of the temple, and are thus similar in many ways to Haggai, though the latter seems to have been a much more practical man than Zechariah. Zechariah was less concerned with the actual work of reconstruction than he was with the theological significance of what was going on. The temple's renovation symbolized in a mysterious fashion God's coming work of renewal among his chosen people; it is this future orientation, prompted by the work on the temple, that links the first part of the book to the second. In chapters 9–14, the rooting in time and place fades into the background, and there emerge on the prophetic screen the outlines of apocalypse. The prophetic message now concerns the eternal struggle between good and evil, which is conveyed in the language of a future war of cosmic proportions among the nations. This apocalyptic battle to end all battles is presented in intimate association with the future fate and ultimate restoration of the chosen people and their holy city. The apocalyptic scene culminates in the conquest of evil persons and nations and the establishment of God's universal dominion of peace.

Apocalyptic language of the kind that predominates in Zechariah 9–14 is always difficult to interpret, and there are good reasons for the difficulty. From a human perspective (that is, setting aside for the moment the self-possessed revelatory quality of the language), the prophet has embarked on a virtually impossible task. In the present world, he perceives the perpetual superiority of violence and evil and the apparent ineffectiveness of the good; it is exemplified in his own broken people and the success and power of evil nations. The present circumstances raise for the prophet the eternal questions facing any person in this world who believes in a God of righteousness and justice. Must evil always triumph? Is there never an end to injustice? Does God really control in some sense the passage of human history?

There are no simple or rational solutions to such problems, but in the prophetic tradition they were resolved in part in apocalyptic language, which in turn is rooted in religious and visionary experience. The prophet projects onto the screen of future "history" a resolution of present dilemmas. The projection is rooted in faith in a God of justice and in the ultimate triumph of good over evil. Because good and evil, whether in personal experience or international affairs, are apparently always in conflict with one another, the future projection is one of battle and the ultimate victory of good over evil. This apocalyptic vision, which we glimpse in the writings of Zechariah and other prophets, is not in any simple sense *prediction*. It is predictive only in the sense of affirming the ultimate victory of God and good over evil; it is not predictive in the sense of being a kind of historical road map in which the predestined events of the future gradually unfold.

The prophetic notion of history is a carefully balanced one. On the one hand, human beings determine the direction of history and human evil in such a way that the horrors of apocalypse are always hovering on the horizon of history. On the other hand, God is sovereign and history will somehow move toward its divinely destined culmination in the triumph of good over evil and of justice over injustice. This delicate balance of human responsibility and divine sovereignty with respect to human history is not easy to maintain. Nor, frankly, is the apocalyptic vision easy to accept, whether in Zechariah's time or our own, for the actual evidence of history, ancient or modern, offers little support to the notion that good will ultimately triumph. But such is the direction of apocalyptic thought and language. It is necessarily mysterious, given its future orientation and unsubstantiated hope. Nevertheless, the apocalyptic vision, for all its warlike character and overtones of violence, is ultimately an affirmation of hope in God and hope for the world. It refuses to accept as the ultimate condition of the world the current supremacy of evil and looks to a better world beyond.

12. The Book of Malachi

The last of the prophetic books, and in most English Bibles the last book in the Old Testament, is that of Malachi. It is also one of the latest prophetic books to be written in the Old Testament period; from the examination of the substance of the book, the date of the prophet's ministry can be tentatively set in the years around 460 B.C. Thus more than half a century has passed since the time of the prophets Haggai and Zechariah, and not long after Malachi's time the religious reforms of Ezra and Nehemiah were to be inaugurated (for further see chapter 10).

The title verse of the book (1:1) provides some very general information about it. Its substance is described as an *oracle,* or *burden,* (see Zechariah 9:1 and 12:1). Some scholars have lumped Malachi together with the two parts of "Deutero-Zechariah" and interpreted them as three anonymous appendices to the collection of prophetic books. But, despite the common use of the word *burden,* it is best to recognize Malachi as a separate and independent work; its substance and form sharply distinguish it from the last chapters of Zechariah. The prophetic message in the four chapters of Malachi is addressed to "Israel," the word's being used in the broadest sense to incorporate all the chosen people of God.

Although the general integrity of the book need not be questioned, the identity of its author has been the source of some difficulty. Reading the title of the work in the English Bible, we may simply assume that *Malachi* is the name of a prophet. But the Hebrew word means "my messenger," and indeed the word occurs elsewhere in the book (3:1) not as a name, but as a noun. Thus there is some difficulty in determining whether we are dealing here with an anonymous prophet who is entitled "my (read God's) messenger," or with a virtually unknown individual called Malachi. In the earliest Greek translation of the book, the word was not translated as a name, but as a title; however, the Greek translates "*his* messenger," raising questions of another kind about the nature of its antecedent Hebrew text. Although the matter cannot be settled, the balance of probabilities is that we should take the word to be simply the prophet's name, and that the use of the same word in 3:1, where it is quite properly translated "my messenger," involves a word-play on the prophet's name designed to communicate his message more effectively.

The book has a distinctive literary form. It contains a series of disputations, or arguments, between God (who speaks through his prophet) and Israel. The disputations have a generally common structure: First, God makes a statement, then the people make a response (or series of responses), which in turn is followed by a further and more detailed response from God through his prophet. It is not possible to determine with certainty whether this disputation reflects an actual life situation, in which the prophet pursues his ministry actually engaged in argumentation and debate, or whether it is simply a literary form designed to convey the prophetic message. The form may be rooted in real life, in which case we should view

Malachi's activity as a teaching ministry, rather than the more conventional prophetic activities of preaching and proclamation.

There are six disputations in the book, and their topics range from theological concerns to more basic social concerns. From a theological perspective, Malachi addressed issues such as the nature of God's love and justice. From a more practical perspective, he addressed current problems such as divorce, the abuse of worship, and the importance of tithing. The focus of Malachi's message indicates something of the difficulties into which his community had fallen. In the mid-fifth century B.C., the Jews were still a colony in the Persian Empire; the times were relatively calm and the Jews were governed in a benign manner. The lack of crisis and the colonial status seems to have functioned like decay in the Jewish community—the ancient faith was casually observed, if it was observed at all. Divorce had become a common practice; men divorced their wives to marry pagan women, and thereby the purity of the ancient faith was undermined. The worship in the temple was maintained, but it was conducted in a half-hearted manner, without care or any genuine spirituality. People still contributed to God in tithes and offerings, but they gave what was left over, the second and third best. All these signs of superficiality and hypocrisy merely pointed to deeper problems—belief in God's love and justice had collapsed.

Malachi, through his disputations, sought to revitalize the religion of his people. He affirmed the importance of the ancient law for their lives and worship; profound belief in God and careful observation of the law in social concerns and in the conduct of worship were essential if the drab years of colonial existence were to be transformed once again into years of fulfillment and faith. The book ends with a short appendix (4:4-6), which not only summarizes Malachi's message, but also that of the prophets as a whole. (Whether the appendix is from Malachi's hand or that of an editor is a subject of continuing debate). Looking back through history, Malachi enjoins the people to remember the ancient Law of Moses which established for all time the dimensions of their relationship to God. But looking forward in time, he alerts the people to the return of the prophet Elijah, whose coming would precede the "great and terrible day of the Lord" (4:5). Moses and Elijah represent, in symbolic terms, the Law and the Prophets, which together constitute the foundation of the nation's faith. But they also symbolize the past (Moses) and the future (Elijah). Moses established the foundations, but the return of Elijah would prepare for the culmination of the Hebrew faith—the day of God which would inaugurate a new world. So Malachi highlights that tension which constantly occurs in the Old Testament writings: The present moment is to be lived with a knowledge of the past and in anticipation of the future. The God in whose mercy the beginnings of the faith had been established would one day bring that faith to its fulfillment.

THE
WRITINGS (I):
PSALMS AND
WISDOM LITERATURE

T HE third major division of the Hebrew canon of the Bible, the *Writings* or *Kethubim,* is the most diverse with respect to the form and contents of the various books comprising the whole. Whereas the other sections, the *Law* and the *Prophets,* have a degree of thematic unity, the Writings can only be described as a miscellaneous collection of books that did not clearly fit into either of the other canonical collections. (This division of the canon is also described in some books as the *Hagiographa,* a Greek expression meaning "sacred books," going back to the early history of Christianity.)

In addition to the miscellaneous character of the contents of the Writings, the order in which the books appear differs considerably from one manuscript tradition to another. We cannot be sure of the original sequence of these books, though we can be reasonably certain that the sequence is of no particular importance. The books can be studied, for the most part, as independent works. Where there is a particular context suggesting that some books should be studied together, it will be noted in the sections that follow in this chapter and in chapter 10. In this chapter, the review of the Writings is restricted to the book of Psalms and to the Wisdom books (Job, Proverbs,

Ecclesiastes). In chapter 9, the remainder is examined: Ruth, Song of Songs, Lamentations, Esther, Daniel, Ezra-Nehemiah, and I–II Chronicles.

1. The Book of Psalms

The book of Psalms served as the hymnbook of ancient Israel. It is not a *book* in the strict sense, but a collection of the hymns and prayers that were employed in the worship of Israel, both public and private. Thus, like several other Old Testament books, it is an anthology. The one hundred fifty psalms come from different authors, some known but most unknown, and were composed at different times and in various places. The collection was later referred to as the "Psalms of David," for King David was remembered as the patron of psalmody in Israel, but David was not the author of the collection as a whole (though a number of the psalms may be traced back to him), which arose rather as the result of a long process of development.

The individual psalms are all written in poetry (as are many sections of the prophetic books), and many of them would originally have had musical settings, though these have not survived. The quality of the poetry varies from one psalm to another. While some psalms are magnificent examples of poetic composition in strictly literary terms (19, 23), others are more uneven in literary terms, but profound when understood functionally in their original context (22). Many of the psalms (one hundred sixteen out of the total one hundred fifty) are prefixed by short titles written in prose; these titles range from a few words to a few lines. There are various types of information contained in the titles: references to a person (David, Asaph), who may be author, collector, or the one to whom the psalm was dedicated; historical references concerning the original setting of the psalm; and liturgical references concerning the type of psalm (*hymn*) and its musical accompaniment. While a few of these titles may have been composed at the same time as the psalm, the majority of them reflect later tradition concerning the use of the psalm in Israel's worship. The psalm titles are, nevertheless, a part of the canonical text of the Hebrew Bible, not merely the notations of a post-biblical editor.

In the nineteenth and early twentieth centuries, the traditional approach to the psalms by biblical scholars was to examine them in literary terms; that is, the book was considered to be a collection of poems and was examined as such. But the literary approach to the Psalms, while it was fruitful in a few instances, failed for the most part to lead to a proper understanding of the individual psalms. As has been noted, many of the psalms are not great works of art, but when they are examined in terms of their function their true significance may emerge. For example, the national anthems of many nations in the modern world contain rather dreary poetry and would win no prizes in a literary competition. When the anthems are sung in the context of an Olympic victory ceremony, however, the dullness of the poetry is lost in the experience of national pride. The analogy is not precise, but it provides a clue to understanding the individual psalms. Just as a knowledge of the setting in which a national anthem is sung will help us to appreciate its power, so too a knowledge of the setting in which Israel's psalms were employed will contribute to a proper understanding of them. Thus the psalms, in most cases, need to be examined in *functional* terms, rather than *literary* terms; in twentieth-century biblical scholarship there has been a major move toward this perspective in the study of the psalms.

The starting point for the functional study of the book of Psalms is the recognition of the importance given to worship, both public and private, in the life of ancient Israel (for further information, see chapter eleven). The books of the Law established the fundamental religious observations in Israel, ranging from the daily and weekly worship conducted in the temple to the great annual festivals of Israel's religion (for example, Passover). In addition to these regular forms of religious worship, initially in the temple and later (after 586 B.C.) in the synagogue, there were particular occasions which involved a religious dimension—for example, the coronation of a king or the departure of the nation's army for war. These public contexts for worship were supplemented by private worship, though of this we have less detailed information; individuals, nevertheless, turned to God in praise or lament when experiencing joy or encountering the crisis of sickness. Some of the more personal dimensions of religious worship may have been conducted in the privacy of the home, others in the context of the temple.

If we are to understand the psalms, then, we must try to envision each one in its appropriate social setting (bearing in mind that a few may be literary creations in the first instance, only later being used in some particular context). The study of the psalms in this functional context has been called *form criticism,* though that label is perhaps too narrow to embrace the variety of approaches employed in contemporary functional studies. In form criticism, an attempt is made in the study of each psalm to determine its *type* (hymn, prayer) and also the *setting* in which that type would be used (worship in a festival conducted in the temple). The *types,* in turn, were thought to be characterized by a distinctive literary form. The detection of the elements of form would lead to a classification of a psalm according to type and a determination of its setting in the life of ancient Israel.

In classical form critical studies in the early decades of the twentieth century, five principal types of psalms were distinguished, to which a number of minor types could be added. The five principal types were: (i) hymn; (ii) communal lament; (iii) royal psalms; (iv) individual lament; (v) individual song of thanksgiving. In more recent study, however, this fivefold classification has been recognized as too general; there are considerably more types of psalms with very diverse settings than was at first supposed. It has also been increasingly recognized that while one may reasonably speak of distinctive types of psalms, there is considerable variety with respect to the aspects of form within a given type. Perhaps the best way to illustrate the functional study of the psalms and the aspects of type and setting is to provide a few examples.

(a) *Psalm 8* is classified with respect to type as a *hymn,* and its setting, initially, would have been an act of worship in the temple. More precisely, it is a hymn celebrating *creation.* Given its substance, therefore, it might be possible to suggest a more specific setting, namely a great festival in Israel's religious year in which God's creation was celebrated (for example, the Festival of Tabernacles), but to be as specific as this is to move further into the realm of hypothesis. What does this analysis mean for the reader of Psalm 8? It indicates that in reading this psalm, while we may recognize from the outset its outstanding literary qualities, we must bear in mind that it was designed for use by a congregation engaged in an act of worship in the temple. To think of a psalm simply as a *poem* will result in missing much of its force.

(b) *Psalm 19* is also a hymn, and from the psalm's title we may infer that this psalm, too, was employed at some point in Israel's worship.

But the literary structure of this psalm and the excellence of its language are so striking that we should allow the possibility that it was in the first instance simply a literary work of art. C. S. Lewis, who taught English in both the University of Oxford and Cambridge University, wrote of Psalm 19: "I take this to be the greatest poem in the Psalter and one of the greatest lyrics in the world" (*Reflections on the Psalms*, p. 56). The psalm may thus illustrate an important point, namely that any given psalm may have several stages in its history. Psalm 19 may have started its life as a work of art, but was later used in liturgy. The following example futher illustrates the point.

(c) *Psalm 6* is commonly classified as an *individual lament*, but it is more precisely a *psalm of sickness*. The language is intensely individual; in its initial usage, therefore, it may reflect a setting in the life of a person who was suffering from a serious illness. The setting may have been private (the home), but was more probably in a ceremony conducted in the temple for a sick person. Nevertheless, for all the individuality of the psalm, its title indicates that later it came to be used more generally in the worship in the temple.

(d) *Psalm 2* is an example of a *royal psalm*, that is a psalm that was related in some way to the role and office of the king in ancient Israel. It is more precisely a *coronation psalm*, and its setting would have been in the context of the ceremonial coronation of a new king in Israel. Thus the notion of a *royal psalm* is a very flexible one and incorporates many different kinds of psalms which have in common some association with royal activities. To provide another example, Psalm 45 is also a royal psalm. It is associated, however, not with a coronation, but with a royal wedding, and its language and imagery are those of romantic poetry.

(e) *Psalm 37,* in literary terms, is an acrostic psalm; that is, its successive verses (though these do not correspond to the verse numbers in the English Bible) begin with the successive letters of the Hebrew alphabet, *aleph, beth,* and so forth. (There are several alphabetic acrostic psalms in the Psalter: 9, 10, 25, 34, 37, 111, 112, 119, 145). The designation *acrostic*, while indicating the psalm's literary character, does not specify its type. In terms of type, it is a *didactic psalm* (or "instructional poem"), and it may have been used for instructional purposes in the "wisdom" schools of ancient Israel. Later in the psalm's history, it came to be used in a more general context of worship, as is implied by its incorporation within the book of Psalms.

The examples provided above, while by no means giving a comprehensive overview of the varity of types and settings to be found in the book of Psalms, do give some indication of an appropriate perspective from which to read the individual psalms. Though a few can be appreciated simply as literary masterpieces, the majority come alive only when we see them against the background of Israel's actual life and worship. There are revealed in the Psalms the various dimensions of both secular and religious life—the joy, thanksgiving, and sometimes sorrow expressed in public worship as well as the more personal emotions expressed in such experiences as sickness and even dying (for example, Psalm 22).

This perspective on the individual psalms indicates that the book of Psalms as a whole is a collection of units, each of which has a separate and distinctive history. The collection of Israel's psalms into a single book is the end result of a long and complex history, only a part of which can be reconstructed. First, the individual psalms were written, some as early as (or earlier than) the time of David in the tenth century B.C., and some from later centuries during and after the exile. Occasionally an author of a particular psalm can be proposed, but the majority must be recognized as anonymous works. Gradually, over the passage of Israel's history, a number of these originally independent psalms were brought together into small collections; a few traces of these early collections have survived in the book of Psalms. There were, for example, collections of "Davidic Psalms" (either psalms by David, or more probably dedicated to David). These psalms are usually designated in the title verse as "a psalm of David" (for example, Psalm 3:1). But in Psalm 72:20 we read that, "David son of Jesse's prayers are ended." The expression probably refers to the end of an early collection of these psalms, for there are further Davidic psalms after 72 (for example, Psalms 138–145). Other early collections may include the "Psalms of Asaph," the "Psalms of Korah," and several others. These early, small collections were gradually gathered together into larger collections, and eventually the book of Psalms as we now have it—a collection of collections—came into existence (perhaps in the fifth century B.C. or later).

Although the process of the formation of the Psalter is important from a historical perspective, it is not of prime significance for the study of individual psalms. The psalms can be studied independently, in the context of other psalms of the same type, and a sensitivity to their function will illuminate their meaning. But there remain further difficulties concerning the psalms, particularly those associated with their proper translations and meanings. The psalms contain many Hebrew words of uncertain meanings, and they are written in a poetic form which entails difficulties of syntax for the would-be translator. In recent decades, a major new thrust has occurred in the examination of these kinds of difficulties in the psalms. The starting point for this new thrust has been the recognition that the resources of biblical archaeology may have something to contribute to the resolution of difficulties in the psalms; in particular, the texts discovered in the archives of ancient Ugarit (see chapter 3) have promised to shed new light on the psalms.

Many of the Ugaritic texts are written in poetry, thus have contributed significantly to an understanding of the character and style of poetry in the Old Testament world. Furthermore, as Ugaritic is a close linguistic relative of the biblical Hebrew language, a knowledge of the meaning of Ugaritic words has frequently contributed to the interpretation of rare and obscure Hebrew words, especially in the psalms. To summarize several decades of pioneering research into the Psalms, it would be fair to say that the study of Ugaritic poetic texts, recovered by over half a century of archaeological exploration, has illuminated many of the former obscurities in the psalms. They can now be translated more accurately and with a sounder knowledge of ancient poetic style and convention than was formerly the case. The fruits of this kind of detailed research can be found in the various modern commentaries on the psalms. (It should be added that the study of Ugaritic texts has contributed to the study of the Old Testament texts as a whole, but perhaps nowhere so dramatically as in the book of Psalms.)

The diverse origins and different types of psalms in the Psalter are such that it is not possible to speak of one single religious perspective emerging from the book. There are, however, certain common themes underlying the diversity of the Psalter, the most distinctive of which is the sense of *relationship* to God which permeates the collection as a whole. The essence of Israel's religion was relationship. The ancient covenant established at Mount Sinai marked the relationship of mutual commitment established between God and Israel, and the sense of national relationship had its individual counterpart in the life and faith of Hebrew persons. In the psalms, the many faces of this relationship with God are revealed to us—joy and sorrow, the sense of presence and the awareness of the divine absence, rejoicing in life and trembling in the face of death. The book of Psalms, as it has survived, is above all a book that was designed to be used; it is not simply a record of ancient poetry. Thus the appreciation of the psalms presupposes the imaginative attempt to understand the role of the words in the lives of human beings. In contemporary Judaism and Christianity, the greatest appreciation of the psalms comes from their continuing use in both private and public worship.

2. The Wisdom Literature

Three of the books within the Writings form the sub-category of Wisdom Literature; they are Proverbs, Job, and Ecclesiastes. This category can be defined in literary and in social terms. In literary terms, its focus is wisdom (Hebrew *hokmah*), a word indicating both the intellectual and moral traditions in ancient Israel, and this focus on wisdom involves in turn a distinctive vocabulary and literary style. In social terms, the wisdom literature emerged from the "wisdom schools" of ancient Israel, thus represents a tradition distinct from that of prophecy or law.

The wisdom tradition in ancient Israel is of such significance that it deserves careful examination in its own right; this larger perspective on wisdom is provided in chapter 11, "The Religion and Culture of Israel." In the present context only the three wisdom books are examined. In literary terms though, it needs to be recalled that in addition to these books, samples of wisdom literature have been preserved elsewhere in the Bible (for example, wisdom psalms in section 1 above, and wisdom passages in both Law and Prophets). The book of Proverbs provides the most basic insight into the wisdom tradition in ancient Israel; the books of Job and Ecclesiastes explore respectively the experiential and intellectual dimensions of wisdom.

(a) The Book of Proverbs

The first of the wisdom books is named after its principal contents (*proverbs*) and after a person (*Solomon*). The word *proverb,* in context, incorporates both brief statements (two-line sayings) and more sustained passages of moral wisdom and instruction. Solomon is named as the author of Proverbs, although (as we shall see in reading the book) he was clearly not intended to be understood as the author of the whole—Proverbs, like Psalms, is a collection of collections. Nevertheless, King Solomon, who was David's successor in the united kingdom of Israel (from around 960–922 B.C.), was a man remembered for his wisdom; the historical traditions of Israel attribute to him some three thousand proverbs (I Kings 4:32), a considerably larger corpus of sayings than has survived in the thirty-one chapters of the book of Proverbs!

Despite the reference to Solomon in the opening verse (1:1), the reader of Proverbs quickly becomes aware that the contents of the book are more diverse than at first they might appear. Chapter 10 begins with a new heading, "the proverbs of Solomon," and 22:17, with its reference to the "words of the wise," appears to introduce a further collection. Other headings appear throughout the remainder of the book: "the sayings of the wise" (24:23), proverbs of Solomon copied by the men of Hezekiah (25:1), the "words of Agur" (30:1) and the "words of Lemuel" (31:1). In summary, the book of Proverbs in its present form is an anthology of various smaller collections of wisdom sayings from ancient Israel named appropriately enough after Solomon, the patron of the wisdom tradition. Although we may reasonably suppose that many of the proverbs go back to Solomon, the tradition has clearly been supplemented over the centuries by the addition of later proverbial sayings. The structure of the book as a whole may be set out as follows:

1. Introduction to the book(1:1-7)
2. First collection (1:8–9:18)—"wisdom poems"
3. Second collection (10:1–22:16)—"proverbs of Solomon"
4. Third collection (22:17–24:22)—"words of the wise"
5. Fourth collection (24:23-34)—"sayings of the wise"
6. Fifth collection (25:1–29:27)—collection of the "men of Hezekiah"
7. Sixth collection (30:1-33)—"the words of Agur"
8. Seventh collection (31:1-9)—"the words of Lemuel"
9. Appendix (31:10-31)—"the virtuous wife"

There are some differences among the various collections. The first, for example, in its subject matter, is much more coherent in literary terms than are the following sections, and thus it is easier to read. The remainder of the collections contain the brief statements of wisdom strung together in an apparently haphazard fashion, but conveying as a whole the essence of ancient Israel's moral wisdom.

The subject matter of the book of Proverbs is perhaps the most international in character of all the Old Testament. Wisdom sayings similar to those of Proverbs are to be found also in the literature of ancient Mesopotamia and Egypt, and a few wisdom texts have been found in the archives of Ugarit in Syria. Some parts of Proverbs have very close Near Eastern counterparts; thus Proverbs 22:17–23:14, from the third collection, is closely parallel to an Egyptian wisdom text, *The Teaching of Amenemopet*. Even within the book of Proverbs the international character of the contents may be discerned. The sixth and seventh collections are attributed to Agur and Lemuel respectively, both of whom are said to have been citizens of *Massa* (30:1 and 31:1), perhaps a country (or tribal territory) in Saudi Arabia (the location is uncertain). The international character of wisdom is in fact recognized in the biblical historical traditions; in Solomon's time, people came from various parts of the world, all no doubt experts in wisdom, to learn from the famous king (I Kings 4:29-34).

The purpose of the proverbial sayings which constitute the major substance of the book was to offer instruction, especially to the young, and subsequently to offer guidance throughout life to those who had absorbed and understood their meaning. They work frequently by means of contrasts—wisdom is better than folly, diligence is better than sloth, or honest poverty is better than unjust wealth. The short (two-line) proverbial sayings were designed no doubt to be memorized, so that their substance could be recalled to the mind in subsequent years to offer moral guidance. In a sense, the proverbial sayings were designed to shape the conscience and character of those who learned them, instilling the fundamental virtues and characteristics of the good life and directing the conscience toward the appropriate decisions throughout life. Given this fundamentally ethical outlook, the international character of the Proverbs and the apparent secularity of many of the sayings are not surprising, for fundamental moral wisdom and ethical norms may transcend national and religious boundaries. Indeed, the wisdom of Proverbs not only has parallels in ancient Egyptian and Mesopotamian wisdom texts, but may also be compared to more distant texts, such as the *Analects of Confucius,* a Chinese text approximately contemporary with the final form of the book of Proverbs.

Nevertheless, for all the commonality of the substance of Proverbs with other wisdom literature, it is given distinctive shape and meaning by its foundational principle in ancient Israel: "the fear (or reverence) of the Lord is the beginning of wisdom" (1:7). This fundamental principle, which reappears in both Job and Ecclesiastes, establishes the basis on which the sometimes secular moral wisdom is built. All the biblical wisdom teaching presupposes not only the existence of God, but also that human beings should "fear," or hold in reverence, the God of Israel. It is this reverence for God which provides the motivating force of the biblical proverbs. In this, the proverbial wisdom is similar to law, which also presupposes reverence for God; whereas Hebrew law is presented as a revelation from God, having within it the divine imperative, Hebrew wisdom is addressed rather to common sense. If you hold God in reverence, you should live an upright and moral life, but how is such a life to be lived? The moral wisdom of Proverbs provides direction, ranging from simple common sense to guidance in sexual mores and advice as to business practice. All of human existence comes within its perspective, and though no moral handbook can be comprehensive, the diversity of the subject matter of Proverbs clearly indicates that no realm of human life is beyond its perspective.

It is not possible to determine with any accuracy the process by which this anthology of collections of Hebrew wisdom came together. There is no reason to doubt that the initial stimulus in the wisdom tradition came in the tenth century B.C., prompted by King Solomon's interest in wisdom and learning. The reference to the work of the "men of Hezekiah" (25:1) indicates that the work of collecting and recording proverbial wisdom continued throughout the late eighth and early seventh centuries B.C. The impossibility of dating the collections of Agur and Lemuel makes it equally difficult to know the period in which the book of Proverbs reached its final form. Nevertheless, the context in which the book was compiled is probably that of ancient Israel's educational institutions; this background to Proverbs is examined in more detail in chapter 11.

(b) The Book of Job

Whereas the book of Proverbs establishes the moral norms of the wisdom tradition, the books of Job and Ecclesiastes address areas of difficulty which go beyond those norms. Proverbs teaches how one should live a moral and upright life and clearly indicates the blessing and prosperity which would accompany such a life. There are two directions from which such basic moral instruction is susceptible to criticism. One is the life of experience, which may indicate that in reality a person who lives a moral life may experience terrible suffering and misery, and the other is the life of the mind, which may call into question the very foundations of moral wisdom. In the book of Job, the problems that may arise from the cruel experience of human living are subjected to examination.

At the outset, it should be recognized that we are examining a superb work of art. From a literary and artistic perspective, the book of Job is not only the superlative work of the Old Testament, but it also rightfully takes its place among the masterpieces from all cultures and all times. Its excellence has many dimensions, ranging from the magnificent power of its poetry to the depth and insight with which it develops its themes. Although the brilliance of this work shines brightest when it is read in its original language, its quality is such that it survives translation into other languages. (In the English language the best rendition of Job from a literary perspective is that of the *New English Bible;* although Hebrew scholars might quibble on numerous technical aspects of this translation, its literary excellence *in English* reflects to some extent that of the original work.) It is important to stress this literary quality of Job at the beginning of the study, for the book of Job has also been subjected to detailed and complex academic discussion; for all the value of careful scholarly investigation, there is the danger of losing sight of the original beauty as the critical knife dissects the parts of the whole.

The book is anonymous, giving no clue as to who its author might be; likewise, it contains no specific information as to the date on which it was written. It is not a book that can be easily categorized with respect to its genre. It is in part a story, especially in the prologue (chapters 1 and 2) and the epilogue (42:7-17). It also contains a lengthy debate, with speeches from Job and his companions (chapters 3-37) and some concluding speeches from God (chapters 38-41); the speeches and the debate are all poetic in form, whereas the prologue and epilogue are in prose. It is not in any strict sense a history, though its insight into the human condition reflects a profound experience of the dilemmas of human and historical existence. The book of Job, in the last resort, defies any simple attempts at classification; it is wise simply to recognize its unique character and to adopt appropriate sensitivity in the approach to interpretation.

A summary of the book's contents will indicate for us the range of its interest and the complexity of its interpretation. The prologue (chapters 1 and 2) tells a simple story which sets in perspective all that is to follow. It concerns a man called Job who lived in the land of Uz. The location of Uz is not known and is of no more importance for the story than is the location of Oz in the story of the Wizard, but it is interesting to note that Uz was not a place that can be identified in the promised land, nor is Job specifically identified as a Hebrew or an Israelite. The story seems to be consciously removed from a national setting or a particular period, thereby accentuating its universal appeal; its message is for all people in all times and in all places.

Job is that rare person who combines riches with righteousness. He had a large family and considerable wealth, but he was a man of integrity who "feared God" (1:1; this is the principle of the Wisdom Literature). But no sooner have we been introduced to Job than the setting of the story shifts from the earthly scene of Job's residence to the heavenly setting of God's council. A conversation develops between the Lord and the "adversary." (Many English translations here specify *Satan,* a proper name, but the Hebrew word *satan* means "adversary" and it is used here with the definite article, indicating it is a noun, not a name. Only later in Jewish and Christian literature do we find *Satan,* without a definite article, used as a name.) The adversary suggests to God that Job's integrity is not all that it might seem to be and that if Job's wealth were to be affected, he would curse God to his face. God, who has confidence in his servant, permits the adversary to test Job.

The scene then shifts back from the heavenly to the human world, and Job undergoes a severe testing. Through a series of disasters, Job loses his wealth and his children die. From Job's perspective, for he does not know of the divine testing, his disasters come from two sources; part of the trouble that befalls him is the work of human enemies and part is the consequence of natural disasters (what insurance companies call "acts of God," such as lightning and storm). By the actions both of fellow human beings and of the forces of nature, Job's world has been shattered, but he does not curse God: "Naked I came from my mother's womb, and naked I shall return; the Lord gave, and the Lord has taken away; blessed be the name of the Lord" (1:21). A second round of testing is permitted, and this time Job suffers physically, being afflicted with a terrible skin disease. Still, he holds on grimly in his integrity: "shall we receive good at the hand of God, and shall we not receive evil?" (2:10). Superficially he has passed the two rounds of testing, but this is not the end of the book; it merely sets the stage for all that is to develop. Three friends—Eliphaz, Bildad, and Zophar—hearing of Job's plight, come to visit him, hoping to offer consolation and advice. When they see him, they are so appalled by his suffering that for one week they merely sit with him in silence. The prose prologue of the book ends in this shared silence, precipitated by the depth of human suffering. Job has lost his children, his health, and his wealth, but he has retained his integrity; yet, during those seven days and nights of silence enormous questions emerge in his mind about God and justice.

The silence is broken by Job's terrible lament (chapter 3), in which he curses the day on which he was born. Better, he thinks not to have seen the light of day at his birth than to come to this sorry estate. But as Job breaks his silence, it gives license to his friends to speak. Each has advice to explain why it is that Job's life has come to this. The next major section of the book (chapters 4–31) contains three cycles of speeches; in each cycle, the three friends speak and Job responds to each (the third cycle is incomplete; whether the text has been damaged or whether the friends at last give up in exhaustion is not clear). The passage concludes with Job's summarizing his case and apparently casting down a challenge to God to face him and explain his ways (chapters 29–31). The substance of these speeches, both Job's and those of his friends, concerns human suffering and the ways of God to human beings. The advice of Job's companions, well-meant but not helpful, is rooted in a simplistic theology apparently derived from the tradition of Deuteronomy and that of Proverbs. The good person will be blessed, they argue, and the evil person will be cursed; from this they deduce that the reverse must also be true, namely that anybody who is suffering is being cursed and, therefore, must have done something wrong. Their advice to Job, boiled down to its essentials, is quite simple: If he would only confess his sin, or the sins of his children, he would be forgiven and restored to his former happy state.

The friendly advice, freely profferred, is not of great assistance to Job. His integrity is such that he will not confess to sins that he has not committed; yet, initially his theology and understanding of suffering do not seem too different from those of his companions. As the debate continues, we perceive a gradual change developing in Job's position; he is testing his theology against both his own experience and his observations of human life, and he finds it wanting. Why is it, for example, that if the good are blessed and the wicked cursed, the wicked in fact seem to prosper (21:7-16), while the righteous seem to suffer so much? In these and other words, Job gives voice to the universal questions of human existence which can find no simple solution to the problems of suffering and despair. Failing to find any solution to his problems in the long-winded speeches of his friends, Job's last hope (by the end of chapter 31) is that a confrontation with the Almighty might resolve his desperate dilemma. He suffers, but if God is truly just, then he can find no explanation for the magnitude of his suffering.

Just when, from a literary perspective, the reader might expect a resolution of the tension in Job's confrontation with God, there comes an anticlimax. Chapters 32–37 contain a lengthy speech from Elihu, who has not been mentioned earlier in the book. Now, Elihu is introduced as a young and learned man (perhaps the ancient equivalent of a graduate student), who has modestly held his peace while his elders debated, but as he listens, he becomes increasingly angry with both Job and his friends. When they finally shut up, Elihu chips in with his "ten cents' worth." He gives a long speech, some of it reflecting sound theology—though it rings of bookish knowledge, wisdom that has not really been absorbed into the understanding— yet Elihu, for all his merits, cannot resolve Job's problems. Indeed, when Elihu finishes at last his long discourse, Job does not respond.

The anticlimactic nature of Elihu's intervention has delayed the book's climax, which comes at last in the divine speeches in chapters 38–41. Addressing Job from the awesome eye of the whirlwind, God sets out before his servant the mysteries and magnificence of creation, indicating thereby the smallness and ignorance of a mortal man in the cosmic scheme of things. Then the divine speech, which began with the unlimited sweep of the universe, focuses on some of the smaller wonders of creation—the mountain goat, the ostrich, the horse—even these mundane things are mysteries ultimately beyond Job's power and understanding. Job, who had earlier been so anxious for this divine confrontation, now tries desperately to stop it (40:3-5), but he discovers that the God who granted the encounter will alone decide when it will end. Job, who through many chapters has demonstrated his capacity for speech, is at last rendered speechless by the divine demonstration.

The book concludes with two quite distinct sections. The first (42:1-6), still in poetry contains Job's verbal response to the divine speeches; they have created in him an awareness of both his own ignorance and of the mysteries inherent in God's creation, but above all Job is a changed man, having encountered the living God face to face. The second (42:7-17), written in prose, states that Job's fortune and family were restored, and that he lived happily to a ripe old age.

The academic study of the book of Job has focused on two separate, but inter-related areas. One of these areas is strictly literary, pertaining to the structure of the book in its extant form. The other pertains primarily to the meaning and interpretation of the book, both in literary and religious terms.

From a literary perspective, various difficulties have been raised. The prose form of the prologue/epilogue has suggested to many scholars that the story of Job had an origin independent of that of the dialogues contained in the poetic sections of the book (3:1–42:6). With respect to the prehistory of the book, it is perfectly possible that the unknown author took an ancient story about Job (reflected in the prologue/epilogue) and adapted it to his larger purpose; nevertheless, in the book's present form the prose and poetic portions are intimately inter-related, and the poetic debates presuppose a knowledge of the prose introduction. The difficulties concerning the sections in prose and poetry, therefore, pertain primarily to the book's prehistory rather than to its extant form. Another area of literary difficulty concerns the Elihu speeches (chapters 32–37); the manner of their insertion into the developing debate, the absence of reference to Elihu at the beginning of the story, and, indeed, the differing perspectives within the chapters have led many scholars to the conclusion that these chapters are a later addition to the original book of Job. Again, although an independent origin in the book's prehistory may be admitted, it is dangerous to label the Elihu speeches as secondary additions. Their removal takes away a feature of the extant book, namely the literary use of anticlimax to heighten the force of the climax when it finally comes. These are only a few of the literary difficulties in the study of Job, but the larger problems of interpretation are even more difficult.

In the interpretation of any great work of art, it is dangerous to claim "This is what it means" or "That is what it means." The imposition of a single interpretation on a work of artistic genius somehow shrivels its greatness and confines its universal appeal. It is better to approach the problem of interpretation on a broad front, identifying the book's principal themes and suggesting directions worthy of reflection. We cannot contain the meaning of Job; like all great works, it speaks in the same words to different people, conveying different levels of meaning and different degrees of enlightenment.

At first sight, the book appears to address the problems of human suffering, specifically undeserved suffering, or more specifically that kind of suffering for which no reason can be found. Thus the book begins with Job on trial; he suffers both physically and mentally, and the reader wonders whether he will have the courage and integrity to survive, and whether any explanation will be given. No sooner are we into the great debate than we realize it is not Job who is on trial, but God. What kind of God is it that can permit innocent persons to suffer so terribly? The atheist and the theist in this world may both suffer terribly, without any evident reason for their agony, but the theist—whose God is supposed to be just and merciful—may suffer the more profound spiritual agony. Is it really possible to believe in a God of justice in a world marked by such apparently unjust suffering? Or can one believe in a God of mercy, when human experience can be so painful and merciless? These kinds of questions raise, in turn, the matter of *creation*, one of the dominant themes running through the book of Job. If suffering without reason is the common human experience in the created world, just what kind of world has God created? Is it an orderly world, as the writer of Genesis suggests, or is it a world of chaos and meaningless pain, as Job's experience indicates?

The book of Job thus raises the most fundamental question of human existence: the issues of human life and suffering, the question about the character of the world in which we live, and the issues concerning the nature of God. These general questions are in a sense timeless, renewed from one generation to another, addressed by philosophers, theologians, novelists, artists, and others. But they are not merely questions of the mind; they are wrung out from the pain of human existence, whether in ancient Uz or modern Vietnam. The universality of the questions points to the timelessness of the book of Job and its perpetual relevance—answers are always sought for such questions. The book of Job offers no simple answers; at most it points in certain directions. One direction is that of religious experience. Although Job never had his dilemmas resolved, he was a changed man after his encounter with God; his awareness of God cast a different perspective on suffering, making it not so much irrelevant as secondary to his knowledge of God. Another direction is what might be called the "theology of mystery"; the wonders of creation revealed in the divine speeches mark not only the boundaries of human knowledge and understanding, but also the mysteries of the universe which will always lie beyond those boundaries. These are only a few of the directions in which the book points; reading and then re-reading this extraordinary work open up new vistas of understanding. But this much is clear—the homespun moral wisdom of Proverbs is supplemented in the book of Job by a more profound wisdom, which in turn understands the limitations of its own ability to perceive all the mysteries of human existence in this world.

(c) The Book of Ecclesiastes (Qoheleth)

The third of the Wisdom books, Ecclesiastes, is named after a person referred to in verse 1 as *Qoheleth*. The word is translated in most English Bibles as "preacher," which is the sense of the Greek title *Ecclesiastes*, but the Hebrew word is of uncertain meaning and occurs only in this book. The author is anonymous, and *Qoheleth* may be either a *nom de plume* or it may designate a position the author once held (not so much "preacher" as "public orator" may be implied by the Hebrew). We are also told that the author was "son of David, king of Jerusalem" (1:1); although in ancient times the rabbis interpreted these words to mean that Solomon was author of Ecclesiastes, few (if any) scholars would hold such a view nowadays. The author may have been a descendent of David's line, or more probably a member of the wisdom tradition that was named after Solomon, its patron and founder. Given the anonymity of the author, it follows that the date of the book must be uncertain. On the grounds of the language employed within the book, it is commonly assigned to the fourth century B.C., toward the end of the Old Testament period; however, as with the book of Job, a knowledge of the date is not essential to an appreciation of the book of Ecclesiastes.

Although the identity of the author cannot be established firmly, a number of inferences can be drawn about him from the substance of his book. It is possible that he was a teacher; this may be implied both by his title (*qoheleth*) and by his membership in the wisdom tradition—one of the responsibilities of that tradition was teaching. It is also very likely that the author, at the time of writing this book, was an old man; it reflects a kind of insight and understanding that is normally acquired only with the passage of years. The writer was also a man of reason, but not to the exclusion of faith. Reason dominates more in the thought of Ecclesiastes than it does in most other Old Testament writings.

The book which this unknown writer has left for us is not a conventional one. It does not have the inner coherence or sense of development that is to be found in the book of Job. It is, rather, a kind of notebook in which have been collected some of the thoughts and ideas of this teacher of wisdom from the ancient world. His thoughts on a variety of topics are recorded in the space of a few verses; sometimes the various musings are linked together thematically, but on other occasions there is no evident inter-connection between the short passages that comprise the book as a whole. A colleague or editor has preserved the book for posterity, adding a short introduction (1:1) and a postscript (12:9-14) to set the work in perspective.

The nature and format of the book of Ecclesiastes have made it in some ways a difficult book to read; it is one of those books which takes on greater significance when, after reading the whole two or three times, one returns to the individual passages and reflects on their meaning. Most readers, when they become familiar with the work, will recognize a certain affinity in the thought of Ecclesiastes. Robert Gordis, one of the most distinguished Jewish scholars of the twentieth century, has expressed well the significance of Ecclesiastes (*The Wisdom of Koheleth*, 1950, p. ix).

Whoever has dreamed great dreams in his youth and seen the vision flee, or has loved and lost, or has beaten barehanded at the fortress of injustice and come back bleeding and broken, has passed Koheleth's door, and tarried awhile beneath the shadow of his roof.

The experiences and thoughts of Ecclesiastes are not unique, but the writer had a gift of capturing them in words and recording them with insight, thus offering wisdom and advice to all others who walk the same difficult path through human life.

Both the world of nature and the world of human experience come within the purview of Ecclesiastes. When the writer observed the world of nature, it was not its beauty but the monotonous repetition of the cycles of nature which grasped his attention (1:4-8), indicating to him the weariness and vanity of all human existence. Observing the world of human affairs, he saw clearly that for all the talk of justice, it was injustice which prevailed; the oppressed continued in their oppression and the oppressors grew more powerful, so that the dead seemed frequently more blessed than those who remained alive (4:1-2). The writer of Ecclesiastes seems to have had a jaundiced eye, always penetrating the veneer of civilization and seeing beneath it the injustice, oppression, and sheer misery that characterize so much of human existence. His reason requires that he see the world as it is; he cannot succumb to the temptation of faith to see the world as it might be. In seeing the world only as it is, life itself became at times hateful to him (2:17), evoking the melancholy refrain of the book: "all is vanity."

This somewhat negative summary of the teacher's musings raises the question of whether he had anything positive to contribute. He had, at first glance, only a little of positive worth to contribute. It was a kind of reductionist theology—(i) He continued to hold to the existence of God, even though there seemed to be little evidence that God was just or good. (ii) He affirmed the legitimacy of seeking a little joy in life, even though the joy of youth would soon be offset by the rigours of old age (11:7–12:8).

It quickly becomes clear to the reader of Ecclesiastes that the book is not only unusual, but also is unorthodox; the question is raised as to why a book such as this was preserved in the biblical canon. (Its inclusion in the canon was, incidentally, a matter of extensive debate). The melancholy skepticism of Ecclesiastes does not at first fit harmoniously with the more cheerful optimisim of Proverbs or with the grand hope of the Hebrew prophets. On the other hand, the thought of Ecclesiastes, though quite different from that of Job, is of a similar sort, and one suspects that had the writer of Ecclesiastes been one of Job's companions, though he could have offered no solutions, he could have offered consolation. Job and the writer of Ecclesiastes had both seen, in their distinctive fashions, something of the misery that human life can bring. Neither would cloak misery in a veil of piety, but faced it head on and described it as it was. Job grappled with human suffering, Ecclesiastes with radical doubt and skepticism, and both protested a quick acceptance of the wisdom of Proverbs—it was not that they rejected the simple moral wisdom of Proverbs; they recognized that, by itself, it was inadequate. Proverbs needed deeper dimensions and more rigor if the young person weaned on proverbial wisdom was to have the strength to face all the harsh realities that human life can bring.

Thus, although in some ways Ecclesiastes can be seen as a protest against the simpler wisdom of Proverbs, in reality it provides more of a supplementary diet. One does not take penicillin except to combat certain forms of illness; one does not always need Ecclesiastes except when the virus of doubt or skepticism attacks the organism of faith. The book thus became a part of the arsenal of wisdom, its contents offering understanding and reinforcement in times of crisis. But like the book of Job, Ecclesiastes does not offer simple solutions to the problems of life and faith which it addresses; rather, it offers consolation and insight of an intellectual kind from one who has seen the world in its harshest realities, and yet has clung through thick and thin to a slender faith.

THE
WRITINGS (II):
OTHER BOOKS

T HE remaining books of the Writings are not examined in any particular order. Although they all belong to the third section of the Hebrew canon, they appear in English Bibles interspersed between the various books of the Former and the Latter Prophets. They vary enormously with respect to style and content—some are poetic in form while others are prose, some are concerned with history while others are closer to prophecy. Despite the variety in these remaining books of the Writings, they contribute to a fuller understanding of the rich panorama of ancient Israel's life and literature.

Five of the books in the Writings were conventionally grouped together in later Judaism and referred to as the *Five Scrolls,* or *Megilloth.* Each of these books was associated with the celebration of a particular Jewish festival. The Song of Songs was associated with the Festival of Passover, Ruth with the Festival of Weeks, Lamentations with the commemoration of the destruction of Jerusalem (the "Ninth of Ab"), Ecclesiastes (a wisdom book already examined in chapter 8), with the Festival of Tabernacles, and Esther with the celebration of Purim. These associations with festivals are for the most part later developments   and,   with   the   exception   of   Esther,   do not represent either an original intent or a particular literary characteristic of the books as such. (Although Esther, as we shall see, was associated from the beginning with the celebration of Purim, and a less certain association may also apply to the book of Lamentations.)

1. The Book of Ruth

For all its brevity, the book of Ruth is one of the most charming volumes in the Writings. As is the case with so many biblical books, Ruth is an anonymous work, and the ancient tradition that it was written by Samuel has little to commend it. Nor is the date on which this little book was written known, though its style of Hebrew prose might suggest some point in the history of the Hebrew monarchy, perhaps between the ninth and seventh centuries B.C. The lack of information concerning the author and date of writing do not detract in any way from the appeal of the book. It has been described with respect to genre in various ways—it may be a short story, a novella, or perhaps even a historical novel. Although the story is set in a distinct historical period, the time of the judges, and although it concerns real persons, its goal is not primarily historical. Through the beautiful telling of a simple story, certain timeless truths concerning Israel's faith emerge for the edification of the reader.

A married couple, Elimelech and Naomi, emigrate from Judah during a time of famine, taking with them their two sons. They settle down and start a new life east of the Jordan Valley in the land of Moab, but soon Elimelech dies. Naomi remains as a widow in Moab with her two sons, who marry Moabite wives, Orpah and Ruth (after whom the book is named). After ten years, the two sons die, and Naomi is left with her daughters-in-law. She is essentially an alien in a foreign land. She returns to Judah, taking with her Ruth, and there the main plot of the story develops. It concerns the devotion of Ruth for her mother-in-law, her marriage to a kinsman of her former husband, Boaz, and the birth of a child, who was named Obed. The development of the story presupposes some knowledge of ancient Hebrew customs, specifically those concerning the redemption and inheritance of land and the responsibility of relatives toward the childless widow of a deceased member of the family. Although these traditions are known only from other portions of the Old Testament, the story is sufficiently self-contained to reveal its general sense even to the reader with little background knowledge.

From a literary perspective, the story of Ruth and Naomi is a work of art and forms a unity in its present form. Only the concluding verses (4:17b-20) have been added by some subsequent editor to set the story in a larger and perhaps more significant context. The primary purpose of the story was to entertain and to edify. As entertainment, it is beautifully told, with economy of words and gradual development of the plot toward the climax. As a means of edification, it operates on two levels, presenting both the exemplary life and a dimension of theological insight. There are no human villains in Ruth; hardship is precipitated only by nature (famine) and by death. But the characters in the story reveal the best faces of humanity. In Naomi and Ruth we perceive the graces of fortitude, faithfulness in human relationships, and loving-kindness. Beyond the exemplary behavior of the human beings, a theological understanding of life's vicissitudes is revealed. The troubles which befall Naomi and Ruth, especially in bereavement, are a part of the mystery of God's ways with human beings. But ultimately beyond the experience of grief and hardship, the courage of Naomi and Ruth is rewarded with blessing. At last, in the birth of a son to Ruth, praise is rendered to God who made such a blessing possible (4:14). This book does not reveal the profound theological wrestling with grief that is reflected in the chapters of Job, but it contains a more homespun theology, a recognition of the value of fortitude and the ultimate mercy of God toward the faithful.

The short appendix to the book (4:17b-20) takes the original story and sets it in a national context. Ruth's son, Obed, was later to become the father of Jesse, who in turn became the father of (King) David. In this new context, the story indicates the providence of God and the working out of the divine plan through the faithfulness of individual persons, even though those persons had no knowledge of the greater goals which would be achieved through their simple faith.

2. The Song of Songs

The full title of this book is "The Song of Songs, Which is Solomon's"; hence, it is sometimes referred to as the Song of Solomon. The expression *Song of Songs* is an example of the manner in which the superlative is expressed in Hebrew—it means "the very best of songs." Whereas the first part of the title is clear, the second part is ambiguous. It could mean "which was written by Solomon," and indeed early Jewish and Christian tradition affirmed the Solomonic authorship of this book. But it could also be translated "which is for Solomon" (in the sense of dedicated to Solomon). As we shall see, the latter sense is more probable.

The eight chapters of the Song of Songs are written entirely in poetry. As one reads the chapters, a couple of unusual characteristics emerge. First, despite the fact that this is a biblical book, there is no mention of God in these eight chapters; they appear to be *secular,* to use a modern term. Second, when read at surface value, the chapters of this little book seem to contain only the verses of romantic poetry; they are neither religious nor nationalistic in theme, and this again may seem curious in a biblical book. The Song of Songs contains the poetry of human love; it ranges from the emotions of lovers to the beauty of the human body in the eyes of a lover, and it taps the beauty of the natural world and its seasons in giving expression to love.

The distinctive character of the Song of Songs has given rise to a certain ambivalence toward it in both Jewish and Christian tradition. Within Judaism its place in the canon was hotly contested, and though it secured a firm place in the Writings, the debate over its eligibility indicates the uncertainty existing in the minds of many as to why such a book should be included in the canon of Scripture. Within early Christianity, the presence of this little book in the canon was the source of considerable anxiety and embarrassment to many of the distinguished leaders of the church. Jerome (fourth–fifth centuries A.D.) preferred young people to confine their reading to the historical writings of the Old Testament lest they be led astray by the substance of the Song of Songs. Origen suggested that nobody read it until first they had "ceased to feel the passion of bodily nature," which on reflection amounts to banning the book completely.

Given this anxiety about the nature and substance of the Song of Songs, it is not surprising that there has been both debate and diversity in the matter of the book's interpretation. One of the oldest theories of interpretation, beginning in early Judaism and adopted with modification in Christianity, is that the Song of Songs should be interpreted as an *allegory.* In Judaism, the description of the love of a young man for a young woman was interpreted as an allegory of

God's love for Israel. Thus where the Song of Songs says "My beloved is mine and I am his" (2:16), the rabbis pointed to a deeper meaning: "Israel says: He is my God and I am his people." For Christianity, a similar approach was taken, though now the allegory concerned the love of Christ for the church. (Remnants of the Christian allegorical interpretation may still be seen in the chapter summaries printed in early editions of the Authorized Version, or King James Bible. Thus the summary of chapter 1 begins: "1. The Church's love unto Christ; 5. She confesseth her deformity; 7. and prayeth to be directed to his flock. . . ." Needless to say, the text makes reference neither to Christ nor the church!)

From the perspective of the history of Jewish and Christian interpretation, the allegorical theory is important, not least because it played a role in the acceptance of the book into the canon of Scripture. In literary and historical terms, the theory is far from satisfactory. The text itself contains no explicit clues to indicate that it was written as allegory or that its author or editor intended it to be read as allegory. Indeed, there is ancient evidence for alternative approaches to interpretation. Rather than allegory, some ancient interpreters viewed the Song of Songs as a *drama*. The dramatic theory takes as its starting point the observation that the Song of Songs is constructed from a series of speeches—or words of "actors"—and considers that the text was once the script for a play. The ancient evidence for this view is found in one of the early Greek translations of the Hebrew text (*Codex Sinaiticus*), in which headings were inserted into the text: "the bride speaks to the maidens . . . the bridegroom speaks to the bride. . . ." (The modern survival of the theory can be seen in some contemporary translations of the Bible, for example, the *New English Bible*.) For all its antiquity, there are numerous difficulties with the dramatic theory of interpretation. Drama was not an art form of either the biblical or the ancient Near Eastern world (though it was in the Greek world). Even more troublesome for the dramatic theory is the absence of a clear story line in the Song of Songs. Numerous moving stories have been "discovered" in the text by various commentators on the Song, most of them quite different from each other, but these stories are not easy to detect without the aid of the commentator! It is safest to conclude that there is no story line unifying the eight chapters of the Song of Songs and that the dramatic theory has little to commend it.

The dissatisfaction with the allegorical and dramatic theories of interpretation has led to a multitude of other approaches in modern times. Of the various approaches to interpretation currently held, the most probable is that which maintains that the Song of Songs must be viewed as an anthology of love poetry from ancient Israel. The biblical analogies for such anthologies are numerous; just as the book of Psalms is an anthology of Israel's hymns and prayers, or the book of Proverbs is an anthology of Israel's wisdom, so too the Song of Songs is an anthology of love poetry, or romantic poetry, from ancient Israel. There are also analogies from the biblical world that are provided by the texts recovered in archaeological explorations. Numerous love songs, secular in form, have been recovered from the civilizations of ancient Egypt and Mesopotamia. Love poetry in the ancient world as well as the modern was a common literary genre.

In the study of the Song of Songs as an anthology, one of the difficulties is that of determining the boundaries of the poems in the collection. Although scholars differ in the analysis of some texts, it is agreed that there are approximately thirty songs or poems in the collection as a whole. The poems are different in kind, reflecting the many faces and dimensions of human love. There are poems of longing and those of fulfillment, poems in praise of the loved one and those in praise of love itself; some of the songs celebrate love's joy, whereas others depict its sorrow and occasional desolation.

An appropriate starting point for reading the Song of Songs is to recognize the book for what it is: a collection of love poetry. In reading the songs which comprise the whole, we will recognize both the book's antiquity and its sense of timelessness. The antiquity and cultural background from which the book emerge are reflected in the words, for the language and imagery of ancient love poetry differ in many ways from the modern forms of poetry with which we are familiar. The expression of love between a man and a woman is essentially timeless, and the beautiful notes struck in this ancient song have not lost their charm in the twentieth century.

Once one has recognized that the Song of Songs is an anthology, however, it is necessary to return to the theory of its being an allegory. It has been argued that neither the poems nor the anthology reflect any allegorical intent on the part of the original authors or editor. Yet, it is a fact that the place of the Song of Songs in the canon was secured in part on the basis of the allegorical theory. There is a further important point to be stressed; the songs of human love could not serve as an allegory of God's love for Israel unless human love itself was recognized as a beautiful and God-given thing. In the modern world we tend to distinguish between the secular and the sacred; the Song of Songs as an anthology is secular, whereas as an allegory it becomes sacred. Yet, with respect to ancient Israel, the secular/sacred distinction is not altogether satisfactory. Since life itself was the gift of God, human love between a man and a woman could equally be celebrated as a God-given gift. It was, in a sense, the sacredness of human love that made it so appropriate a medium, at a later date, to convey an understanding of God's love for his people.

Just when this anthology of love poetry was compiled is not known. Some of the poems may have been written early in the centuries of the Hebrew kingdoms, others later, perhaps during and after the exile. Then some unknown person or persons compiled the collection that has survived. It is a testament both to the value and sanctity of human love and to the insight which might be gained from the experience of love—God's love and the love a person may have for God.

3. Lamentations

Undoubtedly the greatest crisis faced by the Hebrew people during the biblical period was the fall of Jerusalem and the destruction of its temple in 586 B.C. The events themselves were a terrible experience of horror and tragedy, permanently scarring the lives of those who endured them, but more than that, the disastrous turn of events called into question the very foundations of Israel's faith. How could such events happen? Could there be a future for the chosen people beyond the desolation of Jerusalem? Had the ancient religion of Israel also died in the ruins of Jerusalem's temple? The awful events of 586 B.C. called forth not only grief but also reflection. The survivors had to face a question to which there was no easy answer: Was there a future for the chosen people, or had the preceding centuries of faith and hope culminated at last in a dead end?

The little book of Lamentations is one of several documents from the sixth century B.C. that gives us some insight into the manner in which the Hebrews attempted to cope with this turning point in their history. Its author is not known, for the book plunges directly into its subject matter, which is appropriately designated by the title in

English Bibles, *Lamentations.* There is an ancient tradition that Jeremiah was the author of this book; this belief goes back to a reference to that prophet's "lament" in II Chronicles 35:25. Hence, in English Bibles Lamentations follows Jeremiah. While we need not doubt that Jeremiah composed his laments, we can have no certainty that there was any connection between that distinguished prophet and the book of Lamentations. It is safest simply to accept the text at face value and recognize its anonymous character.

The book contains five poems, each poem corresponding to the five chapters of the English translation. The first four chapters have a distinctive literary form; they are written as alphabetic acrostic poems in which the successive verses begin with words employing in sequence the letters of the Hebrew alphabet. (There are similar kinds of poems in the psalms; see chapter 8, section 1 *e.*) The fifth poem (5:1-22), though not an acrostic, contains nevertheless the same number of verses as there are letters in the ancient alphabet, suggesting that its composition was dictated by concerns similar to those lying behind the other poems. Sometimes, as in the case of certain psalms, the acrostic form is used as a device to assist learning and memorization, but such a purpose is unlikely in the Book of Lamentations. It is more probable that here the alphabetic acrostic represents, in literary form, the completeness of suffering and grief from alpha to omega, from A to Z.

Within the overall alphabetic acrostic structure, the poet has employed various other literary and liturgical forms to convey the force of the words. In chapters 1, 2, and 4, for example, there are the overtones of funereal language, echoes of the kinds of dirges uttered at the open grave of one who has died. Chapter 3, on the other hand, is similar to the individual laments so common in the book of Psalms, in which a personal expression of grief is illuminated from time to time with resurgent hope in God's ultimate goodness and mercy. Chapter 5 is similar to the communal lament, in which an entire congregation, engaged in worship, gives expression to its grief and sorrow.

The sense of immediacy which permeates the poems as a whole suggests that the majority of them were written soon after the events that precipitated the mourning. The intensity of the grief, on the one hand, and the vivid illustrations of Jerusalem's plight, on the other, point to an author still living with the memory of the smoke and stench of warfare. Though one cannot be precise in dating a work such as this, a period of composition within a decade or so of the year 586 B.C. is most likely.

The permanent value of the book can be seen against the backdrop of its times. Many people, reflecting upon the wreckage of Jerusalem and its temple, must have abandoned hope and faith; the poet of Lamentations can abandon neither. Although God is recognized as the author of judgment, he is also the one to whom the poet turns in desperation. Although the wrath of God hangs over the devastated city like a dark cloud, the poet refuses to see only wrath: "The Lord is good to those who wait for him" (3:25). The morning after destruction is overcast with the onset of despair, but the poet can but affirm that "his mercies never come to an end; they are new every morning; great is thy faithfulness" (3:22-23). Like fresh flowers springing up on the blackened field of battle, the poet's hope cannot be totally crushed by his load of lamentation. So we see in the book of Lamentations not only the black despair and grief that marked the end of one era in Israel's history, but also the seeds of hope from which eventually a new age was to flower.

4. The Book of Esther

The book of Esther is named after one of the key characters in the story that it tells. The book contains no information about its author, nor can there be certainty as to the date of its writing. The story, nevertheless, can be set in the early decades of the fifth century B.C. (around 485–465 B.C.), and its geographical setting is Susa, a city in Persia in which the royal family maintained a winter palace.

The story is one of intrigues and plots within the royal domain of King Ahasuerus (possibly Xerxes I, as he is more commonly known). Esther, a young Jewish girl, became queen following the deposition of Queen Vashti. Through her position and influence in the royal household, Esther was able to be of assistance to her cousin, Mordecai, and to her fellow Jewish exiles living in Persia. The plot focuses on the ambitions of Haman, a Persian nobleman whose drive for power and promotion led him to plot the death of Mordecai and all the other Jews resident in the Persian provinces. By means of Esther's intervention with the king, Mordecai turned the plot onto Haman; the nobleman's execution was accompanied by the slaughter of thousands of Persians, who had planned to attack the Jews.

Having recognized that a story provides the central focus of the book of Esther, there remains the difficulty of determining the literary genre of the book as a whole. There are some who would argue that the book is essentially a historical volume, depicting a chapter in the history of the eastern community of Jews living in Persia a century after the beginning of the exile. On the other hand, many scholars propose that the book of Esther (like the book of Ruth) should be interpreted as a short story or historical novel. The evidence in support of either theory is ambiguous. Certainly the writer knew a good deal about life and customs in the Persian court, and the work has a general air of authenticity about it; on the interpretation of this evidence, however, it has been observed that both history and the historical novel should be characterized by realism and a thorough knowledge of the setting. Though it is difficult to come to a firm hypothesis, the weight of the evidence is normally taken to lead to the view that the book is a short story. It is historical in the sense that it reflects an authentic Persian setting and the tension and danger of persecution under which the Jews of the exile lived perpetually. Within this authentic framework a story has been told to convey a message and an understanding of certain issues that are crucial to its readers.

There are a number of distinctive characteristics about the story and the final editorial form in which it is preserved. First, like the Song of Songs, there is no explicit reference to God anywhere in the ten chapters of Esther. This is curious not only in a biblical book (which we expect to be "religious"), but also in a book which has such a strong nationalistic theme as does Esther. As a consequence, in part, of this lack of reference to God, the book of Esther is one of those few books whose right to a place in the biblical canon was strongly contested (its place in the canon was also questioned in that it authorized the celebration of a festival not mentioned in the Law of Moses). Although the place of Esther in the canon was affirmed relatively early in Judaism, its place in the Christian canon continued to be debated and its final acceptance was not secured until the fourth century A.D. Centuries later, Martin Luther expressed the wish that neither Esther nor II Maccabees had ever come into existence. In part, the apprehensions about the book were evoked by the account of the slaughter of more than seventy-five thousand Persians, followed by a "day of feasting and gladness" (9:17) celebrated by the perpetrators of this slaughter.

Although the book of Esther does not make any mention of God, it does have an explicitly religious purpose. In 9:20-32, which has the role of an appendix to the book, the explicit purpose of the story is specified. The story served to establish and to authorize the subsequent celebration within the Jewish religion of the Festival of Purim. This festival, no where referred to in the Law of Moses, is given its stuff and substance in the story of Esther. It is a time of joy, of the exchanging of gifts, and of the celebration of freedom from oppression. In the course of the celebration, from ancient times into the present century, the story of Esther is told and retold to each generation. Whether it recounts historical events giving rise to the festival, or whether it was created to give meaning to an already existing festival must remain for the moment the subject of scholarly debate. Likewise the date on which the story was written must remain uncertain; it was probably composed in Persia during the fourth or third centuries B.C., thus is one of the latest books added to the Old Testament.

Despite the secular nature of the story and the uncertainties attached to its value from an early date, it is not without its interest in understanding the development of Judaism and the perennial issues which have been the focus of Jewish thought through the centuries. On the one hand it reveals the survival of a distinct Jewish community in an alien land and culture; the Jews in this story, despite a century of separation from their homeland, retained their identity. On the other hand, the story reveals a dimension of Jewish experience which has characterized their history from the time of ancient Persia to modern times; though the Jewish people retained their identity, they were always vulnerable to attack and persecution. From Haman in Persia to Hitler in Europe, there have arisen over the centuries those who have threatened the survival of the Jewish people. In Esther, the Persian *pogrom* was averted by nationalistic spirit and militaristic activism; yet, it is not this activism which is highlighted in the concluding verses, which establish the continuing celebration of Purim. Rather, the author (or editor) highlights the joy of human liberation, the necessity of remembering a day that was turned "from sorrow into gladness and from mourning into a holiday" (9:22). The book is at once a reminder of the ever-present threat of the persecution of one group of people by another and of the importance of freedom if human life is to be lived with any kind of joy.

5. The Book of Daniel

For the modern reader, the book of Daniel is surely one of the most curious and puzzling books of the entire Old Testament. It is, in its opening chapters, entertaining reading, but much of the substance of the book is taken up with various dreams and their interpretations. The dreams are vivid in their symbolism and substance, but the interpretations do not immediately make their meanings clear. The complexity of the dream-like quality of much of this book is compounded by a further difficulty that is not immediately evident to the reader of the English Bible—it is bilingual. The book begins (1:1–2:4a) and closes (chapters 8–12) in the Hebrew language, but the middle section is written in Aramaic (2:4b–7:28).

The book is made up of two principal parts; it should be noted that the two parts are not coterminous with the linguistic divisions of the book. Part one (chapters 1–6) contains stories written in a third person narrative about Daniel, and his companions. Part two (chapters 7–12) principally contains an account of various visions experienced by Daniel and their interpretations. In chronological terms, however, part two does not follow part one; the visions of part two are interspersed from a chronological perspective at various points in the narrative contained in part one. The book has, therefore, a double-layered character; the initial narrative in part one provides an overall framework for the quite different substance of part two.

Taken at face value, the stories in the first part of the book pertain to a young Hebrew man named Daniel who, with his companions, was taken into Babylonian exile in 605 B.C. some years before the main exile which followed the destruction of Jerusalem in 586 B.C. The stories do not contain a comprehensive history of Daniel's experiences in exile, but relate a series of incidents taking place over several decades beginning in the Babylonian period of the exile and extending to the Persian period (mid-sixth century B.C.). The stories all have a moral and religious flavor to them, exemplifying the wisdom and courage of Daniel and his friends. Despite pressures to conform to local eating customs in Babylon, the young exiles courageously stick to their Jewish dietary laws. Daniel, through God-given wisdom, is able to interpret Nebuchadnezzar's mysterious dreams. Daniel's companions, refusing to participate in idolatry, are cast into a fiercely blazing furnace, but are miraculously rescued by God. Daniel, refusing to abandon the integrity of his faith, is thrown into a den of lions, but again is rescued by the divine aid. In these and other stories in the first part of the book, the writer has portrayed the courage, integrity, and righteousness that typified the behavior of these Hebrew heroes of the exile.

The second part of the book contains an account of Daniel's visions; they are written in the first person form as if taken from a diary or autobiographical statement. The scope of the visions with their somewhat obscure interpretations ranges from the immediate future (when viewed from the sixth century perspective in which the story is set) to a more distant future which incorporates the end of historical time. The imagery is principally that of various beasts and particular animals (ram, goat) which symbolize the kings and kingdoms of human history.

The interpretation of Daniel is extremely complex and fraught with difficulties of all kinds. The debate over the book of Daniel includes both technical questions of a literary and historical kind and issues of a religious nature pertaining to the contemporary relevance of the book. The initial problems faced by the reader are those of the date and authorship of this curious work and the related matters of its literary genre and its bilingual character. In respect to authorship, it must be noted immediately that the book in its present form is anonymous; in this it is typical of many biblical books, as we have already noted. The first person narrative of the second part of the book, however, and the statement that Daniel "wrote down the dream" (7:1) have suggested to many interpreters that Daniel should be considered the author of the book. To this it can be responded that no claim for Daniel's authorship is made at the beginning of the book, the conventional place for such statements, and that the first person character of part two may be related more to issues of literary genre than to the matter of the authorship of the book as a whole. Given the absence of explicit evidence, it is safest to recognize from the outset that we are dealing once again with an anonymous work.

The question of the date at which the book was written is even more complex. The older tradition within Judaism and Christianity maintained that the book was written in the period, or shortly thereafter, reflected in the narrative itself—the sixth century B.C.. A number of conservative scholars continue to champion this view. On the other hand, the majority of biblical scholars claim that the book was written (or at least reached its final form) in the second century B.C. in the period of around 167–164 B.C. The technical evidence for dating is complex, pertaining in part to the nature of the Hebrew and Aramaic languages employed in the book, the presence of Persian and Greek loan words in the Aramaic, and other related matters. (Such technical data are always subject to debate and difference of opinion, but the initial implication of the linguistic evidence might suggest a period later than the sixth century but earlier than the second century, thus not clearly supporting either of the polarized positions in the current debate!)

The debate over the date of Daniel has, in the minds of some interpreters, become an issue of theological significance, not merely a scholarly matter. The dreams of Daniel, if taken as sixth century productions, clearly and accurately predict the course of Near Eastern history down to the middle of the second century B.C. (at least), and are a testimony to the accuracy of God's special revelation to Daniel. On the other hand, it is precisely the concurrence between the substance of the visions and the actual history of the Near East which compels other interpreters to claim that the visions must have been written after the events they describe. When the debate moves into this context, the interpretation of Daniel has become for some a touchstone of orthodoxy and religious faith. Within Christianity, for example, a nineteenth century English scholar, E. B. Pusey, ventured to suggest that the entire validity of the Christian religion depends upon the sixth century dating of Daniel! To place the book later, Pusey claimed, would be to render false the entire substance of Daniel's "predictions." We can see in this example a perennial difficulty in the study of Daniel—it has not always been easy for the book's interpreters to maintain a dispassionate stance in the interpretation of the evidence. It may help, in retaining perspective, to recall that the writer of this book did not see fit to specify the date at which it was written, and this observation warns against the elevation of minor issues to major proportions. The essence of the issue of the book's dating can be summarized as follows: The book does not clearly specify the date of its writing, the internal evidence is complex, the majority of modern scholars date the book at a later period (second century B.C.); therefore, a firm dating of the book remains debatable and difficult.

For all the difficulty of dating the book and the debate that has raged around the question, there is in fact a prior question to be solved, one that is equally complex: *What kind of book is Daniel? To what literary genre does it belong?* The location of the book in English Bibles (between the major and minor prophets) tends to imply to the reader that Daniel is a *prophetic* book, similar to Ezekiel and Jeremiah. Within Judaism and Christianity, this initial impression may be reinforced by other data—in a scroll fragment from Qumran, in the writings of the Jewish historian Josephus, and in the New Testament (Matthew 24:15), Daniel is called a "prophet." However, as we have already noted, the book of Daniel is not included in the second division of the canon, the *Prophets,* but in the third division, the *Writings.* Within the book of Daniel, the hero is *not* referred to as a prophet, nor are his life and work similar to those of the biblical prophets. Thus, although from the perspective of later Jewish and Christian tradition, Daniel was viewed as a kind of prophet, the book named after him makes no prophetic claims. This, in turn, impinges on the debate, noted above, concerning Daniel's "prophetic predictions." If he were not a prophet, at least in the strict Old Testament sense, one should be careful about labelling his visions as prophetic or predictive.

If the book of Daniel is not prophetic literature in the normal sense, then what is it? Most scholars would agree that the book of Daniel is an example of *apocalyptic literature.* We have already observed instances of an apocalyptic flavoring in the prophetic writings (for example, Zechariah in the Book of the Twelve Prophets), but Daniel is the only Old Testament book which can be properly classified as apocalyptic (along with certain post-biblical Jewish works, such as Enoch, and the Revelation of St. John in the New Testament). To describe a book as *apocalyptic,* however, is not to suggest that it belongs to a distinctive literary *genre;* apocalyptic writings differ considerably with respect to format and style, but exhibit certain commonalities of substance and religious thought.

Although no single definition of apocalyptic has been accepted, there are certainly clearly defined characteristics of apocalyptic thought and literature. It involves a way of understanding time and history, with particular reference to the future; although rooted in a particular historical present, it portrays the unfolding of the future within the divine scheme of things. This notion of future history is characterized in many ways by a kind of *determinism*—history does not simply unfold as a consequence of human actions (which is more the emphasis in the prophetic writings), but has in some mysterious fashion been pre-determined by God. Apocalyptic thought is also characterized by *dualism*, an awareness of the eternal conflict between good and evil which is experienced in the present and projected into the future. The resolution of this dualism is to be found in the constant affirmation of the ultimate conquest of the forces of evil by those of good. This resolution is portrayed in terms of human nations, representing human and cosmic evil, aspiring for conquest and victory, but eventually being defeated by the power of God. The language of apocalyptic literature, given its futurity, is necessarily opaque and mysterious, thus draws richly on the strange and sometimes grotesque substance of visions and esoteric symbolism.

From perspectives of these kinds, it is clear that in general terms Daniel can be categorized as apocalyptic. As an example of apocalyptic literature, the book is inevitably difficult to interpret; the rich tapestry of symbolic language and vision is always more prone to understanding by those of an artistic and symbolic turn of mind than it is to the technical scholar or literalist interpreter. One suspects that the very mystery inherent in all apocalyptic writing is a reason for the associated difficulties of determining the book's author and date. In a book which consciously attempts to break the shackles of immediate time and space, inevitably the data beloved by the modern historian will be hard to pin down. We do not grasp the book's relevance by fighting the battles of historical criticism; eventually, the message of this book is revealed to those who would attempt to share its author's vision. We must be careful, too, to avoid the millenarian tendencies of modern times. The book of Daniel is not a "prophetic timetable" of either the ancient world or the twentieth and twenty-first centuries, as some would have us believe. But it does convey a vision which at once embraces human history and divine providence. It affirms a hope, rooted in faith, that the chaos of the present world is not also the culmination of human history; there remains eventually a new world in which God's good shall triumph. Such a hope, whether in Daniel's time or our own, is clearly not a logical deduction for one who observes the progress of history. It is, rather, a prism of faith through which the harsh realities of contemporary history can be observed and which offers some ground for hope in a better future. In the last resort, the future as the apocalyptists viewed it was in the hands of God.

6. Ezra-Nehemiah, I and II Chronicles

The four books referred to in the subtitle of this section are actually two books in the ancient Hebrew canon of Scripture. The first, Ezra-Nehemiah, was only subdivided into the two separate books which now appear in most English Bibles at a late date and, as we shall see, the division is somewhat artificial. The two books of Chronicles were also a single volume originally, as were I and II Samuel and I and II Kings in the Former Prophets; the division into two provides units of more manageable length. In the Hebrew canon, Ezra-Nehemiah precede I–II Chronicles, even though in historical terms the narrative in Ezra-Nehemiah is recognized as following that of I–II Chronicles. Although there is a continuing debate about the relationship between these books, most scholars agree that they belong to a common literary tradition which might be called the "school of the chronicler" or the "Chronistic Historical Tradition."

(a) I–II Chronicles

The initial impression given by the books of Chronicles is that they duplicate material in the Law and the Prophets, especially the historical narratives in Samuel and Kings. There is indeed a degree of duplication, although the particular emphases and insights of Chronicles are distinct from those of the prophetic historical tradition. The Chronicles contain a sweeping view of history extending from Adam to the return of the Hebrews to the promised land in the sixth century B.C., but this massive scope is in fact more restricted than at first it might appear.

The survey begins with a series of genealogies beginning with Adam and the first humans and extending as far as the family of the first Hebrew king, Saul (I Chronicles 1–9). These chapters are heavy reading for one who has little interest in ancient genealogies, and between the long lists of names only a few brief scraps of general information emerge. The character of the book changes radically in the next section (I Chronicles 10–29), in which the history of the monarchy from the time of Saul's death to the time of David's death is told in some detail. In II Chronicles, the first part of the book is devoted to an account of the reign of King Solomon (1–9), and in the remainder of the book (10–36) the story of Judah is traced through the period of the monarchy to the exile; it concludes with the beginning of the return from exile.

For all the duplication in Chronicles, the author has given distinctive character to the work by using both emphases and omissions. The themes which are emphasized include David and the Davidic kingship, the importance of Jerusalem, and the significance of proper worship in the temple in Jerusalem. There is also an individualistic theme in these narratives; individuals who are obedient to God and obey his law prosper, whereas those who do not suffer. The chronicler is not in the least interested in the northern tribes after the disruption of the Kingdom at Solomon's death; he traces the history of the chosen people in Judah under the Davidic kings and ignores the fate of the northern state of Israel.

The chronicler is the kind of historical writer who not only drew upon ancient sources, but also made constant references to the works from which he drew his material. There are frequent references, for example, to the "book of the Kings of Judah and Israel" (for example, II Chronicles 16:11; 25:26; 28:26; 32:32); numerous references are also made to various ancient prophetic works which no longer survive independently, such as the "Words of Nathan the Prophet" (II Chronicles 9:29). Despite the multiplicity of such references, it is clear that a basic source for the chronicler's works was the historical tradition of the Former Prophets; at many points there are word for word similarities between I–II Chronicles and the books of Samuel and Kings. The similarities in narrative, however, are ultimately distinguished in the chronicler's work by the particular historical and theological framework in which they are set.

Just when the Chronicles were written is not known, though traditionally it is argued that they should be dated to the fourth or third centuries B.C. But it is exceptionally difficult to date a work in which there is such extensive use of ancient sources, as is the case with Chronicles. There is a tendency nowadays to argue for a relatively early date for the composition of Chronicles, at least in a "first draft" form; the basic work may have been compiled by about 515 B.C. But if the book were indeed as early as this, then it is important to see it as a part of the "Chronistic Tradition,"and that same tradition over the next century and a half was to have a hand in the production of Ezra-Nehemiah.

(b) Ezra-Nehemiah

The narrative of Chronicles is consciously resumed in Ezra-Nehemiah; indeed, the closing verses of Chronicles (II Chronicles 36:22-24) are repeated in the opening verses of Ezra (1:1-3), suggesting either an artificial division between the books (the last chapter of Chronicles ends in the middle of a sentence!), or a conscious editorial attempt to link them together. Ezra-Nehemiah breaks new ground, carrying forward the story of the chosen people beyond not only the chronicler, but also the narrative in II Kings.

Ezra resumes the historical narrative with an account of the return of many Jews from exile and the beginning of the work of restoring the destroyed temple in Jerusalem. It does not provide a comprehensive history, but focuses on particular events of significance for the newly emerging tradition of Judaism—the reforms of Ezra (Ezra 7–10), Nehemiah's rebuilding of the walls of Jerusalem (Nehemiah 1–7), the reading of the Book of Law under Ezra's direction, and other aspects of the work of Nehemiah (Nehemiah 8–13). The historical focus of these narratives is the latter half of the fifth century B.C., though there are numerous difficulties for the historian in reconstructing the precise sequence of events (see further chapter 10: The History of Israel).

As with the Chronicles, the book of Ezra-Nehemiah has drawn explicitly on various ancient historical sources. Principal among these are the "Memoirs of Ezra" and the "Memoirs of Nehemiah," which have not survived independently. In addition, the author has made use of various official documents and letters, giving the work as a whole the ring of authenticity—various Persian decrees and documents are referred to, as are letters and ancient lists of names. From the various sources and documents, the historian has compiled a relatively coherent account of one of the most critical periods in the history of the chosen people. The focus on Jerusalem and the temple, which was prominent in Chronicles, continues in Ezra-Nehemiah, but there is no longer such an emphasis on the tradition of Davidic kingship, suggesting a slightly later historical perspective than that reflected in Chronicles. The book may have been compiled from its slightly older sources in the fourth century B.C.

THE
CONTENT
OF THE
OLD TESTAMENT

PART IV

THE
HISTORY
OF ISRAEL

A KNOWLEDGE of Israel's history is useful for at least two reasons. First, as has become clear from the survey of Old Testament books, there is a historical thread running through almost all the literature. Sometimes history seems to be a major focus of the books (as in Samuel and Kings), and sometimes it provides only a setting (as in the prophetic books), but there is a distinct historical dimension inherent in the subject matter of Old Testament studies. Second, a knowledge of Israel's history, based upon both the biblical books and the data provided by ancient Near Eastern sources, provides the reader of the Old Testament with a, broader background for understanding the biblical literature and message. Having recognized the importance of Israelite history, however, we must also recognize from the outset that there are various difficulties involved in the study of that history.

1. Problems and Perspectives in the Study
of Israel's History

The study of Israel's history draws upon two major categories of evidence. First, there are the biblical books which provide both direct and indirect information of a historical kind. Second, the biblical evidence must be supplemented by extra-biblical evidence which is largely, though not exclusively, provided by archaeological excavation and discovery. The bibilical texts provide the primary sources; the extra-biblical evidence provides the larger context within which to interpret the primary sources and from which their information can be supplemented. In dealing with both types of evidence, the historian faces numerous problems.

(a) Theological History

The historical narratives of the Old Testament are consistently written from a theological perspective. They contain not only an account of episodes from Israel's history, but the writers also present that account in terms of their faith in God and their understanding of God's participation in the history of Israel and the neighboring peoples. In other words, the Old Testament contains a theological interpretation of history; its fundamental assumptions (or presuppositions) include not only the existence of God, but also the conviction that God is involved in the human historical process. In contrast to this biblical perspective, the conventional approach to historical writing in the modern world is secular; the secular historian may or may not be a person of religious faith, but the modern historian's presentation of history will not normally be theological— except in terms of pointing out the theological dimensions inherent in the ancient sources.

Now, the fact that Israel's history is constantly *interpreted* in Old Testament texts is not a problem; all historical writing involves interpretation and presuppositions, whether done in ancient or modern times. The difficulty has to do with the *theological interpretation,* partly because that orientation is so foreign to the modern approach to history writing, and partly because theological history seems sometimes to be less than "historical" to the modern historian. Thus while an ancient historian may have no difficulty in recounting a miraculous "historical event," the modern historian may seek an alternative explanation of the data. To some extent, therefore, there must inevitably be differences of opinion on some aspects of the historical data in the Old Testament when viewed by modern interpreters of different backgrounds. While a secular historian will be interested in the manner in which the ancient writer has expressed history in theological terms, his own understanding will remain strictly secular. On the other hand, a Jewish or Christian reader, while sharing the interests of the secular historian, may also share the faith of the ancient writer. That is, religious readers may accept the ancient theological understanding of events as much as the historical data themselves.

(b) Incomplete Sources

Neither the primary nor the secondary sources for Israel's history provide complete information for the adequate and detailed reconstruction of events. The biblical writers selected their material and placed their emphases in terms of their religious goals. Thus, for example, we have very detailed accounts of the reigns of David and Solomon, but very little information on Omri. From a religious perspective, this imbalance is quite appropriate, but a detailed secular history of the Hebrew kingdoms would allocate considerable space to Omri's reign. When we recall that Israel's history in the biblical period extends over more than a millennium, we must also remember that only a few of the centuries are known in any detail at all. While it is possible to sketch Israel's history in broad strokes, there must of necessity be large gaps on the historical canvas.

The external sources are also incomplete, despite the vast number of archaeological discoveries made over the last century. Some periods and places in the biblical world are well known; others are virtually unknown. For some periods, there are correspondences between the external sources and the biblical texts; for others, there are none. As a consequence of the nature of the sources for the study of Israel's history, it follows (as we shall see) that there are areas of major disagreement and debate—especially with respect to the early history of Israel, it cannot be said that any consensus of scholarly opinion has been achieved in modern times.

(c) Literary Problems in the Biblical Texts

We have already noted in the survey of the Old Testament books (Part III) that there are major differences of opinion with respect to such matters as the authorship and dating of the books in question.

Insofar as a reconstruction of Israel's history depends primarily upon the interpretation of the Old Testament books, it naturally follows that the disagreements over the literature are balanced by equally intractable disagreements over the history of Israel.

Consider, for example, the books of the Pentateuch. They contain, among other things, insights into Israel's beginnings from the time of the patriarchs until the time after the exodus from Egypt. But how are we to interpret the historical data from these books? If one accepts the hypothesis that the Pentateuch has been compiled from various sources (J, E, D, and P) and that the sources were written down at a distance of several centuries from the period which they describe, inevitably the historian must exercise critical judgment in the evaluation of the historical worth of those sources. Even if one takes a very conservative view of the origin of the books of the Pentateuch, the interpretation of their historical value is still fraught with difficulty. The principal point to be emphasized is simply this: Insofar as there is little common consensus of opinion on the dating and evaluation of certain key Old Testament books, there must continue to be radical differences of opinion in respect to certain periods of Israel's history.

(d) The Major Periods

From a modern historical perspective, in terms of the availability and usefulness of the evidence, the history of Israel can be divided into two major periods; some scholars would describe the periods as prehistory and history respectively. The first period extends from the time of the patriarchs (Genesis) down to the time of the judges. It is prehistory in the sense that it is the period prior to the establishment of the first Hebrew kingdom. It is also prehistory, in the opinion of some scholars, in the sense that none of the Old Testament texts in their present form can be clearly dated within the period and in that there are few correspondences between the biblical texts and external documents (that is, on the basis of external documents alone virtually nothing is known of Israel prior to the establishment of the monarchy). The second, or historical, period extends from the first establishment of the Hebrew monarchy down to the end of the Old Testament story (approximately the fourth century B.C.). For this period, the biblical texts are far more explicit and less contentious, and there are numerous external correspondences between the biblical story and Near Eastern texts (Israel and later the Jews are referred to in numerous texts of this period, which have been recovered through archaeological discoveries).

In the modern study of Israel's history, the second of these two periods is the least contentious, and broad areas of agreement have been reached between scholars of various perspectives. The first period, the so-called prehistory, continues to be the area of massive debate. There are such radical differences between some modern treatments of the early period that it is difficult to believe sometimes that it is the same history that is being studied. To some extent, the differences in approach are to be accounted for in terms of the estimate of the value of the biblical texts. Thus in the more conservative approach to the early period of Israel's history, a high assessment of the worth of the Hebrew texts is balanced by a positive interpretation of the complementary value of archaeological evidence. In this conservative tradition, it is possible to describe with caution the history of Israel from its primitive roots in the time of the patriarchs down to the establishment of the monarchy. Other historians, however, holding a more negative assessment of the worth of the sources, would hesitate to venture much further back than the time of the judges in their study of Israel's prehistory.

In the survey that follows, both the two periods of Israel's history described above are reviewed. The reader should be aware, however, that the comments which follow on the patriarchs, on the exodus and Sinai, and on the Hebrew settlement in the land are all subject to debate and differing interpretations.

2. The Hebrew Patriarchs

Israel's story begins, according to its own religious traditions, with Abraham and his descendants; the story is recounted in the book of Genesis (12–50) and there are frequent allusions to it in other biblical books. For the truth of the story the only direct evidence comes from the biblical text. There are no explicit references to the patriarchs in any of the extra-biblical sources; however, the external sources are not without value, for they provide a general knowledge of the historical and cultural environment in which the patriarchal narratives purport to be set. In addition, the external sources provide a general knowledge of the world of the patriarchs against which the authenticity, or otherwise, of the biblical traditions can be measured.

The essence of the Hebrew traditions is that Israel's ancestors come from the geographical and cultural milieu of northern Mesopotamia. Abraham (Abram), before he set out on his travels, was a resident of the city of Haran (Genesis 12:4); the site is located nowadays in southeastern Turkey, and in ancient times it belonged to the cultural region of Northern Mesopotamia. Leaving the settled life of Haran, Abraham and his successors lived a semi-nomadic way of life which took them south from Haran into the region of Palestine. They were neither bedouins nor nomadic shepherds, but something more like semi-nomadic stockbreeders, whose life-style was well integrated with that of the more permanent residences and towns around which they gravitated. The narratives in Genesis do not make it possible to put firm dates on Abraham or his successors, but the general period reflected in the narratives is approximately 2000–1700 B.C.

Clearly the details of the stories (conversations, marital affairs, human incidents, and the like) lie beyond the immediate purview of the historian. What is of interest to the historian is the religious insight they contain. The patriarchs believed in a single God, the "God of the Fathers (also called the "God of Abraham," or "the God of Isaac," and various other titles). They were not necessarily monotheists in a technical sense; that is, although they believed in a single god, we do not know that they categorically denied the existence of any and all other supposed deities. Their belief in a single god was a distinctly personal one. They had a relationship with their God which made certain demands of them, in religious and ethical terms, and which also offered certain prospects to them. In Abraham, and to a lesser extent in the other partriarchs, one senses a religion with a future and a purpose. The patriarchs expected one day to have a land they could call their own and to become a nation. The patriarchal narratives also portray a religion characterized by a degree of intimacy rarely found in Near Eastern religious texts of the second millennium; their God was not a remote deity, like the state gods of the great nations of that time, but one who was known and worshiped in personal terms by his followers.

Geographically, the patriarchal narratives move from Mesopotamia to Palestine, and then eventually to a new geographical setting in Egypt (in the Joseph story). In other words, the narrative in Genesis traces ethnic and cultural origins (Mesopotamia), a period of semi-nomadic existence (Palestine), and eventual residence as aliens (Egypt). It is in Egypt that the next stage of Israel's story begins—Exodus, followed by the encounter with God at Mount Sinai.

Before we move on, we need to ask what historical weight can be attributed to the patriarchal narratives. At the outset, it must be noted that a number of modern scholars would not attribute any historical worth to the Genesis narratives (at least in a second millennium setting); they would remove the patriarchs from the realm of historical investigation and examine them only in the context of later literary creations. Abraham, Isaac, and the other patriarchs, they would claim, may at most be vague lengendary figures from a distant past. More probably, they are fictional characters, the story about them being told principally for the purpose of religious instruction and edification. Scholars who hold this view would emphasize the late date of the sources of Genesis in which the stories are told, some dating the stories to the sixth century B.C. or even later. In respect to the archaeological evidence, they would claim that it is of little help in authenticating a second millennium date for the patriarchs.

The more conservative tradition, especially in North American scholarship, places more weight on the Genesis narratives; even if it is granted that the sources of Genesis may indeed be late, it is held that they contain traditions very much more ancient than the date of their written form. The conservative approach to Israel's history is also much more positive in its assessment of the value of archaeological sources. For example, the names of persons employed in Genesis fit well into the class of names known from external sources dating from the early second millennium, and many of the customs and cultural insights of the Genesis narrative have parallels in the customs and cultures reflected in second-millennium Near Eastern texts (though the latter topic is one of continuing debate).

How does one decide between two such radically different assessments of the historical worth of Israel's patriarchal origins? First, it should be suggested, in strictly historical terms, that neither position should be held too dogmatically; whichever view one adopts, the real difficulty of the historical data on which the view is based should be recognized. Second, new evidence is constantly coming to light which, when it has been thoroughly examined, may explain some of the difficulties. The archaeological discoveries at Tell

Mardik (ancient Ebla, see chapter 3), for example, should have considerable light to shed on the civilization of Northern Mesopotamia at the end of the third and the beginning of the second millennia B.C. But until that evidence has been published, studied, and digested, it would be unwise to venture an opinion as to which side of the debate (if either one) it might support. The rediscovery of Ebla, in turn, is a reminder of all the other discoveries which remain to be made—by the time we all reach the so-called golden years of our lives, the evidence for or against the patriarchs may be totally different from what it is today.

These comments set a general context of caution in which to view the patriarchal age, but can anything more definite be said? To venture a personal opinion, it seems possible to me to form a positive assessment of this earliest period in Israel's history. Of course one cannot "prove," in historical terms, that the events of Genesis took place in just the way they are described. And one should recognize, even in a positive assessment of the patriarchs, that the narrative of Genesis has, by virtue of its particular interests, simplified a long and complex history. However, the persistence of the traditions, not only in Genesis but also in the other biblical literature, is hard to overlook. The cultural origins in Mesopotamia fit well with much of the later biblical tradition, whose law and literature, despite Hebrew shaping, reflect Mesopotamian origins. The early reflections of religion in the patriarchs can easily be understood to develop into the full bloom of Israel's later religion. It is true that the data can be otherwise explained, but it is too radical an approach to history to deny in the stories of the patriarchs some genuine reflections of the beginnings of Israel's story.

3. Exodus and Sinai

With the story of the exodus of the Hebrews from Egypt and their encounter with God at Mount Sinai, we move gradually from prehistory into a period which was, in Israel's self-understanding, foundational for both its national and religious existence. By the time of Moses (approximately fourteenth century B.C., though this too is debated), the Hebrews are still in Egypt, though they have become slaves in a foreign land. The story is relatively straightforward in the biblical sources (Exodus to Deuteronomy), although it is used as a framework for the insertion of massive detail concerning earliest Israel's traditions, laws, and religion.

The Hebrews in Egypt, finding their servile condition unbearable, are led in what is a kind of slave revolt, resulting eventually in their escape (or exodus) from Egypt under Moses' leadership. They escape to the east into the wilderness area of Sinai. At Mount Sinai, a covenant (or contract) is formed between God and the Hebrews through the mediatorship of Moses. According to the covenant, the Hebrew people are bound to worship God and to obey the divine law. God, in turn, promises to bring his people eventually to a land of their own and make them into a nation. After the encounter with God at Mount Sinai, the people set off once again on their travels through the wilderness region, arriving after forty years at the Plains of Moab, just east of the point where the Jordan River runs into the Dead Sea. From this point, according to the biblical narrative, they will launch their invasion of the promised land. It is here, too, that Moses dies, marking the end of an era.

Even in the brief synopsis of the story which has just been given, some of the potential difficulties which face the modern historian can be discerned. On the surface, it is simply the story of a slave revolt, followed by an escape of the Hebrew slaves from Egypt and their journey back toward Asia from which their ancestors had come. There are historical difficulties of various kinds associated with the interpretation of the story.

(a) If one takes the story at face value, there are the traditional difficulties of miracles. There is a strong miraculous thread running through the early chapters of Exodus, culminating in the crossing of the Red Sea by the Hebrews and the drowning of their Egyptian pursuers. This is not the context in which to address the philosophical or theological issues of miracles; it is enough to note that the many miraculous elements in the story will lead to a skeptical assessment of the value of the texts as historical sources on the part of most modern historians.

(b) Closely related to the difficulty of miracle, there is the difficulty of theology. For example, in the account of the giving of the Law (including the Ten Commandments) at Mount Sinai, the clear emphasis of the story is that the Law is God-given. The historian will inevitably have difficulty in dealing with texts of this kind; they fall more into the categories of theological rather than historical writing.

(c) A further difficulty has to do with the biblical sources. As it is in the treatment of the patriarchal period, so it is that in the examination of the traditions of Exodus and Sinai many scholars find little of historical worth. What they find are documents which reflect the theology and creativity of a later age. Some modern studies of Israel's history attribute little or no historical worth to the books of Exodus–Deuteronomy, at least insofar as they purport to describe the age of Moses. They would, however, give them considerable weight as a description of the religious history of the first millennium B.C.

These are only a few of the difficulties associated with the story of Exodus and the covenant formed at Mount Sinai. It should be added that external sources, though they tell us a great deal about Egyptian history in the fourteenth–thirteenth centuries B.C., do not contain any explicit statements about Moses and his companions. Thus we can begin to see why, in the work of many modern historians, this early period is still firmly within the realm of prehistory; some would remove it from the plain of historical discussion altogether, and others would limit the discussion to an evaluation of the biblical texts as embodying the nucleus of ancient traditions which have nevertheless undergone considerable embellishment over the course of subsequent centuries.

Although one must acknowledge from the outset that there are very grave difficulties in studying this period in the biblical story, it is still possible to make some positive, but cautious, statements about the period, limiting oneself to the essentially historical data (and leaving a discussion of the religious ideas and practices to the following chapters). First, there is no reason to doubt that the Hebrews (or at least some of the Hebrews who later constituted the people of Israel) did indeed spend a long time in Egypt, the latter part of their stay characterized by an existence as forced laborers. Although the sources do not refer to the Israelites in Egypt, they do indicate that the Egyptians made extensive use of foreign (Asiatic) labor in their building schemes and other industries. Second, there are no sound reasons for doubting the authenticity of the Hebrew exodus from Egypt (although historians will reconstruct the actual details of the exodus in different ways, depending on their interpretations of the sources and their historical methods). Although the date at which this exodus took place remains a matter of debate in contemporary scholarship, a date of around 1290 B.C. seems the most likely. Third, the formation of a religious covenant at Mount Sinai seems to be firmly grounded in history, although of necessity the religious aspects of that process are not easily susceptible to historical investigation. (It should be noted that the precise location of Mount Sinai is not known, despite various claims for the authenticity of this or that mountain in the wilderness of Sinai.) Fourth, it is surely unnecessarily skeptical to more or less eliminate Moses from this period of Israel's history, as is done in some modern historical texts. While nothing is known of Moses beyond what is contained in the biblical narrative, his influence and shadow loom too largely through the Old Testament books as a whole for him to be arbitrarily excised from ancient history. From the strictly secular perspective of modern historical investigation, one may be very limited in what one can say about Moses, yet for all the uncertainty of ancient tradition, he is a figure of extraordinary proportions without whose existence Israel might never have come into being.

The reader of this book who may not be well versed in how modern works treat the history of Israel may think that in this and the preceding section I have been exceptionally cautious and too skeptical of the "self-evident" history contained in the biblical texts. On the other hand, many scholars and contemporary historians would judge that I have been far too positive and optimistic concerning what can be said about Israel's early history. My position, as I have said before, is conservative, but governed by what I take to be a sensible approach to historical understanding. Yet, even the cautious position adopted here may be disturbing to some—for example, Jewish or Christian readers of a conservative background. Cannot a more positive statement of Israelite history be made? There are varieties of opinion within historical scholarship, as will already have become clear. But it must also be stated that there is an added dimension which a religious reader, Christian or Jewish, brings to the text. When the text is read from the starting point of faith in God, inevitably that faith informs and illuminates the reading of the ancient text. To deny that added dimension in reading the text would not only be wrong, but would also be a failure to recognize the continuing vitality of the ancient Scriptures in contemporary religion. The perspective of this textbook is consciously a more limited one: What can be known of Israel's history if it is examined in the same way as any other nation's history? The summary presented above is a cautious starting point, although, given the limitations of time and space in this book, it is inadequate and incomplete. It must be supplemented by a reading of the texts themselves and an attempt to appreciate them in both historical and religious terms. (The religious significance of Exodus and Sinai will be reviewed in the following chapter.)

4. The Settlement of the Land

We are still not out of the woods in respect to the problems of historical reconstruction when we come to the next stage in Israel's story. This time the problems lie not only in the complexities of historical research, but also in what seems sometimes to be the conflicting evidence of the ancient sources.

Taken at face value, the texts convey an impression something like the following: After the death of Moses, the Hebrew people under the leadership of Joshua cross the Jordan River and undertake a major military campaign designed to give them control over Palestine, their "promised land." By means of a series of swift and decisive attacks aimed at the northern, central, and southern regions of the land, Joshua and his troops secure the land that is eventually to become the Hebrew nation—this is the general drift of Joshua 1–12. On the other hand, the summary account of this period of conquest and settlement given in Judges 1 conveys a slightly different emphasis; the reality of the conquest as portrayed in Judges seems to have been a much longer and more drawn-out affair. Cities said to have been conquered in Joshua's time still seem to retain their independence at the beginning of the period of the Judges. Despite Joshua's famous victories, certain key areas in the promised land retained their independence from the Hebrews for a century or more; the city of Jerusalem, for example, held out against the newcomers in the land until the time of King David.

If the historian's task were simply to resolve the tensions inherent in the biblical narrative, it might not be too difficult. It could be argued that the books of Joshua and Judges give complementary, but considerably oversimplified, pictures of the Hebrew conquest and settlement. Joshua provides the overview, an account of a major military campaign which brings the Hebrews into the promised land. It secures a foothold in the land, but the initial victories are not consolidated and Hebrew control of the land is restricted to a few areas. The summary at the beginning of Judges and the narratives which follow portray the longer and more drawn-out process of actual consolidation and securing the initial toehold in the land achieved by Joshua. Even this kind of summary of the biblical narrative, which is not without difficulties of both literary analysis and historical reconstruction, is subject to major debate and disagreement in contemporary biblical scholarship. Although at the surface level the biblical narrative clearly describes a military invasion of Palestine, followed by a long period of consolidation and settlement, a number of other hypotheses have been proposed to account for the presence of the Hebrews in Palestine prior to the formation of the first kingdom.

The end point of this historical period is clear; the problem concerns how one reaches it. The end point upon which there is common agreement is that by the middle of the eleventh century B.C. there was a group of persons in Palestine, sharing a common faith and (apparently) ethnic heritage, who formed the basis of the Israelite monarchy soon to be established under King Saul (discussed in section 5). The problem concerns who those people were and how they got there. As we have seen, the implication of the biblical narrative, taken at face value, is that they were the Hebrews who had escaped from Egypt under the leadership of Moses, penetrated the land in Joshua's time, and gradually consolidated their hold on the land during the period of the Judges. A number of scholars have found this kind of interpretation either too simplistic (and it must be admitted that the process was obviously much more complex than the telescoped narrative of the biblical books) or too naïve a reading of the biblical texts. One of the major alternatives to the conventional view is that the Hebrews arrived in the land, not by means of military conquest, but by means of gradual infiltration and settlement. The conquest narrative is interpreted as an idealized account by a later writer, who drew upon ancient stories of little historical value. The reality of the matter is that the Hebrew tribes occupied Palestine gradually over the course of centuries, for the most part assimilating the local population and only occasionally being engaged in local conflicts.

Still another hypothesis that has recently gained considerable attention proposes an alternative to both conquest and peaceful infiltration. The hypothesis has been argued with different emphases and from different scientific perspectives, but its essence is that the Hebrew people emerged as an identifiable group and eventually a nation as a consequence of a peasants' revolt. Rejecting the feudal and hierarchical structures represented in the city-states of Palestine, the peasantry shook off the old social structures and established a new society with its own distinctive religio-political basis. This hypothesis, like that of peaceful penetration, requires a critical re-reading of the literary sources of the period and an essentially sociological analysis of the texts in the attempt to reconstruct the origins of Israel.

Now, at the outset it should be stressed that when faced with such different hypotheses concerning Israel's origins the interpreter of the ancient texts cannot simply choose one hypothesis over another, not at least without extensive critical examination of what is being rejected. It must be recognized from the beginning that the period from the exodus to the establishment of the Hebrew monarchy, a period of more than two centuries, was a time of extremely complex historical change; the books of Joshua and Judges provide useful insight into this period, but they certainly do not provide a full and comprehensive account. The various hypothesis, based after all on the same data (though examined from differing scientific and methodological perspectives), may each have something to contribute to an understanding of the period as a whole. What then can be said with reasonable certainty about the emergence of the Hebrew people on the path to nationhood?

First, there are no solid grounds for altogether rejecting the traditions of military invasion, conquest, and a subsequent protracted series of military campaigns. The sheer weight and unanimity of the biblical tradition concerning the military character of the Hebrews' arrival in the promised land is too great to set it aside altogether, and it is a tradition not without archaeological support. Thus the archaeological excavation of several sites in southern Palestine indicates that certain cities, listed in the biblical texts as conquered by the Israelites, were in fact destroyed in the latter part of the thirteenth century (such cities as Debir and Lachish; see Joshua 10:31-39). However, the examination of the archaeological evidence introduces a note of caution in the attempt to understand this period. While some cities were destroyed in the thirteenth century, for other cities (for example, Jericho and Ai) mentioned in the biblical narrative there is no clear evidence of destruction.

In addition to the military invasion and settlement, one may suppose that there was also a degree of peaceful penetration and assimilation. The Hebrews who escaped from Egypt traced their origins to northern Mesopotamia, and before going into Egypt had spent a considerable amount of time in Palestine. Perhaps many persons had remained in Palestine when others went into Egypt, and through kinship and common religious traditions, they had joined the Hebrews from Egypt on the latter's arrival in the land. The biblical narrative itself also gives evidence of the gradual absorption of some local persons into the Israelite community (for example, the Gibeonites in Joshua 9). It is perhaps impossible to untangle all the thin threads of history from the few extant sources, but there is little doubt that in addition to military strength, the Hebrews grew in size as a consequence both of some peaceful infiltration of persons of similar faith and background and also by means of assimilation of people already in the land.

The theory of peasant revolt is in some ways the most difficult to accommodate within the conventional approach to an understanding of Hebrew origins. It is a theory based upon a sociological analysis of the sources and a somewhat deterministic view of history; therefore, simply on grounds of the viability of academic method, it has met with considerable challenge. Nevertheless, it is important to recognize that Palestine, between the thirteenth and eleventh centuries, was undergoing a period of radical social change; in larger socio-cultural terms, it was the transition from the end of the Late Bronze Age to the beginning of the Iron Age. In Palestine, this transition was marked by the gradual breakdown of the old Canaanite city-states, followed by a period of social chaos before the emergence of new socio-political structures. This time of change may perhaps be characterized as a period of peasant revolt, but it was also a time of international upheaval and change; international events had repercussions in the geographical region of Palestine which had little or nothing to do with the peasants. The great Hittite Empire to the north (in the region of modern Turkey) had collapsed; the Egyptian Empire to the south was in a period of gradual decline and as a consequence was loosening its hold on Palestine; and the whole eastern Mediterranean world was being shaken by the gradual assaults of the Sea Peoples from the Aegean region and southeastern Europe.

In other words, the Hebrews were moving toward nationhood in a time of international change and chaos, when old orders were collapsing and new socio-economic structures were beginning to emerge. In the larger historical scheme of things, the emergence of the small state of Israel from the Hebrews in Palestine may seem relatively insignificant. From the perspective of the study of Israelite history, the difficulties involved in the sources and the problems inherent in understanding Israel's emergence as a nation fit well within this larger perspective of chaotic change in Near Eastern history.

5. The United Monarchy

By the middle of the eleventh century B.C., the Hebrew people in Palestine comprised a loose federation of tribal groups, recognizing ties of common kinship and faith. They were united from time to time by one of the judges (in effect a military leader) to face a common or regional threat, but they did not have any form of central government, nor was their society closely integrated. They possessed fairly extensive territories to both west and east of the Jordan Valley, but they did not control them absolutely; there remained pockets of the original Canaanite inhabitants and a number of city-states that had retained their independence. The loose confederation of Israelite tribes had worked well enough up to a point; the principal enemies of the Israelites, the Canaanites, had no more central organization than the Israelites did. Thus the Hebrews were able to survive without central government, but their control of the territory as a whole was loose and gradual, and the picture of conditions in the region that emerges from the book of Judges is one of social chaos. Eventually the settlers were pressed by external conditions to change their style; they were not the only ones vying for control of the land. Whereas, according to the biblical narrative, the Hebrews initiated their bid for the possession of the land from the east, another group of foreign people was attempting to take control of the land from the north and west—these were the Philistines. Around 1050 B.C., the Philistines defeated the Hebrews in a major military campaign near Aphek. Before that, Philistine settlements had been confined for the most part to the territory along the Mediterranean coast. After 1050 B.C. they began to extend their control eastward, pressing inland into the regions loosely held by the Hebrews. The confederacy of Hebrew tribes, during this period of Philistine expansion, could easily have collapsed; it was held together through the leadership and encouragement of Samuel, but it had become clear that if the Hebrews were to continue to survive the increasing pressure from the Philistines, they would have to shift to some centralized form of government andmilitary control. The *ad hoc* responses to external threats, which had worked after a fashion in the past, would no loner suffice.

It was largely in response to this external pressure from the Philistines that Hebrew society began to undergo a gradual transformation from tribal confederation to monarchic state. There emerged from the older tribal society a united kingdom (uniting both the separate tribes and the various geographical regions), which was to survive for approximatey a century (see figure 32).

Figure 32. THE UNITED MONARCHY

Monarchs	Approximate Reigns
King Saul	1020–1000 B.C.
{ Eshbaal - north / David - south }	1000—998 B.C.
King David	998—961 B.C.
King Solomon	961—922 B.C.
922 B.C. The Division of the Kingdom	

The first king was Saul, a member of the tribe of Benjamin, whose qualification for office were principally of a military nature. The appointment of a king did not go without resistance among the Hebrew people; the whole nation of monarchy was alien to the tribal traditions, and for some it may have seemed alien to the faith. But the

Philistine threat was such that some drastic action had to be taken; in this sense, Saul was well equipped for the office to which he was appointed. For the entire period of his reign (though we do not know it in any detail), Saul seems to have been engaged in a series of military actions. In military terms, his rule was successful; he was able to assemble an army from all the tribal groups, and he won a number of significant victories over the Philistines. He did not remove the Philistine threat, but he re-established Israel's control over its traditional territories and rescued his people from the possibility of total annihilation.

With respect to the larger history of Israel, Saul's reign was very much a transitional period. He created a degree of unity, especially in the face of external threats, where formerly there had been little unity. This achievement was accomplished in good part as a consequence of his gifts of leadership, his military skill, and his genuine intelligence and courage. Yet Saul attempted to make no fundamental changes in the society to which he belonged; although it had passed from a loose tribal confederation to a primitive monarchy, society as such had changed very little. There developed none of the administrative machinery or bureaucracy commonly associated with a state, nor were there any national programs, for example, in matters such as taxation. Given the novelty of kingship in Saul's time, little thought seems to have been given as to what would happen after his death. In other parts of the Near Eastern world, kingship as a hereditary matter passed on from one generation to another; Saul, on the other hand, had been appointed to office largely on the basis of his charismatic gifts and military skills.

The latter part of Saul's reign was characterized by tragedy, both personal and national. For all his splendid personal gifts, he was a man of unstable temperament (or else the pressures of office had reduced him to this unhappy state). With the passage of time, his periods of brilliance and leadership were interrupted more fre-quently by fits of despair and paranoid depression; by the time of his death, one cannot be certain that he had retained much hold on sanity. His later years were also distorted by a quite irrational jealousy of, and hatred for, one of his nation's young military heroes, David. Saul died eventually under tragic circumstances in a battle with the Philistines, who were once again regaining their strength; yet, for all the flaws in Saul's personality, he had completed the task for which he had been appointed; he had saved the young nation of Israel from annihilation.

Following Saul's death, there was a brief hiatus in the nation's history, indicating just how fragile was the unity he had created and how unclear was the notion of kingship in Israel. Eshbaal, a son of Saul, was made king in the territories Israel controlled in Transjordan, and he claimed that his rule extended over most of Israel's northern territories; he could have been the rightful successor to Saul, had kingship been commonly accepted as a hereditary office. In Hebron, to the south, David was made king of the southern region, and his claim to the office was based more on the charismatic qualities of leadership which had won Saul the office in the first place. After only two years, Eshbaal was murdered by two of his officers, and David became king over the entire nation of Israel.

David held the throne of Israel for approximately forty years, and the changes which took place during this period of Israel's history were extraordinary and far reaching in their consequence for the future. First, in a series of military campaigns, he destroyed for all time the Philistine threat, thereby extending the lands controlled by Israel and securing its western borders from further military danger. He then conquered the ancient city of Jerusalem, which up to that time had been held by the Jebusites and had resisted all efforts to capture it. In this city, which was centrally located but had no particular associations with any of the older tribal territories, David established his capital city and (in a preliminary fashion) the center of the nation's faith. His military campaigns over the following years took him further afield, and by means of a series of victories he acquired control of vast territories to the north, east, and south. If one were to describe David's kingdom in terms of land held by modern nations, it would have included not only the modern state of Israel, but also extensive regions that today belong to the states of Lebanon, Jordan, and Syria. Israel in David's time extended its borders to the furthest limits, an accomplishment which has never been repeated down into the present century. And, in the tenth century B.C., Israel could be said for a short time to have become one of the world's most powerful nations.

It is clear from this brief summary of David's accomplishments that Israel, as a nation, was rapidly going through a series of radical social changes. Whereas at the time of Saul's death, the old tribal structure of society had changed very little, during David's reign it developed quickly into a monarchical state. The sheer size of David's empire required the development of a massive administrative system. The somewhat rustic character of Saul's court was exchanged for the splendor of David's newly constructed palace in Jerusalem. Out of the welter of different tribal traditions, David had formed an extraordinary degree of national unity and purpose. Yet, for all the significance of his achievements, they were to a large extent the consequence of his personal skills and leadership; there was not a deep-seated unity holding together the disparate components of this new nation that would have the strength to survive through the subsequent centuries.

One old problem which had not been adequately solved was the matter of succession to the throne, whether it should be on the basis of hereditary or charismatic (God-given) gifts. In the king's declining years, the peace of the kingdom was disturbed by several rebellions, whose goal was to secure the throne following David's death. Eventually, one of David's sons, Solomon, was appointed as successor, and after a short period of co-regency he inherited David's throne. A quite different man from his father, Solomon was nevertheless a person of considerable gifts, particularly in the areas of administration, business, and trade. Where David's achievement had been the expansion of the kingdom, Solomon sought primarily to consolidate what he had inherited; he was to a large extent successful, but by the time of his death the fragile unity which had been carved from the old tribal confederacy was on the verge of collapse.

Solomon was not a warrior as his father had been, but in modern terms he would have made a very successful Secretary of Defense. He enlarged Israel's armed forces, increased military strength (through the massive development of chariot forces), and built a series of military strongholds to protect Israel's extensive territorial holdings. In the area of trade, he developed Israel's wealth by means of involvement in, and control of, trade routes to the north, south, and east. A merchant fleet operated through the Red Sea and beyond, expanding commerce with Africa and probably also India. The ancient overland routes, plied by camel traders, were developed through Arabia to the south and to the ancient kingdom of Saba (Sheba); traffic also flowed northward via Syria to Anatolia and

Mesopotamia. This massive development of trade, being essentially a royal monopoly, brought considerable wealth into the kingdom.

Despite the acquisition of wealth in Solomon's reign, it was still insufficient to cover the costs of the expansive programs undertaken at home. In addition to military expenditures, Solomon built at enormous expense the great temple in Jerusalem, which was to become a central symbol of Israel's faith. Programs such as these required extensive physical resources, a large labor force, and a massive bureaucracy. Thus there developed in Solomon's time not only a burdensome taxation system, but also a system of enforced labor; neither of these measures was destined to bring a broad base of popular support for the monarchy and its aspirations for grandeur. When—after approximately forty years of rule over the united kingdom of Israel—Solomon died, there had appeared in the fragile unity of that kingdom a number of deep divisions. His death marked the end of a united history of the people of Israel, and the single kingdom of Solomon broke up into two separate states.

6. The Kingdoms of Israel and Judah

The history of the two kingdoms over the next centuries is known in some detail from the biblical texts (the books of Kings and Chronicles), supplemented by the extensive resources of biblical archaeology. We cannot recount that history in detail, tracing the reigns of the individual kings in each of the two states, for space does not permit. It must suffice to give an overview of the history of the two states which emerged after the crisis at the end of Solomon's reign.

On the death of King Solomon, the inner problems which had grown gradually during the long course of his reign came at last to the surface. There was unrest for a number of reasons, not least as a consequence of the heavy taxation and the forced labor imposed by the crown. In some ways, these immediate causes of unrest merely brought to the surface more deep-seated problems which could be traced in turn to Israel's pre-monarchical period. Before Saul's time, there had never been a profound sense of unity within the confederacy of Hebrew tribes. Saul had held the tribes together for a while, but it is significant that after his death Israel had split, temporarily, into two regions; the north under Eshbaal and the south under David. Unity had been restored again by David and maintained by his personal leadership and genius, but his successor, Solomon, though he maintained the national unity, imposed severe pressures upon it by means of his development and fiscal policies. When he died, the kingdom came apart. The northern tribes formed a separate kingdom of their own, Israel, and what was left of Solomon's empire continued in the south as the state of Judah (see figure 33).

(a) The Northern Kingdom: Israel

The northern region, having seceded from what had been Solomon's empire, had to start from scratch; it had to establish its own monarchy, develop a system of administration and government, and form some foundation for its religion distinct from the temple and worship functioning already in Jerusalem. Its territories were larger than those of the southern state and potentially richer, and in economic terms they provided a sound foundation for the formation of a small state. Following the secession, the sheer magnitude of the internal problems facing Israel was such that the new state quickly lost many of the adjoining territories to the north and east that David had brought within the circumference of his empire. Thus the new Israel, after Solomon's death, was considerably smaller than the northern region which had formerly been controlled by the united kingdom. Israel's southern border lay on an east–west line to the north of Jerusalem; to the north, its holdings extended just north of the Sea of Chinnereth (Galilee) and it retained land to the east of the Jordan River. It was a state of considerable size, though very much smaller than the former empire.

The first king of the northern state was Jeroboam I, and during the twenty or so years of his reign a new apparatus of government was gradually patched together. What is striking about the relatively short history of the northern kingdom is the lack of inner continuity in its principal institutions. In the matter of the new monarchy, for example, the northern people had rejected the principle of hereditary succession to the throne when they refused to acknowledge Solomon's son, Rehoboam, as king. Thus through the two centuries of Israel's history, the monarchy was characterized by constant change in dynasty. At the risk of oversimplification, it is fair to say that on the death of any given king the crown became fair game for the one with the strength and leadership to capture it; three times

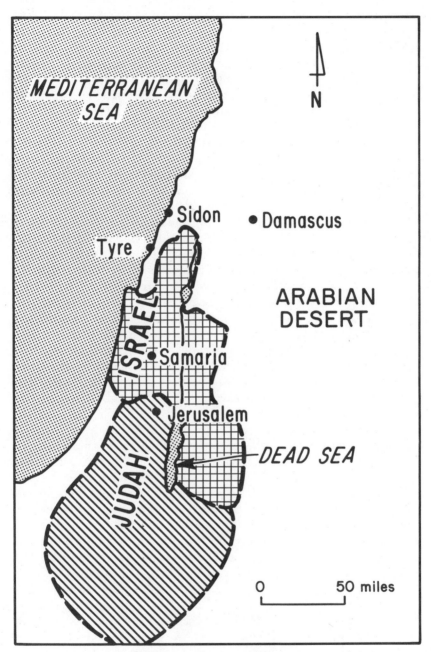

Figure 33. Map of Israel and Judah

in the first half-century of Israel's existence, the throne changed hands as a consequence of violence. Occasionally a strong king came along (such as Omri) who was able to establish a dynasty for several generations, but the principle of dynastic succession was never firmly established or commonly accepted in the north (see figure 19). Likewise, the northern state never had the same sense of continuity as the south, with respect to its capital city. Whereas in Judah Jerusalem remained the permanent capital, in the north it changed from time to time, being first at Shechem, later at Tirzah, and eventually at Samaria—a splendid city built by Omri and his successors. The discontinuity in both king and capital reflects in some ways the older tribal traditions from the period before Saul. The north seems to have tried to hold in a delicate balance the older notions of the tribal confederacy and the charismatic leader with the newer ideas of monarch and state; for the most part, it failed to do this effectively.

In the time of the united monarchy, David and Solomon had ruled one of the greatest states of the ancient world; without wishing to denigrate the achievements of those two men, it must be admitted that their powers and influence had been possible in large part because of a period of general decline in the traditional imperial powers in the Near East. But during the northern state's two centuries of history, the external world was changing once again; the slumbering giants were re-awakening. The Aramean states immediately to the north of Israel, having regained their freedom following Solomon's death, were growing in strength and were a constant threat on the nothern border. Judah lay to the south—in theory no threat, though in practice the relations between Israel and Judah fluctuated over the centuries; sometimes they were at peace with one another, and at other times in conflict. But the principal threat to Israel's security was the great Assyrian Empire, located in northern Mesopotamia. At the end of the second millennium, it had been one of the greatest powers in the Near Eastern world, but had entered a period of decline before David and Solomon's time. During Israel's monarchy, Assyria was growing again, and its imperial plans knew no limits; it was eventually Assyrian military expansion which brought to an end the short history of Israel. In about 722 B.C., the Assyrian armies dealt a final blow to Israel and destroyed its capital in Samaria; that defeat, for all practical purposes, removed the northern kingdom permanently from the annals of Hebrew history.

Figure 34. KINGS AND PROPHETS IN ISRAEL

Approx. Dates	Kings	Prophets
922–901	Jeroboam I	
901–900	Nadab	
–900 B.C.		
900–877	Baasha	
877–876	Elah	
876	Zimri	
876–869	Omri	
869–850	Ahab	
–850 B.C.		} Elijah
850–849	Ahaziah	
849–843	Jehoram	
843–815	Jehu	} Elisha
815–802	Jehoahaz	
802–786	Jehoash	
–800 B.C.		
786–746	Jeroboam II	
		Amos
–750 B.C.		Hosea
746–745	Zechariah	
745	Shallum	
745–737	Menahem	
737–736	Pekahiah	
736–732	Pekah	
732–724	Hoshea	
722	Fall of Samaria →	

Figure 35. *Lamassu (guardian spirits of the gate), palace of Ashurnasirpal II at Nimrud, one of the Assyrian royal capitals*

Although the political and economic history of Israel is not a particularly distinguished one, the two centuries during which the northern state survived are of interest to the historian of religion. The traditional religion of the Hebrews continued in its own distinctive form in the northern kingdom; it was maintained as the official cult of the monarchy and the state and observed in worship at such ancient shrines as Dan and Bethel. The state religion, however, was prone to decline, not least as a consequence of the inroads of Canaanite religion; the religion of Baal, an agricultural kind of religion, had its own intrinsic appeal to human nature. Foreign forms of worship in Israel were strengthened from time to time as a consequence of the monarchy; Ahab's foreign wife, Jezebel, to take one example, was influential in promoting alien religion in the northern state.

Figure 36. The Black Obelisk of Shalmaneser III, showing King Jehu of Israel prostrating himself before the Assyrian King bringing tribute

It was the periods of decline in the religion of the northern state, whether as a consequence of foreign influence or simply loss of faith, that produced some of the most distinguished religious figures in biblical history. The prophetic ministries of Elijah and Elisha during the ninth century B.C., as recorded in I–II Kings, provide evidence for the continuity of a vigorous form of ancient Mosaic faith in the north. These two prophets were outspoken in the condemnation of alien inroads into the pure and ancient faith of Israel and were totally opposed to any compromise with the religion of Baal. It was in the eighth century B.C., during the last few decades before Israel's collapse, that other distinguished prophets arose. The ministry of Amos reveals a devastating critique of the social decline and the unjust society that had emerged in Israel before its end. The prophecies of Hosea reveal the nation's spiritual collapse, its accommodation to the religion of Baal, and its lack of love for Israel's God. But for all the distinction of the prophetic tradition in the north, nothing could avert the nation's downward career; when Samaria was destroyed in 722 B.C., it must have seemed to many to be simply a fulfillment of the prophetic warnings.

(b) The Southern Kingdom: Judah

Whereas the northern kingdom had to build up a brand new government in 922 B.C., the southern kingdom was simply the continuation of what had once been a great empire. Jerusalem, the traditional capital of the united monarchy, remained as the capital city of Judah. Solomon's son, Rehoboam, became the first king of Judah, and throughout the nation's history, which extended over almost three and a half centuries, a king of the Davidic line occupied the throne. The temple which Solomon had built remained the focal point of Judah's worship in the nation's capital. In these and other ways, Judah passed through the disruption of the old kingdom much more smoothly than did its northern neighbor.

The new state of Judah was much smaller than Israel; its territories extended southward from Jerusalem into the Negev, and from time to time included land lying to the east of the Arabah in the region of the ancient state of Edom. Judah was not only smaller but also considerably poorer than Israel, having few natural resources to bring it wealth. The loss of empire and influence, which had accumulated such wealth in Solomon's time as a consequence of international trade, meant that the small state of Judah had few means of supplementing its own meager natural resources.

In some ways, Judah's military position was rather better than Israel's. Its southern location placed it slightly farther away from the northern superpowers which threatened Israel, and the rough, hilly terrain of its territories made the nation more easily defensible than the north. In particular, its capital in Jerusalem was a city that could normally be firmly defended against external enemies. However, Judah was still not secure. Early in Rehoboam's reign (about 920 B.C.), a military campaign of the Egyptian Pharaoh Shishak (or Sheshonk I) devastated Judah's territories, and penetrated into the northern Israelite territories. Although the Egyptians did not follow up the campaign and consolidate their hold on Judah, it was a reminder to the populace that mountainous territory and defended cities offered no guaranteed security. When, in 722 B.C., the northern kingdom fell to the Assyrians, even Judah's northern border seemed particularly vulnerable to external enemies.

The tradition of Davidic kingship in the southern state gave it a much more stable internal history than was experienced in Israel, but the simple fact of consecutive reigns by members of a single dynasty did not guarantee good government. Judah had its share of incompetent or irreligious rulers, and despite the fact that the monarch was, in theory, the patron and defender of the ancient faith, it fell to the prophets to uphold the ancient traditions of the Hebrew faith. There was a long line of distinguished prophets in the south, some fairly well known from the books named after them, and some scarcely known at all beyond the brief references in the historical literature (see figure 37). Among the best known of Judah's prophets were Isaiah and Micah in the eighth century B.C., and Jeremiah, Zephaniah, and others in the seventh century B.C. (see chapters 6 and 7).

Judah, like its northern neighbor, was perpetually vulnerable to the changing tides of fortune in the history of the Near East's most powerful nations. At the end of the eighth and beginning of the seventh centuries B.C., it was threatened by Assyria, which had become the world's dominant power. Judah was for a while simply a vassal state of the Assyrian Empire. When, in the middle of the seventh century B.C., Assyria's power began to decline, there were those in Judah who thought that their nation's future prospects looked brighter. But Assyria's decline and eventual collapse (around 612 B.C.) was a consequence of the re-emergence of other nations. Egypt was regaining its strength once again, but much more significantly, the Babylonians (in Assyria's southern Mesopotamian territory) were growing and eventually conquered their former Assyrian masters, taking over much of what had once been the Assyrian Empire. It was

Figure 37. KINGS AND PROPHETS IN JUDAH

Approx. Dates		Kings	Prophets
922–915		Rehoboam	
915–913		Abijah	
913–873		Asa	
	–900 B.C.		
873–849		Jehoshaphat	
	–850 B.C.		
849–843		Jehoram	
843–842		Ahaziah	
842–837		Athaliah	
837–800		Joash	
	–800 B.C.		
800–783		Amaziah	
783–742		Uzziah	
	–750 B.C.		
742–735		Jotham	Isaiah
735–715		Ahaz	Micah
715–687		Hezekiah	
	–700 B.C.		
687–642		Manasseh	
	–650 B.C.		
642–640		Amon	
640–609		Josiah	Zephaniah
609		Jehoahaz	Nahum
609–598		Jehoiakim	Jeremiah
	–600 B.C.		Habakkuk
598–597		Jehoiachin	
597–587		Zedekiah	
587		Fall of Jerusalem	Ezekiel
586		Beginning of exile	

the Babylonians, around 586 B.C., who after several years of military campaigns in Palestine, and after more than a decade of loose control over Judah, at last brought the southern state's existence to an end. Judah had survived more than a century longer than had Israel, but by 586 B.C. Judah's territories were ravaged by the Babylonian armies; Jerusalem was conquered and its once splendid temple lay in ruins.

Figure 38. *Cylinder of Nebuchadrezzar inscribed with three columns of text (ca. 586 B.C.) found buried in the foundation of a temple in Babylon*

Although Judah was in some ways simply a pawn in the international affairs between the great nations, there is nevertheless little doubt that its final collapse was partly of its own doing, as the prophets and others had recognized. When the inner cohesion of a nation has been lost, when the national faith has been abandoned and replaced by injustice and social disintegration, a nation has neither the will nor the strength to resist external threats. As we have seen already, the prophets perceived this inner weakness in their nation and anticipated eventual defeat, interpreting it as divine judgment on their nation's evil. A few of the better kings in Judah also perceived the importance of a vital faith for the nation's welfare. King Josiah, a little more than thirty years before Judah's collapse, initiated a great religious reform in Jerusalem (around 622 B.C.), attempting to restore the ancient religion to its original purity. The reform may have been assisted for a while by the prophet Jeremiah, but it was too little and too late. Following the death of Josiah, the brief resurgence of faith and spirit declined, and there was little internal strength left in Judah to avert the final crisis when it came in 586 B.C. The fall of Judah marked the end of the short Hebrew history of independent statehood (until the reemergence of the modern state of Israel in the twentieth century).

7. Exile and Restoration

The events leading up to Judah's collapse in 586 B.C. had the potential of being even more devastating. The immediate disaster was comprehensive: The small state of Judah was ruined, its capital city with its defensive walls had collapsed, and the once splendid temple, which for centuries had symbolized Judah's faith, lay in ruins. Judah had suffered setbacks before, but nothing on so grand a scale as this. The natural conclusion to draw from the wreckage of 586 B.C. would be that not only had Judah's history come to an end, but also that her religion, too, must have terminated; that religion, after all, had been the state religion of Judah, and the collapse of the state signalled the end of the religion. As we shall see, however, the religion survived, though in a fundamentally altered form.

The Judean population was decimated in 586 B.C. Large numbers had been slaughtered in the military invasion. A further large number (perhaps between ten and fifteen thousand) had been taken to Babylon, there to live as exiles in internment camps. Although those taken into exile constituted a relatively small percentage of the population as a whole, the effect of the deportation on the homeland was devastating. The Babylonians, for military reasons, deliberately deported the cream of Judean society—the leaders of government, religion, and the intelligentsia—thereby removing from the conquered territory the possibility of future rebellion. Thus those who remained in Judah after the conquest were for the most part a miserable lot, lacking in leadership and struggling to survive in an impoverished land. Nevertheless, although the spirit of the ancient faith seems to have burned very dimly in the conquered Judah, it was kept alive among those in exile; the words and ministry of the prophet Ezekiel, for example, illustrate the struggle of a few faithful souls to keep the ancient faith alive.

The newly powerful Babylonian Empire, whose armies had terminated Judah's national history, was in itself a state without solid inner strength. Within a few decades of its defeat of Judah, the empire was on the verge of collapse, threatened by the speedy growth of the Persians in the eastern regions of the empire. By 538 B.C., a Babylon already severely weakened fell to the Persian conqueror Cyrus, and all western Asia came under Persian control to form the newest great empire of the ancient Near East. In matters of internal imperial administration, the Persians pursued far more humane policies than had their Babylonian predecessors; although the lot of the Judeans, both at home and in exile, remained that of a subject people, their prospects for the future improved immeasurably.

In 538 B.C., Cyrus issued a decree permitting the return of the Judean exiles to their homeland. It was a decree in harmony with his general policy of permitting a degree of regional autonomy and religious freedom within the overall imperial control. So, a number of those in exile, under the leadership of Shesh-bazzar, returned to Judah and set about the difficult task of restoring Jerusalem to some semblance of order. Unfortunately, all too little is known of this (and the subsequent) period of Judah's history, but from the evidence that has survived, it seems that the first of those to return home from exile had very limited success in their attempt to restore the shambles of Jerusalem.

Almost twenty years later, during the reign of a new Persian emperor, Darius I, a little more progress was made. Under the leadership of the civil governor of the Judean province, Zerubbabel, and its chief priest, Joshua, a start was made in the task of completing the restoration of Jerusalem's temple. Although the work was undertaken under the auspices of the civil and religious authorities, beginning in 520 B.C., the inspiration and encouragement for the task seem to have come primarily from two prophets. Haggai and

Zechariah (chapter 1, section 8), whose works have survived, provided the religious incentive and vision that were to contribute largely to the successful restoration of the temple by 515 B.C. It can hardly have been so splendid a temple as the original constructed in Solomon's time, but the achievement was significant, nevertheless, in religious terms. While the old temple had remained a ruin, it symbolized, appropriately enough, the ruin into which Judah's faith had fallen. The restoration of the temple indicated, symbolically at least, the beginnings of the restoration of Judah's faith, which, prior to 520 B.C., had come precipitously close to its demise.

The history of the Judean community is relatively obscure in the decades following 515 B.C. A little more than half a century later, if it is correct to date the book of Malachi to this period, the religious community of Jerusalem appears to have sunk into a state of despondency. The temple was functioning and worship was conducted in a half-hearted fashion, but future hopes had almost died. The anticipation of a return of Davidic rule and national independence, held by a few people in the time of Haggai and Zechariah, had proved unfounded; the faith of the community survived, but it had all but lost hope for any significant future.

It was not until the last half of the fifth century B.C. that the fortunes of the Judean community around Jerusalem were to be radically transformed. The two principal human agents in this transformation were Nehemiah and Ezra. A brief account of their work and accomplishments has been preserved in the book of Ezra-Nehemiah; unfortunately, although that work contains some detailed insights of the period 445–400 B.C., it also contains some complex historical problems which are not susceptible to easy resolution. Nehemiah's work in Judah can be fixed with reasonable certainty as taking place in the period 445–425 B.C., but the relative timing of Ezra's work in conjunction with that of Nehemiah is one of the most intractable and debated problems of Old Testament history. Some claim that Ezra pre-dated Nehemiah, and some that he worked in Jerusalem at the same time as Nehemiah, and some that he served several decades after Nehemiah (see figure 39). Although any view must remain hypothetical, a date of around 428 B.C. for Ezra's principal mission in Jerusalem seems probable.

Figure 39. THE EXILE AND RESTORATION

Approx. Dates	Significant People and Events
—600 B.C.	
586	Beginning of exile
	Babylonian exile (586–538)
—550 B.C.	
539	Cyrus defeats Babylon
538	Beginning of the return from exile
520–515	Restoration of the Temple
—500 B.C.	
	Prophets: Haggai and Zechariah
—450 B.C.	
	Ezra and Nehemiah (Jerusalem)
—400 B.C.	PERSIAN PERIOD
—350 B.C.	
333 B.C.	Invasion of Alexander the Great
—300 B.C.	GREEK PERIOD

Nehemiah, a Judean who rose to a position of considerable seniority in the Persian court, was able to obtain permission from the emperor to go to Jerusalem. His mission was to rebuild the city's walls and, in effect, to become the local governor of the territory around Jerusalem. His personal agenda included the desire to restore to some vitality the declining religion of the native Judean community. The natural ability which had enabled Nehemiah to rise so high in the Persian government stood him in good stead in his new task in Jerusalem. During his first term as governor (he had two terms, extending over more than a dozen years), he was successful, against considerable local opposition, in rebuilding Jerusalem's walls and in providing a degree of security to the citizens of the city and to the worship conducted in the temple. He was successful, too, as governor, providing some coherence to a disorganized and disillusioned people, though it is difficult to tell the extent to which he was successful in bringing about religious reform.

Whatever success Nehemiah may have had in religious terms, it was Ezra who succeeded principally in restoring the vitality of the religious community in and around Jerusalem. He had been given a mandate from the Persian emperor to teach the ancient Hebrew Law to the Judean community and to reform the life of that community by bringing it into harmony with the law. Precisely what constituted Ezra's law is a matter of debate; of various possibilities that have been proposed, the most likely is that the Pentateuch, or Five Books of Moses, constituted the legislative and religious basis of Ezra's reform. Although too few of the details are known with any precision, it is fair to say that the religion, whose future had hung in the balance since 586 B.C., was given a firm foundation in the work of Ezra. From the ancient religion tied intimately to the state of Judah, there had emerged after a period of transition the basic forms of Judaism; under Ezra's leadership, a central role in Judaism was to be played by the Torah (or Pentateuch).

After the time of Ezra and Nehemiah, very little more is known of Israelite history in the Old Testament period. A few of the biblical books may have been written in the following century or so (Esther and perhaps Daniel), and others may have reached their final forms. But in historical terms the period after Ezra and Nehemiah marks a new beginning: The history of Israel gives way to the history of Judaism (this is examined briefly in a subsequent chapter).

THE
RELIGION AND FAITH
OF ISRAEL

T HE brief survey of Israel's history in the preceding chapter has provided some insight into the experience of the Hebrew people over the course of more than a millennium. But historical surveys alone cannot do justice to some of the deeper questions about Israel's existence: What was it that held the Hebrew people together over the centuries? What was it that has made their literature more than simply ancient manuscripts that survived from a bygone age? What was the distinctive contribution of the Hebrews to human thought and civilization? It is evident from the outset that the Hebrew contribution was very different from that of ancient Egypt or Mesopotamia. Although archaeological remains of Israel's history are of interest to the specialist, the Hebrews did not make their mark on history with structures like the extraordinary pyramids of Egypt or the palaces of Nineveh or Babylon. Nor did they achieve particular distinction in, for example, mathematics or medicine, as did their neighbors. Although they left us great literature, the book of Job for example, their literary achievements were matched elsewhere, as in the magnificent *Epic of Gilgamesh* from ancient Mesopotamia. It was above all in the realm of faith and religion that the Hebrews made their most distinctive contribution, and that faith in turn has left its imprint on the pages of the books that have been preserved in the Old Testament.

When we study the religion of Israel and its related culture (for religion pervaded every aspect of Hebrew life, so that one cannot really distinguish between the sacred and the secular), we are engaged potentially in a twofold task. At one level, it is a study of ancient institutions and of the religious faith of the persons who created and maintained those institutions. This is, in the narrow sense, the study of the history of religions, but there is another level to the study of Israel's religion. To study it only as a phenomenon of the ancient world, without reflecting on the fact that the ancient texts continue to survive and to stimulate faith in the modern world, would be to see only a part of the picture. The first of these levels will provide the substance of the present chapter: the study of religion and faith, as they were in ancient Israel. The second level, involving an attempt to appreciate the ancient religious texts in the modern world, will be the substance of the next (and last) chapter of this book.

It is wise to recognize from the outset that the study of ancient Israel's religion is a complex task. We have only the surviving biblical texts, supplemented by the meager archaeological resources, at our disposal; these are less than the ideal resources in an attempt to penetrate those areas of human life which are so closely related to the human spirit and the inner world of faith. We cannot interview any of the participants in the religious ceremonies that used to be conducted. We cannot engage in debate with the theologians and thinkers. We can only view the ancient religion and culture through the lens provided by the extant texts; therefore, our understanding must be incomplete and somewhat superficial. Although we cannot always identify the authors of the biblical books, we may surmise that for the most part they come from among either the religious authorities or from persons of peculiar gifts and remarkable insight, such as the prophet. Very little is known of what the ordinary person on the street believed and how the faith of Israel influenced his or her life.

There is a further problem of a more practical nature. Over the span of more than a millennium, the religion and culture reflected in the pages of the Old Testament underwent considerable change. The simpler faith of the patriarchs was transformed to the complex cult of Solomon's temple. The royal religion of Judah, in turn, was subsequently transformed to a different kind of faith, divorced in effect from its royal ideology. The changes in the forms of religion were naturally balanced by a developing theology. The notion of God in the earliest period of Israel's history had been made broader and deeper by the end of the biblical period. The recognition that change and development took place over the passage of time makes any account of Israel's religion and culture a complicated task; it becomes even more complex when that account is reduced to the confines of a single chapter! Inevitably, the summary which follows has had to be simplified, and all the modifications that occurred through the centuries (in both religious practice and faith) cannot be fully documented or described. Nevertheless, for all the limitations imposed upon the enterprise, the paragraphs that follow attempt to provide some overview of religious practice, religious faith, and the general culture that flourished in Israel in Old Testament times.

1. The Basic Religion of Israel: Cult

The word *cult,* in popular and modern use, has taken on new (and sometimes negative) connotations. It is used, for example, to describe forms of religion which are marginal to "mainstream" religion, and it may have negative connotations in expressions like *false cults.* But in the historical study of religion, the word cult is used in its more classical sense: It designates the social worship of a deity, involving various rituals and symbols, in which the relationship between the deity and the community is given expression. Thus in the study of Israelite religion a study of the cult involves an examination of the formal and communal structures of religion—the forms of worship, the places of worship, the festivals of the religion, and so on. The task is complicated, as has already been indicated, by the development and change that took place through the period of biblical history—Abraham's worship and that of Solomon differed radically, despite the threads of continuity linking the two. The task of reconstruction is even more difficult. Much of the information about the temple and worship is contained in books like Leviticus; as we saw in chapter four, the dating of Leviticus is much debated, hence it is not easy to place it in the history of Israel's religion. Recognizing these difficulties, it is possible, nevertheless, to give a general account of Israel's cult.

Fundamental to the cult was Israel's acknowledgment of the existence of God and of the implications of that acknowledgment for Israel. Israel, by virtue of the special knowledge of God granted to it, was to engage in the worship of God. We shall explore some of the theological dimensions of this requirement of worship in the following sections of the chapter; for the moment, it is sufficient to note that worship required certain formal activities on the part of the community. While God could not be confined to a particular place, nevertheless, normal and formal acts of worship were to be conducted in a particular place, though initially that place was not given a fixed geographical location.

The patriarchs worshiped at different regional shrines in the various places through which they traveled; the Hebrews, after the exodus and before the settlement, also worshiped in various places. Nevertheless, there emerged after the exodus and before the settlement a symbol of God's presence, and where that symbol was located became the principal place for the offering of worship. The symbol was the *ark,* variously called the "ark of the covenant," the "ark of the testimony," or the "ark of the Lord." It was, strictly speaking, a small box (approximately three and one-half feet long and about twenty-seven inches wide and twenty-seven inches deep). It purportedly contained the tablets of the ancient law given to Moses. The ark, in turn, was initially housed in a tent shrine, the tent becoming the place at which worship was to be offered, for the ark symbolized God's presence among his people.

In the time of David, the ark was transferred to Jerusalem, and in Solomon's time it was moved into the newly constructed temple. Thus the temple, which during and after the monarchy came to be the focal point of religion in the south, was the place in which God was held to be symbolically present; it was in the temple, therefore, that Israel, and later Judah, engaged in formal worship. In the northern state of Israel, after 922 B.C., obviously a different tradition emerged (for there was only one ark), but the notion of a particular place for worship persisted; although the cult was practiced in different places in the north, perhaps concurrently, such shrines as Bethel seem to have had particular significance. Nevertheless, the main tradition of the biblical narrative, extending from the united monarchy, through

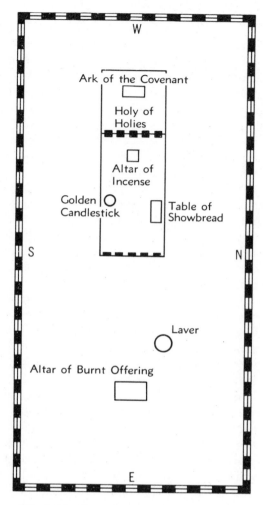

Figure 40. Plan of the tabernacle and its courts

the kingdom of Judah, and into the post-exilic community in which Judaism emerged, focused upon Jerusalem and its temple as the proper place in which the worship of God was to be offered. Practices in northern Israel were viewed, for the most part, in Judah as aberrations; until the destruction of the temple in the first century A.D., Jerusalem became the focal point of all formal worship. The synagogue as a place of worship developed much later than did the temple; although the synagogue's origins are obscure (and not mentioned in the Old Testament), it is possible that it arose as an institution among those in exile cut off from home and temple.

Within the temple, worship was conducted by a body of professional priests who were trained in the religious laws and traditions pertaining to their tasks. Although worship in the temple was a daily activity, it assumed distinctive forms and ceremonies on particular occasions. The daily services in the temple were supplemented by special services on each sabbath and on the first day of each (lunar) month. In addition, there were particular services conducted from time to time in the temple, having to do with national or family events or crises. The year as a whole was punctuated by the great religious festivals, in which the foundations of life and of Israel's faith were celebrated (discussed below). Thus worship in the temple was a day-in and day-out affair, though the participation of the people as a whole in this worship was much more restricted. For many people, their principal involvement in temple worship may have been limited to the great annual festivals.

Various components make up the substance and activity of worship; one of the most important of which is sacrifice. Various kinds of sacrifices involving the slaughter of animals are specified in the ancient ritual laws—the four principal kinds being the burnt offering, the peace offering, the sin offering, and the guilt offering. Although the texts provide a certain amount of detail as to how these sacrifices were to be offered, the symbolism and deeper meaning of the rituals is frequently obscure. In the burnt offering, for example, the animal was slaughtered, its blood was drained off and thrown against the base of the temple's altar, and then the beast itself was burned. Precisely what purpose the sacrifice served is less than clear in the texts.

In the case of the peace offering, the symbolism is more evident. As before, the animal is slaughtered and its blood cast on the base of the altar. Then certain portions (entrails and kidneys) are burned on the altar as a symbolic gift to God; other portions are assigned to the priests for eating, and a third portion is eaten in the sanctuary by the group (perhaps a family) which brought the sacrificial offering to the temple. The symbolism here is that of the sacrificial meal, in which the food offered in sacrifice is shared both by the worshiper and God; it

Figure 41. *Front view of a model of Solomon's Temple, with "molten sea" at left and altar of burnt offering at right*

indicates the relationship and companionship that may exist between worshipers and the God whom they worship. Certain sacrifices were accompanied by the offering of grain and meal, representing on the one hand the goodness of God to his people in the provision of food, and on the other hand the return of thanks to God and the sense of sharing God's presence in the temple meal. The sacrifices as a whole reflect, no doubt, various levels of meaning and symbolism, and although the precise sense of a given sacrifice may be difficult to determine, the overall range of meaning becomes evident from the texts. Sacrifices may reflect such things as the awareness of failure or acts of evil on the part of the worshiper, but the most common element seems to be that of thanksgiving to God.

Worship involved not only ritual and symbolic acts, such as sacrifice, but also the words whereby the assembled persons gave expression to their acts of worship. In understanding this dimension of Israel's religious practice, we have at our disposal many of the hymns and prayers that comprise the substance of the book of Psalms. As we have seen already in the survey of the Psalms, it is not always easy to pinpoint the precise setting in worship in which a given psalm might have been used. Some hymns, for example, may have served for use in general worship, whereas others may have been specified only for use in the great annual festivals. Some of the prayers and laments may have been used in communal acts of worship, whereas others were designed for use in individual or family rituals in the temple (for example, rituals designed for those who were sick or threatened with death). For all the difficulties of interpreting the psalms in their ancient cultic setting, nevertheless they provide a window through which we can see more clearly the inner and spiritual dynamics of Israel's worship.

The passing of a year in ancient Israel followed a religious calendar, and the year was punctuated by special days set aside for particular celebration and acts of worship. These annual festivals were no doubt moments of particular significance for the ordinary people, and set before them the fundamental truths of Israel's religion. Unfortunately, the texts from which we must reconstruct these festivals are subject to considerable debate among literary scholars, and there are, therefore, uncertainties about some of the ancient festivals, their original meanings, and their relationship to one another. The three principal festivals in ancient Israel were: (a)

Unleavened Bread/Passover, (b) Feast of Weeks, and (c) Feast of Booths; a fourth occasion, considered by many scholars to be a later development, was (d) the Day of Atonement. At the very end of the Old Testament period, there developed also (e) the Festival of Purim. (The Festival of Hanukkah is a post-biblical development, its origins being described in I Maccabees in the Apocrypha.)

(a) *The Festival of Unleavened Bread* (Matzah) and that of Passover may originally have been independent celebrations, but from an early date they seem to have been celebrated concurrently. They became in Israel a great pilgrimage festival (as did (b) and (c) below) in which adult males were required to go to Jerusalem to participate in the national act of worship in the spring of the year. Although Unleavened Bread may have been originally an agricultural festival, its linkage to Passover meant inevitably that the celebration of the joint festival had its focus in the past, specifically in the commemoration of Israel's liberation from Egyptian slavery. It was thus a festival of rejoicing in freedom, but at the same time a reminder of the agonies of human bondage; God was praised as the one who had brought, and continued to bring, his people from human slavery into the freedom of God.

(b) *The Feast of Weeks* (or "First Fruits") was also originally an agricultural festival celebrated in the spring in the context of another pilgrimage to Jerusalem. (It was to be celebrated seven weeks after the Festival of Unleavened Bread.) Although the festival may have originally celebrated the completion of the wheat harvest, it came to have historical associations in Israel's religion, as did Unleavened Bread/Passover. It was during this festival that God's gift of the law to Israel at Mount Sinai was recalled and celebrated, so that it was in some sense a covenant festival. It may be that the ancient ceremony of covenant renewal, originating in the time of Moses or shortly thereafter, came to be associated with the Feast of Weeks (see Deuteronomy 27:11-26 and Joshua 8:30-35).

(c) *The Festival of Booths* (or "Tents," or "Tabernacles," or "Ingathering," all being names of the same event) was the harvest festival *par excellence* and was celebrated in the autumn. In ancient times, it seems to have been recognized as the most important of all the festivals and celebrated with corresponding enthusiasm. At one level, it involved thanksgiving to God for his provision for the sustenance of human life in the produce of harvest. But at another level, there was once again a historical dimension to the celebration; it was a time to remember the past, when their ancestors had wandered in the wilderness with only tents for shelter and no land to call their own.

(d) *The Day of Atonement* (Yom Kippur) was a day of an altogether different kind and could perhaps be regarded as the most solemn occasion in the religious year. It was a day on which the people as a whole engaged in solemn reflection and fasting while special sacrifices were offered to secure the cleansing of the temple, the priests, and the people from the impurities and evil of the preceding year. On the Day of Atonement, the past, with all its sins and failure, could be set behind and a new beginning was made in the nation's relationship with its God.

(e) *The Festival of Purim* was established at the very end of the biblical period (see the notes on the book of Esther in chapter 9).

The sketch of Israel's formal worship and holy days provides only a partial picture of Israel's religion. Lying behind the communal gathering for worship and the enacted rituals, there is a set of beliefs embedded in the traditions and literature which have become a part of the biblical text. It is to the substance of religious belief that we must now turn, for an understanding of that will in turn help to make sense of the formal worship that has just been summarized.

2. Religious Belief and Ideas

A knowledge of the cult in ancient Israel must be balanced by some awareness of Israelite theology; that is, its knowledge of God and the implications of that knowledge for an understanding of human beings and the world in which they live. The word *theology*, in this context, can only be used with caution; it is derived from Greek and means "science of God" or "science of divine things." If we take the word in its more scientific sense, with implications for example of propositional statements about God, clarified and defended in rational and/or philosophical terms, then it would be wisest to recognize that, for all practical purposes, there is no theology in the Old Testament. Indeed, some of the profoundest "theological" statements in the Old Testament were written in poetry (Psalms, Job), and poetry conveys more of the mystery inherent in truth than it does its rational structure. If by *theology* we mean simply the study of the

Old Testament's expression of the knowledge and experience of God, then we can use the term cautiously.

There is another area in which caution must be taken if we are to review Old Testament theology. Many books which bear this title are in fact Christian theologies of the Old Testament that attempt to understand the ancient text through Christian eyes, more specifically through the lens of the New Testament. Similar books may be written from a Jewish perspective, in which the theology of the ancient biblical texts is viewed through the lens of the later rabbinical writings. Now, both these approaches to the biblical text are fully legitimate in the context of contemporary Jewish or Christian religion; they will be touched on briefly in the final chapter. But the immediate enterprise is a more limited one. What are the essential theological perspectives of the Old Testament *per se,* examined as a religious document in its own right?

The very nature of the Old Testament, as a collection of different books, is such that we would not expect a single and unified perspective penetrating the whole collection. Despite the diversity of theological perspective within the whole, there are certain overarching themes which give the Old Testament a theological unity. The unity of thought must not be overstressed so that an artificial and bland orthodoxy emerges; the theological perspectives of the writers of Deuteronomy and Ecclesiastes, for example, are in many ways radically different. Yet, for all that, there are some fundamental theological norms, and if we can grasp these, we are in a better position to read the biblical books with understanding.

As a principle of organization, it is important to recognize that religion in ancient Israel was essentially a form of *relationship.* It primarily concerned the relationship between God and Israel, but from that flowed an understanding of the relationship between God and individual human beings. The context of the relationship is this world, and an understanding of the world in religious terms is, therefore, a necessary component of the theological spectrum. Hence, in the summary that follows the subject is treated in the following order: (a) God; (b) mankind; (c) the world; (d) relationship and covenant. The theology is distinctively *Israelite;* that is to say, it pertains primarily to an understanding of God's relationship to his chosen people. But in sections (a) to (c), especially, much of the insight is drawn from Genesis 1–11, which is more universal in scope and application, predating the election of Israel (in terms of theological perspective, though not with respect to the time of its writing). In other words, part of the theological summary that follows is rooted in a general understanding of God and of mankind that was not intended to be limited in its application to the community of Israel alone. No summary can do justice to the diversity of religious thought in ancient Israel; at best, it can only open the door to further study and reflection.

(a) God

The modern reader of the Old Testament, well versed perhaps in the substance of classical and modern philosophy, may find it both disturbing and surprising that the Old Testament writers launch directly into their subject matter with the assumption that God exists. They do not attempt to prove that existence; they take it for granted, as an article of faith or a self-evident truth. We may think that it was easier for them to believe, living as they were in a world which was not permeated, for the most part, with radical philosophical thought. The writers of the Old Testament books had not been exposed to either the classical philosophical arguments *against* God's existence or even to the weakness of the various arguments (the ontological, the cosmological, and others) *for* God's existence. Thus, from our modern perspective, there may appear at first to be a certain naïveté to the biblical books—God exists, and that is that!

Certainly it must be acknowledged that the Old Testament writings emerged from a cultural and intellectual world very different from our own. Specifically, their world was not one dominated by rationalistic philosophy, although the emergence of classical philosophy was taking place in the Greek world in the latter half of the Old Testament period. Having recognized the different cultural world in which the biblical texts emerged, however, we must also recognize that their writers held a theology radically different from that prevalent in their surrounding culture. Furthermore, it was not a naïve view, whatever else one may think of it; in particular, the writers of Job and Ecclesiastes, as we shall see, betray a profound awareness of the problems of human understanding precipitated by their faith in God. Nevertheless, the general perspective summarized above is faithful to the texts—from the first verse of the first book of the Bible,

God's existence is affirmed and assumed. It is indeed an article of faith, and we may suppose in addition that it is deeply grounded in religious experience, both communal and individual, though this dimension of the affirmation of faith is more difficult to examine.

The Hebrews affirmed the existence of a *single God,* though in the earliest period their religion was not necessarily *monotheistic,* in a technical sense. Thus in the earliest period the texts reveal allegiance to one God as the God of the community, but there is little indication that they went out of their way to deny the existence of all other gods, which would be the essence of monotheism. Nevertheless, the early religion was an incipient kind of monotheism, and certainly by the age of the classical prophets, the so-called Second Isaiah (Isaiah 40–55), for example, it had developed into a full-fledged monotheism: There is one God, and there are no others! It is this monotheistic character of the Hebrew religion that immediately sets it apart in the context of Near Eastern religions in the biblical world. Religious traditions as a whole, from Egypt to Mesopotamia, were polytheistic; that is, they involved belief in, and worship of, a variety of deities. Only in Egypt, a short time before the age of Moses, was there a brief emergence of a limited kind of monotheism in the ancient world. The remarkable Pharaoh Akhenaten appears to have maintained a faith which was essentially monotheistic, but it was short-lived. Various attempts to link Akhenaten's monotheism to that of Moses have not proved successful. When we recognize this essentially monotheistic character of the Hebrew theology, we perceive that it was certainly not naïve in the context of its own world. The belief in a single God was sharply at odds with the surrounding culture, and as the prophetic writings make clear, there was a constant tendency in the Hebrew tradition to abandon strict monotheism and to embrace the gods (Baal, for example) of neighboring religions.

The Hebrew notion of God differed in other remarkable ways from the views held by their neighbors. The deities of the Near Eastern religions represented, for the most part, aspects of the natural world—rain, storm, heaven, earth, grain, and the like. They were nature deities and reflected, in turn, a view of the world as being in itself divine in some sense. In contrast, the Hebrews affirmed a God who was not part of the world, or part of nature; he was Creator of the world and Lord of nature, and yet distinct, transcending the world as we know it. The distinction between God and the natural world is one of the reasons lying behind the opening of the Ten Commandments, which prohibits the representation of God in the form of an image or idol (Exodus 20:4). Any image or idol would tend to remove the distinction between God and the natural world. In this, too, the religion of the Hebrews differed radically from that of neighboring nations, in which images and idols were used to symbolize the gods. For the Hebrews, all such symbols and attempts at representation were inadequate.

Various words are used in the Hebrew language to designate the deity. The most common general noun is *Elohim,* which is translated in the English Bible as *God* (where it refers to the God of Israel), or *gods* if the reference is to other deities. The most significant word in the Bible for the deity is not a simple noun, but a proper name: *Yahweh.* In English Bibles, this is conventionally rendered LORD (capitalized), but to render *Yahweh* as LORD is a circumlocution, not a translation. The word *Yahweh* is a proper and personal name. (Its meaning is much debated, but the sense may be: "He who causes to be"). The personal name of God was made known to Israel in Moses' time, according to the tradition, as an act of special grace on God's part (see Exodus 3:13-15 and 6:2). In later Jewish tradition, the sacredness of God's name was such that it was not pronounced, even in reading the Torah (with the exception of the Day of Atonement, when the priest uttered the name), and the circumlocution "Lord" was used instead. From the point of view of Old Testament theology, the fact that God revealed to Israel his personal name is more important than attempting to determine etymologically the sense of the name; it was the knowledge of the name that made possible a relationship of intimacy between God and Israel.

The essence of ancient Hebrew theology is that God could be known in relationship with humankind. The implications of this emphasis are various. On the one hand, there is little speculative or philosophical dimension to Hebrew thought, and little attempt to define the nature and existence of God in abstract terms. On the other hand, the kinds of words used to qualify the attributes of God are primarily relational—God is merciful, kind, loving, patient, and so on. Even such conceptions as God's *holiness* are developed in relational terms: He loves goodness, hates evil, and requires of human beings justice and righteousness.

These, then, are some of the basic aspects of the Hebrew notion of God, but the picture is still incomplete; the fully rounded notion of God does not emerge until we see it in conjunction with the notion of humankind, the world, and covenant.

(b) Human Beings

According to the narrative of creation (Genesis 1), human beings are the creatures of God; they receive the gift of life from the Creator. (Genesis 1, as will be argued further in the section (c) below, is primarily a *theological* narrative, not a page from an early scientific textbook.) Furthermore, human beings, both male and female, are created "in the image of God," and their creation is described as "good" (Genesis 1:27-31). The notion of the "image of God," with respect to human beings, has been discussed and debated at length over the centuries, and no single interpretation can do justice to the conception. But at least a part of the sense seems to be this: The image of God, which distinguishes human beings from the rest of creation, is in part the capacity of human beings to have a relationship with the God whose image they bear.

A preliminary picture of human beings, as it emerges from the biblical text, would thus go as follows: Human beings are the creation of God and as such are good. A part of the mysterious meaning of their existence is to be found in the divinely given capacity to have a relationship with their Creator. Beginning with the Garden of Eden, and extending the survey down into the twentieth century, it is clear that any view of human beings which portrays them simply as "good" requires a little modification. Thus the story of Adam and Eve in the Garden of Eden portrays a more developed view of mankind; the narrative begins with two good humans in relationship with their Creator, but it ends with two sinful human beings cut off from their God. Therefore, the theme of the goodness of the creation of human beings is balanced by an awareness of the potential for evil in human beings, and the ideal of relationship with God is balanced immediately by the reality of human alienation from God. As we shall see, this tension of relationship and alienation is one of several threads running through the Old Testament as a whole. Human beings, who may discover the meaning of their existence in relationship with God, are nevertheless alienated from God by their own exercise of will and freedom and their pursuit of evil. The first three chapters of Genesis thus portray not only a theological understanding of Israel's whole history, but also of the common experience of humankind.

Space does not permit a complete account of the Hebrew understanding of human beings, but there is one further aspect of the Hebrew Bible which requires some elaboration. The theological language about God in the Old Testament is necessarily *anthropomorphic;* that is, it ascribes human form or attributes to the deity. Many textbooks use the term *anthropomorphic* only to illustrate the more picturesque accounts of God (for example, God taking a walk in the Garden of Eden), but in reality almost all biblical language has to be anthropomorphic, to a greater or lesser extent. In order to describe God, only language drawn from the human experience of being and reality is available. This can be illustrated by reference to the language of *love* in the Old Testament.

It is said that God chose the people of Israel to be a special nation because he *loved* them (Deuteronomy 7:8). The principal duty of the Israelites, in turn, was to respond to God in *love* (Deuteronomy 6:5). The theological elaboration of this relationship of love belongs in section (d), below; what is significant in the present context is the manner in which an essentially human attribute can be employed, anthropomorphically, in a theological context. Human beings, whose life as we have seen is a gift of God, have the capacity to love; this is not, in itself, a remarkable insight, and it is present in many cultures and religions. The Hebrews celebrated this capacity for human love, in its romantic form, in the Song of Songs, which as we have already seen is an essentially secular collection of love poetry. What is important, however, is that the assumption of the Song of Songs is that love is essentially good, or a part of the goodness of God's gift of life in creation. (This view is in marked contrast to one stream of later Christian thought, which viewed love as if it were evil, at least in its romantic form, and sought to avoid the obvious sense of the Song of Songs.) The goodness of love is such that not only may the language of love be transferred to the realm of theological expression, but also the experience of love might be used for theological understanding (as in the later allegorical interpretation of the Song of Songs). Conversely, the abuse of human love—for example, in adultery and unfaithfulness—can become a vehicle for expressing the abuse of the relationship with God, as both Ezekiel (chapter 16) and Hosea (chapters 1–3) make clear. What this theme as a whole illustrates is the manner in which an understanding of the biblical conception of human beings is related intimately to Old Testament theology.

(c) The World

At first sight, the world (or cosmos) might not seem to be an essential part of Old Testament theology; yet, in fact, it is vital and is raised as an issue in the first chapter of Genesis and returned to frequently in the subsequent biblical books. The starting point for our discussion must inevitably be Genesis, chapter 1, with its narrative of creation. Now, as every reader will be aware, the interpretation of the creation narrative in Genesis is not only a difficult task, but it is also a frequent subject of debate and dissent in contemporary society. Taken at face value, Genesis 1 describes the creation of the world in six days and God's rest on the seventh day. Is it, as some would have us believe, a history of the beginning of the world and an early scientific account of the origins of matter and of the species? Or is it a kind of theological writing which has more religious issues to address?

I do not have the space to argue my position in detail; I can only state it in outline form. First, it seems that the creation story is a profoundly theological piece of writing; its basic concerns are neither historical nor scientific. (Indeed, the fascination concerning the relationship between Genesis 1 and modern science and history is a relatively new phenomenon, emerging only in recent centuries. The earliest readers of the text may have sensed more easily than we can the theological intent of the writing.) As a theological narrative, Genesis 1 employs forms of language, superficially simple, by which to convey truths ultimately beyond human understanding. Second, the theological intent of Genesis 1 is to address three of the most fundamental questions any human being can raise: (i) What is the nature of God? (ii) What is the nature of mankind? (iii) What is the nature of the world in which human beings live? (Incidentally, these three questions are reflected in the ordering of knowledge in the older universities, which involved the study of *theology,* the knowledge of God, the *humanities,* or the knowledge of mankind, and the *natural sciences,* namely the knowledge of the world. The same general perspective survives in many contemporary universities.) We have seen already something of what the creation narrative has to say about God and mankind; now we must view its perspective on the world in which human beings live.

From a theological and religious perspective, the kind of knowledge required about the world is quite different from what might interest a scientist or a historian. How and when it all began are less relevant theological issues than the nature and character of the world in which human beings live (although the questions may ultimately become related). As human beings reflect upon the world in which they live, they are faced with a tension, or perhaps a polarity of evidence. Some of the evidence suggests that the world is ordered; some suggests it is characterized by chaos. Season follows season in an orderly fashion, but then there are the times of drought, of famine, of flood, or of plague, which evoke only a sense of the chaos of the world. This sense of the polarity of order and chaos is present, to a greater or lesser extent, in all the Near Eastern creation stories; it is also present in the opening words of Genesis.

Although the evidence of the world, when viewed by its citizens, reflects this polarity of order and chaos, the theological affirmation of the creation narrative is that the fundamental and God-given character of the world is one of order. The reality of chaos is recognized in the opening verses of the narrative (Genesis 1:1-2). The essence of creation theology is that God established order out of primeval chaos, and this affirmation of faith, in turn, has implications for human living. What kind of world do we live in? One in which the imprint of divine order has been established, and therefore one in which a meaningful human existence can be had in relationship with God the Creator.

The creation narrative is, nevertheless, a theological statement, and like most theology its substance may be called into question by the experience of life itself. Thus Job's encounter with human misery and suffering called into question the very essence of creation theology; if the actual encounter with the world reveals only its character as chaos, with the subsequent suffering chaos brings, how can one affirm faith in creation? Although the answer to such a question is not easy to articulate, one can begin to see why creation is the central theme in God's answer to Job's anguished cry (Job 38–40). Sickness, death, plague, hurricane, misery—these are the things which, in human experience, raise the question of the character of the world in which we live, hence they raise the question as to the possibility of living a meaningful life in that world.

In summary, the foundations of Hebrew theology are these: There is one God. Human beings are the creation of God and may find the meaning of their existence in relation to God. The world in which human life is lived is marked by God's order, even if at times that order may be difficult to discern. From these essential foundations, the distinctively Israelite theology emerges, in which the specific nature of the relationship between God and Israel is given expression.

(d) Relationship and Covenant

Running through the Old Testament story is the theme of God's special relationship with his chosen people. It begins with Abraham, is developed further in the time of Moses, is amplified fully in the reign of David, and continues through the last decades of history reflected in the biblical books. The principal word used to describe this relationship is *covenant,* and although a few biblical scholars in recent years have attempted to argue that the notion of covenant was a late development in Hebrew thought, the overwhelming weight of the biblical evidence makes such a hypothesis unlikely. There is nevertheless a development and refinement in the notion of covenant over the centuries. The theme begins with a relatively simple covenant between God and Abraham (Genesis 15); it receives its most comprehensive expression in the age of Moses, with the covenant between God and Israel established at Mount Sinai (especially Exodus 19–20). In David's time, the covenant takes on a more royal character, and thereafter God's relationship with his people is established through the royal family, the Davidic line.

The word *covenant* implies a relationship between two persons or parties in which mutual obligations are implied or stated with respect to the covenant partners. (The Hebrew word can be used, for example, to describe a *treaty* between nations or a marriage contract.) The covenant, in religious terms, was the relationship which existed between God and his people; it involved for them mutually recognized obligations, these being freely offered by God and voluntarily accepted by Israel. From a theological perspective, the covenant expressed the divine promise. To Abraham, God promised posterity and the eventual formation of a nation in its own land. To Israel at Sinai, God promised a land and the rich blessing of God in the Hebrews' future existence as a nation. The promise of God in the covenant relationship required, in turn, a response from the people. They would become a "kingdom of priests" (Exodus 19:6), representing the world's nations before God, but they would acquire this role through obedience to the God-given law. Thus the laws in the Old Testament, specifically the Ten Commandments (Exodus 20; Deuteronomy 5) and the detailed law codes in the Pentateuch, were part and parcel of Israel's covenant. They were the gift of God to his people; obedience to those laws would lead to the experience of God's blessing in the covenant relationship.

The notion of covenant, however, for all its theological dimensions, was not a religious abstraction but a political reality. Thus the covenant of Sinai, with its accompanying law, was not merely a religious experience, something to be remembered through later generations; rather, it was the constitutional foundation of a new nation, and the law was to become the law of the nation. For example, the Ten Commandments, which we tend to think of nowadays as an ethical and religious summary, served in ancient Israel as the primary law of the state, in effect its "Criminal Law Code." From the early period down to the time of Judah's defeat in 586 B.C., Israel's covenant was given its external expression in the nation state—covenant religion was national religion. After 586 B.C., however, with the demise of the state, the covenant faith became rather the religion of a community, Judaism, and what were formerly state laws gradually moved into the realm of the laws of a religious community.

Although the external form of the covenant changed quite radically through the centuries of biblical history, its fundamental character remained the same. It constituted the relationship between God and Israel, and at a more personal level, the relationship between God and the individual members of the community. It required of its members respect for law, justice in human relationships, and ethical behavior. It established the foundations for religious practice and worship, the *cult* (described in section 1, above) being an essential part of covenant life. The rituals of the cult sought to maintain spiritual health within the covenant community (for example, the forgiveness and removal of evil, which disrupted the community's relationship with a holy God). The community's worship, which was given both ritual and vocal expression, expressed the communal response to God's goodness and provision. But the reality of Israel's history was such that frequently the covenant stipulations were broken or ignored; a part of the response to Israel's failures in its relationship with God can be seen in the work of the Hebrew prophets.

3. The Prophetic Dimension

We have already seen the review of the contents of the Old Testament that the prophetic writings constitute a substantial proportion of the entire collection. In addition to the books named after the major and minor prophets, several prophetic figures (Elijah and Elisha, for example) occupy places of importance in the historical books. It remains, however, to set the writings and thoughts of the prophets firmly in the context of Hebrew religion as a whole.

It is important initially to dispel certain popular misunderstandings about prophecy, widely circulated in the modern world, which mitigate against an appreciation of the phenomenon of prophecy in ancient Israel. It is common in the modern world for the prophets to be described as the *predictors* of the ancient world, whose principal task was to foretell future events. From this general perspective, there have emerged many contemporary books which have attempted to interpret the prophetic sayings in the light of the history of many other centuries). One of the strange side-effects of this attempt to make the prophets relevant in our own world is that it has portrayed them as essentially irrelevant figures in their own world. While it is true, as we shall see, that the prophets did speak about the future and on occasion offer predictions, prophecy as such cannot be defined in narrow terms.

Prophecy may be defined in its most basic form as the public proclamation of God's word. The prophet's role was that of proclaimer, or the messenger of God. The substance of prophecy may be as diverse as the intent of God's message to Israel through the prophets; thus it may address the past, the present, or the future. It always has some relevance to the present, that is to the present life and circumstances of the persons to whom the message was declared. But the prophetic word frequently had a broader application, and the preservation of so many prophetic words and writings in the canon of the Old Testament is testimony to the fact that the enduring message and relevance of the prophets was perceived at an early date. The principal relevance of the prophets beyond their own time stems not from the fact that they addressed future generations, but from recognition of the fact that they claimed to speak the divine word. The prophetic material is, for the most part, a record of spoken revelation, an account of words addressed by God to Israel through the medium of prophecy.

Prophecy was not unique to ancient Israel; the phenomenon is also attested, for example, in ancient second millennium B.C. texts discovered at Mari, in northern Mesopotamia. But the distinctive character of Israelite prophecy is based on the religion of which it is a part; the Hebrew prophets declared the word of *Yahweh,* Israel's God, and in this they were unique. Some prophets would be called in modern terms *professional clergy;* that is, like the priests, they were the officials (or employees) of the temple cult. Whereas the priests represented the people in their worship before God, the prophets brought God's word to the assembled people. Although the priesthood was a closed profession, passed on by hereditary tradition, prophecy seems to have been more open; many prophets (perhaps the majority of those whose names are still known) were for practical purposes amateurs, or non-professional persons, not engaged in the service of the temple. Indeed, the principal distinguishing feature of the classical prophets is not heredity, but *vocation;* prophets like Isaiah (chapter 6) and Jeremiah (chapter 1) sensed the divine call and responded to it, thereby becoming prophets by virtue of declaring the prophetic word.

Very little is known of the professional, or cult, prophets, whose daily tasks were undertaken for the most part within the temple's precincts. The classical prophets, especially those after whom books have been named, may have had on occasion a high profile in the social context of ancient Israel and Judah. Men like Micah, Amos, Isaiah, and Jeremiah, whose messages were declared in public and who were frequently in the center of controversy, must have become well-known public figures. The fame they achieved in their own time, together with the substance of their messages, led to the preservation of their words, and sometimes biographical fragments, for subsequent generations.

The prophetic sermons and speeches were as diverse in content as were the times and occasions in which the prophets ministered. But for all the diversity of the prophetic messages, it is possible to trace some themes and concerns common to the majority of them, although differently emphasized and expressed in the words of each prophet.

(a) *God:* All the prophets speak from the perspective of a profound awareness of the reality of God; sometimes the awareness of some particular attribute of the deity will give distinctive shape to the prophetic utterance—God's love (Hosea), justice (Amos), or holiness (Ezekiel, Isaiah).

(b) *Sin and evil:* The prophets denounced both the general practice of evil among the chosen people and the particular sins, that is failures or shortcomings in the context of God's law or covenant stipulations.

(c) *Syncretism:* Many of the prophets—Hosea and Jeremiah, for example—condemn the syncretistic practices of their people; that is, the fusion of Israel's faith with elements of pagan religion, such as the worship of Baal, and the adoption of the practices of idolatry.

(d) *Judgment:* One of the most common prophetic themes is the proclamation of the coming of judgment as the divine response to sin or syncretism. Although the message of judgment may indicate an act of God in punishment of the people, at a deeper level it is usually perceived as the natural consequence of practicing various forms of evil. Judgment, in other words, is the culmination of a life, whether individual or national, in which evil has been chosen rather than good. In the prophetic proclamation, judgment is not proclaimed as an abstract notion, nor even as something occurring beyond death; it is a this-worldly kind of reality, and it is expressed in essentially historical language. Judgment may involve disaster, defeat in war, sickness, drought, and eventually the end of the nation of the chosen people.

(e) *Repentance:* There is considerable scholarly debate as to the extent to which repentance (turning from evil and back to God) was a major theme in the prophetic proclamation. Some prophets explicitly called their people to repentance and to a return to God, whereas others seem too preoccupied with the proclamation of doom to give much time to repentance. Yet, even where it was not explicit, the prophetic message seemed to imply a call for national and/or individual repentance, and the awareness of divine wrath was balanced by an awareness of God's mercy and loving-kindness. Even when the prophets seem overwhelmed with the inevitability of doom, they did not release their grasp on the sense of God's patience and mercy and the eventual triumph of loving-kindness over judgment.

(f) *Hope:* Even in the bleakest of prophetic books, there are rays of hope for the future, although sometimes (as in the case of Amos) these may have been added by a later editorial hand. The prophetic sense of hope balances the judgmental message, though it does not replace it. That is, the prophetic hope for the most part is not that judgment will be averted, but that beyond the ruin of judgment there remains hope for the people of God. It was largely this sense of prophetic hope that enabled the chosen people to survive the crises of 586 B.C.—the destruction of Jerusalem, and the life in exile. It is in the expression of hope that the prophetic sayings take on their most futuristic coloring. Yet, the language of the future, involving as it does a world lying beyond the immediate experience of historical reality, is necessarily mysterious and symbolic; it cannot be interpreted literally, but an attempt must be made to discern the more spiritual nature of the message it conveys.

(g) *The nations:* Most of the prophets addressed various foreign nations in their public and written proclamations. The message to foreigners has certain similarities to that addressed to the chosen people; it pinpoints evil and injustice and anticipates God's judgment on the foreign nations concerned. But the prophetic address to the nations illuminates the breadth of the prophets' concerns and their conception of God. Although they shared the nationalistic tradition of their people, namely that God was specifically the Lord in Israel, their notion of God was universalistic; God was concerned with the behavior and fate of all human beings and nations, and he was sovereign in the international world.

The above summary cannot do justice to the diversity and richness which characterizes the prophetic corpus as a whole, but it does indicate something of the principal thrust of the prophetic tradition. There is a further dimension to prophetic thought already evident in the summary: The prophets had a theology of history, which not only permeated their own words, but also gave a distinct perspective to many of the Old Testament books. Israel's history was not a random process, nor could it be understood simply in the secular sense of cause and effect. On the one hand, Israel's history could be understood, in part, in terms of the nation's relationship to God. When they maintained the ancient faith, they could expect the divine blessing, but when they abandoned the faith, as was so frequently the case, they were inviting judgment and disaster. In part, then, history could be understood in moral and religious terms, in the context of the behavior of the chosen people. On the other hand, Israel's history could be understood, in part, in terms of the sovereign purpose of God. Despite the judgment and disaster which the people brought upon themselves, in the last resort history had a goal; God would bring his people at last to the culmination of all history, namely the salvation (or deliverance) of Israel.

The prophetic contribution, both to the history of Israel and to the Old Testament, is an enormous one. In a historical sense, the survival of Israel in and beyond the exile was largely a consequence of the ministries of the great prophets. They gave to their people an understanding of both themselves and of God which made survival possible. Beyond that, they contributed through the biblical literature a vision of Israel's story which lifts it above the mundane level of historical narrative. Their vision is one which vividly portrays the tragedy of human evil and perversity, but which nevertheless can speak of hope, for it is rooted not in any liberal notion of the human capacity for reform and goodness, but in a sense of God as both merciful and forgiving.

4. The Tradition of Wisdom

According to the biblical texts, there were three groups of persons in ancient Israel who held positions of responsibility in the context of the nation's religious life (Jeremiah 18:18 and Ezekiel 7:26). Two of these groups we have already observed, the priests and the prophets; both served within the context of the temple and its worship, although there was greater diversity within the ranks of the prophets, some of them serving in effect as "amateurs," without any formal links to established religion. The third group of persons consisted of the *wise men;* this was an official group within Israelite society, not merely a collection of persons who were intellectually sharper than their fellow citizens. In modern terms, the role played by the wise men would seem for the most part to be more secular than that of their colleagues in the other two groups although only a little is known about the wise men, they did not appear to have close ties to the temple or to established religion.

So far as we can determine, the principal responsibilities of the wise men lay in the areas of government and administration. Though there were no doubt wise men in the earliest Hebrew community, the positions held by the wise men probably only reached a developed form in the time of kings David and Solomon; particularly during the latter king's reign, the Hebrew Empire had grown to such considerable proportions that a large civil service was required to manage it. The wise men thus assumed positions of responsibility in the general machinery of government and administration. The senior officers served as a part of the king's immediate staff, and the junior rank and file spread out through the land in positions of regional authority. They were responsible for taxation, local administration, the implementation of government projects, and many similar things. The wise men, by virtue of the nature of their jobs, would require extensive skills (one of the meanings of the Hebrew word *wisdom* is *skill*). They would have to be able to read and write; they would require competence in mathematics and accounting; they would need managerial skills; and some would have to be bilingual. The wise men, in other words, would require a thorough education to prepare them for their tasks.

With respect to the education of the wise men, the surviving evidence is at best indirect. It is reasonable to assume that there were wisdom schools, perhaps originating in the time of Solomon. Although there are no explicit references to schools in the Old Testament, there are references to teachers and students, and there is also evidence from beyond Israel of wisdom schools in the ancient Near East. Whether there was something like a small "college" in Jerusalem, or whether education was carried on in a more informal fashion (perhaps an apprenticeship model), must remain largely a matter of speculation. It is clear, nevertheless, that many of the wise men must have held positions not only in government and administration, but also in education. As educators, the wise men had a dual function: First, they had to provide their pupils with the necessary skills for the administrative responsibilities they would assume, and second, as we shall see, there was a moral and religious component to their educational task.

What has been summarizd so far indicates a largely secular role for the wise men in ancient Israel. Nevertheless, there were dimensions of their responsibilities which were decidedly religious. Their administrative responsibilities were conducted in the context of a religious state whose laws and traditions had religious origins and authority. They served a king who was not only head of state, but also the patron and defender of the nation's faith. In other words, the very nature of Israelite society was such that the secular and the sacred could not be kept apart; therefore, *de facto,* the wise men were a part of the leadership of a religious community, even though their responsibilities were entirely different from those of the priests. The theological perspectives of the wise men, although they were integrated into the faith of the nation as a whole, were distinctive, having emphases of a more intellectual and moral kind than those of the priests and prophets. The wisdom tradition, in addition, is the most international and cosmopolitan in the entire Old Testament. The Hebrew wise men had many close similarities to that of their fellow wise men in Egypt and Mesopotamia, but the Hebrew wise men are given distinctive coloration by the substratum of Hebrew religious thought upon which they are based.

As we have already seen (chapter 8), one of the categories of biblical literature has been called *Wisdom Literature;* it is distinguished from other Old Testament literature both in literary forms and by virtue of its intellectual and theological foundations. It should not be assumed, however, that wise men produced only one category of literature, namely the wisdom books and other passages which have survived. The positions held by some wise men in the royal court, for example, make it probable that they were responsible for compiling chronicles of royal activities of the kind referred to as source materials in several of the Old Testament historical writings. The wisdom literature that has survived in the Old Testament, especially the wisdom books (Proverbs, Ecclesiastes, and Job), should probably be traced in its origins to a special group within the wise men, those having particularly intellectual concerns and responsibilities for education.

The biblical wisdom literature falls into two general types: (a) writings of proverbial character, probably designed specifically for

3 1 7

instructional purposes (the book of Proverbs and many of the wisdom psalms); (b) writings of a more sustained and intellectual character, addressing the problems and issues of wisdom (Ecclesiastes and Job). Both types are found in parallel Near Eastern literature.

In Egypt, wisdom texts of the proverbial kind have been found which date as early as the third millennium B.C.. From the biblical period, there is the famous *Wisdom of Amenemopet,* which has close parallels to a portion of the book of Proverbs. Similar instructional material existed in Babylonian wisdom literature. In a second millennium B.C. text entitled the *Counsels of Wisdom,* a man's "son" (probably a teacher's pupil) is warned against such potential dangers as dishonesty, unsuitable companions, and bad wives.

In the category of more theoretical wisdom literature, the Egyptian *Song of the Harper* raises issues similar to those of Ecclesiastes, and the *Protests of the Eloquent Peasant* reflects fundamental issues of justice and injustice. A second millennium B.C. Babylonian text, *I Will Praise the Lord of Wisdom,* recounts in the form of a monologue the plight of a man suffering terrible illness who feels that all his traditional beliefs and values have been turned upside down; the text has certain similarities to the book of Job, though little of the beauty and profundity of the latter.

There are thus close parallels to the biblical wisdom literature in the external sources, but what gives the biblical books their distinctive character is the theological foundation upon which they are based: The fear (*reverence*) of the Lord is the beginning of wisdom (see Proverbs 1:7; Job 28:28; Ecclesiastes 12:13). Despite the strong intellectual threads running through the literature, all of it presupposes a theological anchoring in faith. The wisdom of Proverbs is essentially moral, much of it having no explicit reference to God; yet, all of it presupposes God's existence and reverence for God on the part of human beings.

The educational role of the wise men was that of preparing young persons for a career as wise men in government and administration. Information on the professional curriculum has not survived, though it must have included training in language, mathematics, and administration. From external archaeological sources, a number of *school texts* have been discovered which illustrate the work of students in copying out the alphabet and writing practice letters, as for example, in some of the clay tablets recovered from ancient Ugarit

(Ras Shamra). It is perhaps not surprising that the professional elements of the curriculum have not survived, for they have little enduring worth beyond their own time, but portions of the curriculum for moral education have survived in the book of Proverbs. This book illustrates the appropriate breadth of the ancient educational philosophy; education involves more than just training in the essential technical skills and must involve a moral dimension. It was not enough to know how to make a living; one must also know how to live. So in the wisdom of Proverbs one can perceive an approach to maturity and morality quite different from that contained in the Law and the Prophets. It is in part a condensation of common sense, taught in such a way as to inform the conscience and establish clearly the outlines of right and wrong. It balances the technical aspects of education with a sense of perspective and with an awareness of fundamental human values. For the young students who understood and assimilated the wisdom of Proverbs, it would have stood them in good stead in dealing with the human and moral dimensions of the tasks which they were to assume.

For all the strength of proverbial wisdom, there were at least two directions from which its moral insight and basic theology were vulnerable. From the one side, it could be undermined by thoroughgoing skepticism; from the other, a person's experience of life's suffering and misery could be such as to cast doubt on the very foundations of proverbial wisdom. The book of Ecclesiastes deals with the attack on proverbial wisdom from the direction of doubt and skepticism; in keeping with the intellectual tradition to which it belongs, it is characterized more by rational thought than by the exercise of faith. The writer does not abandon the basic wisdom of Proverbs, nor does he renounce the theological foundation of the wisdom school, but he sets the whole tradition to which he belongs in a somewhat different light; he removes the naïveté of proverbial wisdom as it might be understood at a superficial level. He sees that justice and truth, although they form admirable goals for human endeavor, are rarely achieved in human society; conversely, poverty and oppression, although they are reprehensible, are rarely eliminated. The one who has read Ecclesiastes with understanding will enter life and work with eyes wide open; duty must be done, but only with an awareness that when all is done, nevertheless it may seem to be vanity, a grasping after wind. The writer of Ecclesiastes has not abolished doubt and skepticism, but has entered this perspective and has pursued them rigorously with the exercise of reason. He offers not a critique of the skeptical position, but the consolation and understanding of one who has stood where all doubters and skeptics stand. Thus his greatest contribution is the gift of maturity to those who are weaned intellectually in the wisdom tradition.

Whereas Ecclesiastes describes the world's grief and the temptation to doubt from the perspective of a rational observer, the author of Job grasps the problems from within, from the perspective of a sufferer. The life-experience of the suffering Job calls into question much of the substance of proverbial wisdom and ethics. The reality of human life seems to be that an upright and moral life offers no guarantees against disaster and suffering. The difficulties of the moral person are compounded by the recognition that immoral persons seem frequently to prosper and succeed into the years of old age (Job 21:7-15). Indeed, the terrible grief and suffering of a man like Job call into question the very notions of creation; in what sense can this world be thought of as marked with the orderly imprint of God's hand, when the experience of life can be as miserable as Job's? The writer of Job again penetrates the facade of superficial theology and thought; there remains always a mystery in God and in God's ways that eludes the grasp of human understanding. Wisdom is in part the pursuit of the knowledge of God, but wisdom as intellectual knowledge can never grasp ultimate truth in all its depth, for God is always greater than the human mind and the human capacity to understand. Thus the book of Job, although it emerges from a profoundly intellectual tradition, reminds its readers of the centrality of religious experience. There are aspects of the world and of God's dealings with human beings which the mind cannot grasp; religious experience does not replace intellectual inquiry, but it may supplement the limited knowledge acquired by the mind. There is an element of understanding, though it cannot be articulated in human language, which emerges from the encounter with God; the person who grasps this dimension to wisdom again finds that the fundamental moral insight of proverbial morality is set in a deeper and more meaningful context.

In summary, there were may facets to the religious and cultural life in ancient Israel; the different traditions and groups within Israelite society contributed largely to the diversity of thought and faith embodied within the Old Testament books. The priests, the prophets, and the wise men were all a part of the tapestry of Israel's national life, and their words and work illustrate the practice of religion, the challenge of faith, and the exercise of reason in the society which has left as a legacy for subsequent generations the books of the Old Testament.

EPILOGUE

PART V

THE
STUDY OF
THE
OLD TESTAMENT

T HE preceding chapters of this book have presented a compact survey of the Old Testament with its background, growth, and contents. But it will have become clear to the reader that the discipline commonly called "Old Testament Studies" is an enormous one; it encompasses a large collection of texts of varying literary types, a historical span of more than a millennium, and a range of disciplines, including archaeology and literary criticism, in addition to many others. The purpose of this concluding chapter is to provide some perspectives and guidance for the further study of the Old Testament. Together with the annotated bibliography which follows, these paragraphs may open the door to a rewarding field of study, whether viewed from an academic perspective or from the perspective of personal understanding and enjoyment.

1. Jewish and Christian Perspectives

It was noted at the very beginning of this book that the *Tanak* (Old Testament) was a Jewish collection which subsequently became a part of both Jewish and Christian Scriptures. The interpretation of the biblical books differs very considerably at a number of points between Judaism and Christianity, even though a common text is shared by both faiths. The perspective from which the survey in the preceding chapters has been presented is that of contemporary biblical scholarship; as such, it has been deemed inappropriate to highlight the distinctive ways in which the texts might be appropriated or interpreted within the contemporary religions. Thus, to take only one example, in Christian interpretation many Old Testament texts are interpreted as foreshadowing in some manner the coming of Jesus Christ. Judaism, in contrast, has quite different messianic notions and interprets the same texts in a fashion quite different from Christianity. Contemporary scholarship stands back, for the most part, from such differences in the appropriation of the message of the ancient texts; rather, it seeks to determine the historical setting of the texts and the meaning inherent in them in their original form. Yet, such an approach, for all its merits in academic terms, must be less than fully satisfactory to Jews and Christians respectively. Likewise, the objective and impartial approach for which scholarship strives is less than fully satisfactory for Jews and Christians who, in their distinctive fashion, seek to hear the voice of God in the ancient Scriptures. While most Christians and Jews can accept the approach to the Old Testament implicit in modern scholarship, the majority of them will also find it to be inadequate taken alone.

Within Judaism, the *Tanak* does not constitute the entire *Torah* or the sum total of divine revelation. For all its pride of place, it must be supplemented by the *Mishnah*, the written form of the ancient tradition of oral law which is believed (along with the *Pentateuch*) to trace its origins to the time of Moses. The Mishnah, in turn, must be supplemented by the *Talmud*, which adds to the text of the Mishnah the later interpretative tradition of the rabbis. Thus it would be wrong to view Judaism as being a religion based solely (in terms of scripture) on the books of the Hebrew Bible; Jewish scripture is broader than that. In addition, the roles of Mishnah and Talmud within Judaism are such that they shape the manner in which the biblical books are read and interpreted. Hence a Jewish approach to the biblical books, while it may initially share the methods of contemporary biblical scholarship, must continue where a scholarly and secular approach leave off. Not only must it reflect on the meaning of the books of the

Hebrew Bible in the light of the later Talmudic tradition, but it must also continually address the question of the authority of the entire Torah in matters of contemporary faith and practice.

It is also the case that within Christianity the Old Testament does not constitute the entire Scripture (although it was the only Scripture in the earliest decades of the Christian church); it is balanced by the New Testament. For Christians, a knowledge of the New Testament shapes the way in which the Old Testament is read and understood. In positive terms, the content of the New Testament is so penetrated with quotations from, and allusions to, the Old Testament, that it contains an implicit perspective of its own for the interpretation of the older Jewish scriptures. In negative terms, the rejection within Christianity of the rabbinical tradition of Judaism as embodied in the Talmud meant inevitably that the two religions went their own and different ways in the interpretation and appropriation of a common Scripture.

For all the differences between Judaism and Christianity, the modern scholarly study of the ancient Hebrew scriptures does provide an area of common ground between the two faiths. Setting aside the confessional differences in the interpretation of particular passages, Jews and Christians alike may share common ground in the historical and literary study of biblical books. In the professional context of modern biblical scholarship, one of the most refreshing characteristics of the discipline is the manner in which scholars from both faiths work together toward the common goal of understanding the ancient text. But there comes a point at which Christians and Jews, whether scholars or students, must recognize the limits of their shared task and agree to go their different ways. The Tanak has a distinctive role to play in Judaism, as does the Old Testament in Christianity; the shared Scripture should enhance the degree of mutual understanding between the two faiths, but it must nevertheless retain its distinctive position in each.

For Christian and Jewish students of the Hebrew scriptures, the recognition of the dividing line between the objective academic approach and the confessional approach of faith is an important one. The two perspectives and approaches need not be seen as opposed or antagonistic to one another, but as complementary approaches. Insofar as the writings and history of the Hebrew Bible are rooted in time and place, they are susceptible to examination by the modern scientific methods of historical and literary research. But insofar as the biblical writings are rooted in faith, then if they are to be appreciated as Scripture as well as ancient texts, faith must also be brought to bear on the part of the reader.

2. The Academic Study of the Old Testament

While it recognizes the interests of Judaism and Christianity, the academic study of the Old Testament proceeds on different grounds as to both the *why* and as to the *how* of Old Testament study.

The reasons for the large-scale investigation of the Old Testament in the modern and secular world are many and various. In the broadest sense, Old Testament studies are part of the general drive for knowledge and understanding which has characterized our own and preceding centuries. In the rise of modern Old Testament studies, a number of reasons have emerged. In part, the secular and academic study of the Old Testament is analogous to the study of the classics; Jerusalem, as much as Athens and Rome, has shaped the Western world; therefore, the scriptures that have come to us from ancient Jerusalem are worthy of study and reflection. A similar perspective, though broader in scope, is to be seen in the general search for knowledge of the human past, whether pursued through archaeology or history; the Old Testament offers one avenue to a bygone world and, therefore, illuminates the development of human life and faith on this planet. Again, in the study of ancient languages and literatures, the Old Testament offers important evidence. In the discipline called "history of religions," no approach to understanding Judaism, Christianity, or Islam can avoid recognizing that the Old Testament is the necessary starting point for further investigation. But all these approaches are fairly narrow and technical and all are, or perhaps should be, parts of a larger quest, namely the study of the humanities. The humanities, in modern colleges and universities, reflect upon the age-old questions concerning the nature of humankind; the arts, literature, and various intellectual products of genius provide a means toward gaining insight into the nature of human beings. No study of the humanities can ignore the Old Testament, not simply because it is a tapestry of ancient life and letters, but principally because it is an extraordinary monument to *faith in God* as offering a way of human understanding.

The diversity of reasons for studying the Old Testament in the modern world is matched by an equal diversity of methods and approaches. The principal approaches to the Old Testament in modern study have been via the avenues of literary and historical research, frequently combined as literary–historical criticism; the approach is a natural one, for the evidence has survived in literary form and pertains to persons, places, and events that have historical settings. The literary-historical approach to Old Testament studies may be supplemented by many sub-disciplines—sociology, anthropology, archaeology, and psychology to name a few, although the extant evidence often permits only a limited application of such modern approaches. The classical methods are frequently being refined and broken up into sub-disciplines. Literary criticism, for example, must take into account the possibility of a pre-literary form of some texts, which introduces the method of oral criticism (or oral-tradition history). The recognition that some texts reached their present form only after a long period of development introduces such methods as *redaction criticism,* the attempt to study the work of redactors (or "editors," loosely defined) in compiling a work from various sources and imprinting on the whole a new and distinctive shape.

The bewildering variety of modern approaches to the study of the Old Testament makes it clear that anyone who plans to pursue the study of the biblical books beyond the introductory level is in for a challenging task. For those who would venture further, a few guidelines are suggested.

(a) *Reading.* For all the massive production of scholarly writings about the Old Testament books, there can be no substitute for reading the texts themselves. The Old Testament is so long, and in places so complex, that this can be a formidable task. But it can be done initially on a selective basis; if one wishes to understand the exodus from Egypt and the covenant at Sinai, then at the very least, Exodus 1–24 should be read in addition to modern books on the subject. Certainly, I am only stating the obvious, but the size of the Old Testament seems so formidable to some, that they would rather read about it than read it!

(b) *Language*. Ideally one should have a knowledge of Hebrew to come to a full and profound appreciation of the ancient text. Nevertheless, excellent translations are available, and though they cannot convey the atmosphere of the original text, they are faithful renditions of the sense of the original. Of the many valuable translations available, the *Revised Standard Version* (Old Testament, 1952) and the three-volume work completed by the Jewish Publication Society in 1982 (*The Torah, The Prophets,* and *The Writings*) are very valuable for study purposes.

(c) *History of Scholarship*. It is useful to understand the present state of biblical scholarship in the context of the development of scholarship over the last century or longer. An awareness of the history of scholarship highlights the problem areas in the study of the Old Testament and gives some indication of those matters on which there is common consensus and those matters which remain the subject of debate (see the Bibliography).

(d) *Methods*. The diversity of different methods, some of which are exceedingly complicated and technical, can be confusing to the beginner in the field. There are various volumes available (see the Bibliography) which explain the methods, and illustrate their application in the study of the biblical text. It is also important to realize that methodology is in a perpetual process of flux and change, thus the overall value of some of the more recently introduced methods (for example, structuralism) in biblical studies remains the subject of debate.

The above are only a few of the steps which might help to prepare the way for a fuller and more worthwhile study of the Old Testament. They are only preliminary steps; students within Judaism and Christianity, for example, would benefit from broadening their understanding of the traditional and contemporary roles of their ancient Scripture in the contemporary synagogue or church. However, if I may end on a partial note, the study is worth pursuing; the Old Testament may not be the easiest of works to study, but it repays study and reflection with wisdom and understanding. As the writer of Proverbs put it:

> My son,
> do not forget my teaching,
> but let your heart keep my commandments;

EPILOGUE

for length of days
and years of life
and abundant welfare
will they give you.

(Proverbs 3:1-2)

AIDS FOR THE
STUDY OF THE
OLD TESTAMENT

A N N O T A T E D   B I B L I O G R A P H Y

---

1. Translations of the Old Testament

Of the many English translations available, two were recommended (chapter 12) as particularly useful for study purposes: *The Revised Standard Version* (Old Testament, 1952) and the three-volume translation produced by the Jewish Publication Society, completed in 1982, and published in Philadelphia: I. *The Torah*; II. *The Prophets*; III. *The Writings*. There are, however, many other useful and reliable translations available; a guide to the variety of modern translations may be found in the following works:

Bailey, Lloyd R. *The Word of God: A Guide to English Versions of the Bible.* Atlanta: John Knox, 1982.

Kubo, S. and Spech, W. F. *So Many Versions? Twentieth Century English Versions of the Bible.* Grand Rapids: Zondervan, 1975. Revised edition, 1983.

2. Introductions to the Old Testament

Old Testament introductions fall generally into two categories, (a) those designed for teaching, introducing the subject matter at various levels of complexity, and (b) technical introductions which may involve original research or serve more as reference works. The books in category (a) are essentially teaching works, some covering the same ground as the present volume, but in more detail or from a different perspective. The books in category (b) are most suitable for more advanced study.

(a) *General Introductions*

Anderson, B. W. *Understanding the Old Testament.* Englewood Cliffs, N.J.: Prentice-Hall, 4th edition, 1986. A classical introduction for the more advanced student.

Hayes, John H. *An Introduction to Old Testament Study.* Nashville: Abingdon Press, 1979. This book is particularly valuable for its account of the methods of Old Testament study.

LaSor, W. S., Hubbard, D. A., and Bush, F. W. *Old Testament Survey; The Message, Form, and Background of the Old Testament.* Grand Rapids: Eerdmans, 1982. A very thorough introduction written from a conservative Protestant perspective.

Orlinsky, H. M. *Understanding the Bible through History and Archaeology.* New York: KTAV, 1972. A concise and readable introduction, superbly illustrated, by a distinguished Jewish scholar.

(b) *Technical Introductions*

Childs, B. S. *Introduction to the Old Testament as Scripture.* Philadelphia: Fortress Press, 1979. A clearly written and highly original introduction from the perspective of "canonical criticism."

Eissfeldt, O. *The Old Testament, An Introduction.* Translated by P. R. Ackroyd. Oxford: Blackwell, 1965. A very thorough introduction, representing the best of European scholarship.

Fohrer, G. *Introduction to the Old Testament.* Translated by D. E. Green. Nashville: Abingdon Press, 1968 (German edition, 1965). A clearly organized and comprehensive introduction, with extensive bibliographies.

Harrison, R. K. *Introduction to the Old Testament.* Grand Rapids: Eerdmans, 1969. A massive work (1,215 pages), written from a conservative Protestant perspective, with a wealth of material on the history of interpretation.

3. Bible Atlases

Aharoni, Y. and Avi-Yonah, M. (eds.). *The Macmillan Bible Atlas.* New York: Macmillan, 1968.

May, H. G. (ed.). *Oxford Bible Atlas*. London: Oxford University Press, second edition, 1974.

Wright, G. E. and Filson, F. V., eds. *The Westminster Historical Atlas to the Bible*. Philadelphia: Westminster Press, revised edition, 1956.

These atlases include illustrations and narrative, in addition to maps; they may be usefully supplemented by geographical works (below).

4. The Geography of the Old Testament World

Aharoni, Y. *The Land of the Bible. A Historical Geography*. Translated by A. F. Rainey. London: Burns and Oates, 1966. A detailed and original study, covering both physical geography and historical geography.

Baly, D. *Geographical Companion to the Bible*. London: Lutterworth, 1963. A very readable book, written by a professional geographer with an intimate knowledge of the land.

Smith, G. A. *The Historical Geography of the Holy Land*. Original edition, 1894. London: Collins, 1966. Although now dated, Sir George Adam Smith's book is a classic, beautifully written, and richly informed by the author's immense knowledge of his subject.

5. Bible Dictionaries

The multi-volume Bible dictionaries listed below will not only provide concise information on any biblical subject being examined, but they will also provide useful bibliography for further study. All are illustrated and include maps.

Buttrick, G. A., ed. *The Interpreter's Dictionary of the Bible; An Illustrated Encyclopedia*. Nashville: Abingdon Press, 1962. Four volumes. Supplementary volume (K. Crim, ed.), 1976.

Douglas, J. D., ed. *The Illustrated Bible Dictionary*. Wheaton: Tyndale House, 1980. Three volumes. A revised and expanded version of *The New Bible Dictionary* (1962).

Bromiley, G. W., ed. *The International Standard Bible Encyclopedia*. Grand Rapids: Eerdmans. Four volumes. Vol. I, 1979; Vol. II, 1982. A completely revised version of the dictionary first published in 1915.

6. Commentaries on Old Testament Books

An enormous number of commentaries have been published on each of the Old Testament books, some very technical and some written at a popular level. The best way to locate commentaries on a particular book (other than browsing in the library) is to refer to the bibliographies in the Introductions (especially B. S. Childs, *Introduction to the Old Testament as Scripture,* in section 2, above) and to the concise bibliographies in the articles on particular books in the Dictionaries (see section 5, above). As a general introduction:

Laymon, C. M., ed. *The Interpreter's One-Volume Commentary on the Bible.* Nashville: Abingdon Press, 1972.

7. Near Eastern Civilizations

(a) *General Introductions*

Moscati, S. *The Face of the Ancient Orient; A Panorama of Near Eastern Civilizations in Pre-Classical Times.* New York: Doubleday, 1962.

Ringgren, H. *Religions of the Ancient Near East.* London: SPCK, 1973. Translated by J. Sturdy.

Wiseman, D. J., ed. *Peoples of Old Testament Times.* Oxford: Clarendon Press, 1973. A series of essays on the peoples and nations of the Old Testament world.

(b) *Near Eastern Texts in Translation*

Beyerlin, W., ed. *Near Eastern Religious Texts Relating to the Old Testament.* London: SCM, 1978. A selection of Egyptian, Mesopotamian, Hittite, Ugaritic, and North Semitic texts.

Pritchard, J. B., ed. *Ancient Near Eastern Texts Relating to the Old Testament.* Princeton: Princeton University Press, 3rd edition, 1969. An enormous collection of texts, including myths, laws, historical texts, hymns, and many others from the literature of Israel's neighbors.

Thomas, D. W., ed. *Documents from Old Testament Times.* New York: Harper Torchbook, 1961 A concise and readable collection of texts (cuneiform, Egyptian, Moabite, Hebrew, and Aramaic); this is the most useful introductory volume.

8. Archaeology and the Old Testament

(a) *General Introductions*

Gray, J. *Archaeology and the Old Testament World.* Edinburgh: Thomas Nelson, 1962.

Thomas, D. W., ed. *Archaeology and Old Testament Study*. Oxford: Clarendon Press, 1967. A summary account of the excavation of the principal archaeological sites in the Old Testament world.

Thompson, J. A. *The Bible and Archaeology*. Grand Rapids: Eerdmans, 1964. 3rd edition, 1982.

Wright, G. E. *Introduction to Biblical Archaeology*. London: Duckworth, 1960.

(b) *Works with a special emphasis on archaeology:*

Aharoni, Y. *The Archaeology of the Land of Israel; From the Prehistoric Beginnings to the End of the First Temple Period*. Translated by A. F. Rainey. London: SCM, 1982.

Albright, F. W. *Archaeology of Palestine*. Harmondsworth: Penguin Books, revised edition, 1960. A book by the most distinguished American archaeologist of the twentieth century.

(c) *Books about the archaeological sites described in some detail in chapter 3.*

Craigie, P. C. *Ugarit and the Old Testament*. Grand Rapids: Eerdmans, 1983.

Cross, F. M. *The Ancient Library of Qumran and Modern Biblical Studies*. New York: Doubleday, 1961.

Matthiae, P. *Ebla; An Empire Rediscovered*. New York: Doubleday, 1981.

Pettinato, G. *The Archives of Ebla. An Empire Inscribed in Clay*. New York: Doubleday, 1981.

9. The History of Israel

Ackroyd, P. R. *Israel under Babylon and Persia*. The New Clarendon Bible. London: Oxford University Press, 1970. A very clear account of the latter period of Israel's history in Old Testament times.

Bright, J. *A History of Israel*. Philadelphia: Westminster, 3rd edition, 1981. The classical exposition of the "American" approach to Israel's history, with a positive assessment of Israel's earliest historical period.

Herrmann, S. *A History of Israel in Old Testament Times*. London: SCM, 1974; revised edition, 1981.

BIBLIOGRAPHY

Jagersma, H. *A History of Israel in the Old Testament Period.* London: SCM, 1982.

Noth, M. *History of Israel.* London: A. and C. Black, 1960. The classical "German" approach to Israel's history, a counterbalance to the interpretation of Bright (above).

Ramsey, G. W. *The Quest for the Historical Israel.* Atlanta: John Knox, 1981. Examines the difficulties faced by the historian in the study of Israel's earliest history, and reviews critically recent trends in this area of study.

10. The Religion of Israel

Anderson, G. W. *The History and Religion of Israel.* The New Clarendon Bible. London: Oxford University Press, 1966. A concise and clearly written account, representing a balanced interpretation of the subject.

de Vaux, R. *Ancient Israel: Its Life and Institutions.* London: Darton, Longman and Todd, 2nd edition, 1965. A comprehensive volume, with detailed examination of Israel's culture and religious institutions.

Kaufmann, Y. *The Religion of Israel: From its Beginnings to the Babylonian Exile.* Translated by M. Greenberg. Chicago: University of Chicago Press, 1960. This is an abridgment of the first six volumes of Kaufmann's major study (in Hebrew) of the history of Israelite religion.

Ringgren, H. *Israelite Religion.* London: SPCK, 1969.

11. The Theology of the Old Testament

Clements, R. E. *Old Testament Theology; A Fresh Approach.* London: Marshall, Morgan, and Scott, 1978.

Hasel, G. *Old Testament Theology: Basic Issues in the Current Debate.* Grand Rapids: Eerdmans, 1972.

McKenzie, J. L. *A Theology of the Old Testament.* London: Fowler Wright, 1974. A concise and non-technical summary of the basic religion and theology of Israel.

12. The Text and Manuscripts of the Old Testament

Weingreen, J. *Introduction to the Critical Study of the Text of the Hebrew Bible.* Oxford: Clarendon Press, 1982.

Wurthwein, E. *The Text of the Old Testament; An Introduction to Biblia Hebraica.*

Translated by E. F. Rhodes. London: SCM, revised edition, 1980. Particularly useful as an aid to reading the critical edition of the Hebrew Bible in its original language.

13. History and Survey of Old Testament Scholarship

Anderson, G. W., ed. *Tradition and Interpretation*. Oxford: Clarendon Press, 1979. A collection of essays by members of the British Society for Old Testament Study, giving a thorough review and assessment of the current state of research in the principal areas of Old Testament Studies.

Clements, R. E. *A Century of Old Testament Study*. London: Lutterworth, 1976; revised edition, 1983. A very useful survey of one hundred years of scholarship, focusing principally on the study of Old Testament literature.

Hahn, H. F. *The Old Testament in Modern Research*. Philadelphia: Fortress Press, 1954; revised and expanded edition, 1966. Although now somewhat dated, this is a very useful survey of Old Testament scholarship according to the different *methods* employed by scholars.

Rowley, H. H. ed. *The Old Testament and Modern Scholarship*. Oxford: Clarendon Press, 1951. This volume is in the same tradition as that edited by G. W. Anderson (above); despite its date, it is still a very useful guide to Old Testament scholarship.

14. Methods in Old Testament Study

Some of the volumes already listed will provide a helpful understanding of the methods employed by contemporary Old Testament scholars; see particularly John H. Hayes, *An Introduction to Old Testament Study* (section 2, above). In addition, a series of slender, but useful, study guides can be recommended: G. M. Tucker (general editor), *Guides to Biblical Scholarship: Old Testament Series*, published in Philadelphia by Fortress Press. The separate guides explain such methods as literary criticism, form criticism, tradition history, textual criticism, and biblical archaeology.

15. Journals for Old Testament Studies

For more advanced study of particular issues in Old Testament studies, the reader must turn to the professional journals in the field; the following list refers to just a few of the principal journals.

Journal of Biblical Literature. Published, quarterly, by the Society of Biblical Literature (U. S. A.). Covers both Old and New Testament Studies.

Journal for the Study of the Old Testament. Published by the Department of Biblical Studies, University of Sheffield, U. K.

Vetus Testamentum. Published (in Holland) for the International Organization for Old Testament Studies; articles are principally in English, French, and German.

Zeitschrift für die alttestamentliche Wissenschaft. Published in Germany this journal carries a number of articles in English in each issue. It also includes in each issue a very useful review of all newly published articles and books in Old Testament Studies.

The above are only a selection of numerous journals in the field; further guidance will be found in the bibliographical guides (below).

16. Bibliographical Tools

In addition to the review of books and articles in the German periodical (listed above), there is one regular bibliographical guide in English:

Vawter, B., ed. *Old Testament Abstracts.* Published thrice yearly by the Catholic Biblical Association in Washington, D.C. Each issue contains abstracts of recently published articles and books, arranged according to topic.

There is, in addition, an international bibliography, published annually, which (despite its German title) lists items in a variety of languages, including English:

Internationale Zeitschriftenschau für Bibelwissenschaft und Grenzgebiete. Published by Patmos Verlag, in Dusseldorf, Germany.

A very useful *Book List* is published annually in the U. K. by the *Society for Old Testament Study,* which contains a comprehensive listing of newly published books, together with abstracts, arranged topically.

INDEX OF
OLD TESTAMENT
REFERENCES

GENERAL INDEX

Abdon, 132
Abraham, 48, 50, 51, 58, 108, 114, 119, 259-60
Abram, 260, *See also* Abraham
Achaeminid Dynasty, 73
Acrostic poetry, 194, 215-16, 240
Adam, 107, 249
Agriculture, ancient, 50, 54
Agur, words of, 219, 220
Ahasuerus, King, 241
Ahijah, 140
Ai, city of, 129, 269
Ain Feshkha, 92
Akhenaten, Pharaoh, 303
Akkadian, 55
Alexander the Great, 61, 73, 74
Alexandria, Egypt, 33-34, 76
al-Kifl, 165
Amalekites, 122
Amariah, 198
Amaziah, 182
America, early civilization in, 50
Amorites, 72
Amos, book of, 180-83

Amos (prophet), ministry of, 180-81, 189, 198, 282
Analects of Confucius, 221
Anathoth, 158
Anthropomorphic language, 306
Aphek, 270
Apocalyptic thought, 200, 205-6, 247-49
Apocrypha, 18, 24, 30
Arabah, 112
Arabic language, 25-26
Aramaic language, 24-25, 29-30, 244, 246
Aramean, Arameans, 72, 278
Archaeology, biblical, 79-112 passim, 121, 268-69
    definition, 81-82
Ark of the covenant, 136, 294
Aristotle, 74
Asaph (psalmist), 212, 216
Asia Minor, 73, 74
Assur, 54
Assyria, Assyrian, 48, 58, 61, 76-77, 174, 193, 194, 198-99, 278, 283
Athens, as classical symbol, 40-41